Connected Minds, Emerging Cultures

Cybercultures in Online Learning

D1473821

a volume in
Perspectives in Instructional Technology and Distance Education

Series Editors:
Charles Schlosser and Michael Simonson
Nova Southeastern University

Perspectives in Instructional Technology and Distance Education

Charles Schlosser and Michael Simonson, Series Editors

Connected Minds, Emerging Cultures

Cybercultures in Online Learning

edited by

Steve Wheeler
University of Plymouth

Information Age Publishing, Inc.
Charlotte, North Carolina • www.infoagepub.com

Library of Congress Cataloging-in-Publication Data

Connected minds, emerging cultures: cybercultures in online learning / edited by
Steve Wheeler.
    p. cm.—(Perspectives in instructional technology and distance
education)
   Includes bibliographical references and index.
   ISBN 978-1-60752-015-3 (pbk.) — ISBN 978-1-60752-016-0 (hardcover) 1. Internet in
education. 2. Cyberspace—Social aspects. 3. Learning, Psychology of. I. Wheeler, Steve.
   LB1044.87.C64 2009
   371.33'44678—dc22

                              2008042394

Printed in the United States of America

CONTENTS

PART III.
CYBER PERSPECTIVES

PART IV.
NARRATIVES AND CASE STUDIES

FOREWORD

Howard Rheingold

If user-generated content was the engine that drove Web 2.0, student gen-erated learning is what might drive Education 2.0. Forget about the tech-nology involved, for the moment—the One Laptop Per Child and ubiquitous broadband networks, the content management systems, and chatrooms. The technologies are only enablers for human-generated phe-nomena that are psychological and social, not just technological. The tools by themselves are insufficient to transform existing educational institutions—new methods, new attitudes, and new distributions of power are necessary for these tools to go beyond doing old tasks more efficiently and begin doing entirely new kinds of tasks that were never before possi-ble. Because a thousand-year-old power structure is threatened by truly participative pedagogy, however, do not expect existing educational insti-tutions to flock to adopt these methods. Universities might be locked into proprietary content management systems, but that is a long distance from actively enabling, requiring, and guiding students to teach each other their own syllabi.

Introducing participative media to students, if done properly, is not a slick new way to deliver knowledge. Its explodes, inverts, and mashes up educational activities with the same cultural practices that students engage in when they hang out online, tag a Flickr photo, and upload or

Connected Minds, Emerging Cultures: Cybercultures in Online Learning
pp. vii–ix
Copyright © 2009 by Information Age Publishing

comment on a YouTube video. And that is a good thing, because "delivering knowledge" does not work any more. The kinds of collaborative inquiry and social knowledge creation that wikis, forums, and blogs afford can challenge much of the structure of education as we have known it, including the power structure. Instructors no longer are limited to delivering knowledge, but have new opportunities to catalyze, model, participate, and guide inquiry driven by the students themselves

I was involved in cybercultures long before anyone thought to call them cybercultures. We knew that important issues about identity, community, media power, collective action were involved in the nascent digital publics of the 1980s, but all evidence in our arguments at that time was anecdotal. There was no empirical work, no cyberculture theory. Notions of distance learning and telecommuting were in vogue, but I do not think anyone forecast the consequences of Wi-Fi and laptops in classrooms. That is where that thousand-year-old power structure comes into play.

Before Gutenberg, books were rare, precious, and chained to the lectern. Universities started when young men flocked to cities to hear readers read Aristotle aloud. And brilliant lectures will not—should not—go away. But the not-so-brilliant lecturers, recycling old material, perhaps punctuated with bullet-point laden PowerPoint presentations, are no longer looking into the eyes of hundreds of students who might or might not be listening. They—we—are looking at hundreds of students, most of whom are looking at their laptops. Many of them are taking notes and searching out references and definitions online. And many of them are battling monsters in World of Warcraft, pimping out their MySpace pages, IMing their buddies, twittering, and engaging with silent but fervent enthusiasm in a million other seductive attractions that mind-wandering doodlers of past millennia did not have at their disposal. Talk about your cybercultures; at this moment, professors around the world are dealing with students immersed in cybercultures.

Sometimes, and more rarely than most of us think, it is proper to tell them to close their laptop lids. Attention-training—or at least elementary mindfulness of where one's attention is deployed from moment to moment—is a necessary element of the curriculum if you are going to allow the Web into the classroom. A more radical task is to step down from the lectern, pull the chairs into a circle, and invite true inquiry. But how? In what ways, specifically, can learners be encouraged to construct knowledge together, rather than receive it from above? How might that fervent enthusiasm they put into MySpace or World of Warcraft be enlisted in the joy of learning? How can educators learn to stop delivering knowledge and begin facilitating inquiry?

The authors in this volume have directly challenged the questions I have raised. The only way to find out what works when mixing learners, teachers, and technology is to try. Herein are helpful reports from the pioneers—hints to the rest of us about how we can foster collaboration with wikis, encourage the development of public voice with blogs, and show the way to social knowledge production with tagging and bookmark-sharing. This is not just lore; it is part of the key to using the technologies at hand to help students learn to live in a world where the basis of governance, commerce, and culture is unreliable, rapidly changing, socially constructed knowledge.

INTRODUCTION

Steve Wheeler

The contributing authors of this volume represent diverse backgrounds and disciplines, drawing on their experience and knowledge from psychology, education, philosophy, sociology, business, computer science, and linguistics. It should come as no surprise then, that this broad mix of individuals has produced such an eclectic, disparate, and sometimes contradictory spectrum of writing styles, arguments, and perspectives. In a sense, the range of ideas represented in this book is analogous to the content found on the social web—the patchwork or bricolage of ideas and artifacts we might refer to less eloquently as the "mashup." Well, it is our hope that this mashup of commentaries and narratives will offer the reader much food for thought. If there is one unifying feature of the book however, it must be the central theme of cybercultures. As the title indicates, this book highlights the shifting and emergent features that represent life online, specifically in and around the territory of e-learning. Cybercultures in themselves are complex conglomerations of ideas, philosophies, concepts, and theories, some of which are fiercely contradictory. As a construct, "cyberculture" is a result of sustained attempts by diverse groups of people to make sense of multifarious activities, linguistic codes, and practices in complicated and ever-changing settings. It is an impossibly convoluted field. Any valid understanding of cybercultures

Connected Minds, Emerging Cultures: Cybercultures in Online Learning
pp. xi–xviii

can only be gained from living within it, and as Bell (2001, p. 2) suggests, it is "made up of people, machines and stories in everyday life."

Although this book contains a mix of perspectives, as the chapters progress, readers should detect some common threads. Technology-mediated activities are featured throughout, each evoking its particular cultural nuances and, as Derrick de Kerckhove (1997) has eloquently argued, technology acts as the skin of culture. All the authors are passionate about their subjects, every one engages critically with his or her topics, and each is fully committed to the belief that e-learning is a vitally important component in the future of education. All of the authors believe that digital learning environments will contribute massively to the success of the information society we now inhabit. Each is intent on exploration of the touchstone of "any time, any place" learning where temporal and spatial contexts cease to become barriers to learning, and where the boundaries are blurring between the formal and informal.

Drawing together an edited volume about cyberculture, or about hypertextual environments, or about e-learning—all of which provide the backbone of this volume—has been an interesting and challenging task. It prompts me to echo the sentiments of David Bell (2001) who sees the book as an anachronism in the era of the World Wide Web. Standard texts such as this are linear and finite—they have a beginning and an ending. Hypertexts by contrast, are nonlinear and infinite—they are always a work in progress and, with the inception of Web 2.0 open structures, are receptive of contributions from all. Readers may consider it somewhat curious then, that such a topic should be presented in a manner that is anachronistic. This volume can be considered a remnant of the old culture of textuality and paper-based artifacts, which still have a role to play in the modern culture of communication. I believe that it will continue to maintain a significant place in our culture, because old technologies generally form the foundation for new and emerging technologies. This can be witnessed in almost any modern classroom, where overhead projectors sit comfortably alongside fully interactive whiteboard technologies. The traditional sits comfortably with the new. In this linear book, we have tried the impossible—to represent the nonlinear characteristic of the Web within a linear artifact. So see this book for what it is: a small, handheld, paper-based repository of ideas, commentaries, and discourse around a concept that is largely already beyond its reach, but which is still inexorably intertwined with it. If all else fails, you can create your own hyperlinks by dipping into the book randomly.

Each of the authors invited to contribute to this book were keen to participate, and all have stories to tell of how they have traveled on their own personal cyberculture journey. As the editor of this book, I am fortunate to have encountered many of the authors over the last 2 years, either personally or through their writings and Web-based publications, and each of them has gained my respect. Each, I believe, has contributed significantly toward our developing understanding of the way in which cybercultures are emerging from the world of e-learning and how digital identities and microcultures are being shaped as a result.

This book is divided into four sections. In Part I, which has been titled "Digital Subcultures," we begin an exploration of "culture" and attempt to locate the learner within a number of digital subcultures that have arisen around new and emerging technologies such as mobile and handheld devices, collaborative online spaces, and podcasting. The chapters in this section represent attempts by the authors to demonstrate that there are many subdivisions present on the Web, and that online learners cannot and should not be represented as one vast amorphous mass of "Internet" users.

In the first section there are four chapters about digital subcultures, the first of which focuses on learning within the collaborative online spaces increasingly popular in education. The chapter showcases some of the recent research into the use of wikis in higher education and I approach this topic armed with an extensive data set derived from the discussion group postings of my online teacher trainee groups. I conclude that wikis are a powerful and as yet relatively untapped online collaborative tool that has the potential to promote deeper engagement with learning.

The second chapter, by John Traxler, dwells on the realities and possibilities of the mobile culture, made possible by cellular and wireless technologies that are now pervasive in the Western world and in the process of becoming a global phenomenon. Although the future of mobile technology seems robust, Traxler raises a number of important questions about its impact on learners, teachers, communities, and society in general. He offers to evaluate this impact through an exploration of the impact of mobile technology on culture, community, discourse, identity, and their educational implications. The author attempts to reconcile the perception that discrete mobile subcultures exist with the perception that all cultures are somehow transformed by mobility.

Chapter 3, written by Palitha Edirisingha, reveals that a "listening" subculture has grown up around the increasingly popular podcasting technologies. In his chapter, Edirisingha traces the development of podcasting through media, entertainment, and technology industries and the transformation of a broadcast tool into a learning tool. He identifies a variety factors that have an impact on the formation of such a listening culture. He highlights some of the lessons learned from empirical studies, predominantly from an international study called IMPALA. Edirisingha concludes by offering insights into how podcasting can be effectively used for learning, with a focus on higher education.

Part I concludes with chapter 4, in which Mark Kramer explores the ways students are beginning to harness mobile networked-enabled technologies to create new cultures of learning and collaboration. Kramer argues that these new movements can best be understood as a ubiquitous and pervasive learning culture in which anyone can engage in a form of learning that takes place independent of time and location. He concludes by suggesting that this new culture of ubiquitous and pervasive learning is inevitable, but warns that it may take time to become established in education.

Part II, which has been designated "Roles and Identities," covers a range of ideas about how the individual copes within the new cyber landscape. Several key questions are addressed: How do learners maintain a constant identity in an ever-shifting digital world in which multiple identities and roles are possible? Do they adopt alternative personae as easily as they create new avatars within multi-user virtual environments? Does the creation of an avatar create something new within the identity of the individual? And are real life identities influenced by what the individual does whilst within a cyber-identity?

Hugh Miller and Jill Arnold open this section with an investigation into cyber-identities and the presentation of self within online environments. They show how social rules governing presence in virtual environments are as important as those that apply in embodied life. Miller and Arnold argue that people construct and reconstruct themselves in cyberspace in ways that are subject to cultural restrictions on both sides of the screen, as well as being influenced by the affordances offered by new media. They suggest that to learn not only requires gaining a new understanding of the world, but it also requires a readjustment of one's *self*.

In chapter 6, I take the reader on a journey through the various digital tribes and virtual clans I believe are emerging due to intensive and sustained use of new technologies. I argue that new tribes and clans are emerging as a direct result of sustained interaction with technology. I contend that tribal identity shapes individual identity in cyberworlds, and that digital tools and networks provide ideal environments within which new cultural transmission propagates. Clans tend to emerge within tribes as cultural definitions and the generation of artefacts become more pronounced. Finally I assert that there may be one single "digital tribe" in the broadest sense of its meaning, but analysis of the many social activities found on the Web indicates that many subsets of this large digital tribe exist—the "virtual clans."

In a robustly written chapter on the digital gaming cultures, Nicola Whitton explores how games can be positioned in higher education. Chapter 7 considers the acceptability of computer game-based learning in the context of university education. Whitton discusses the potential of computer games in relation to theories of learning and examines the conceptions of a cognitively different type of learner. She challenges the notion that these learners find computer games the ideal environment in which to learn. Whitton discusses student game preferences in terms of genre and the types of computer game that may be more appropriate for learning, and aspects of computer game design that may influence student use. The chapter concludes with a consideration of the benefits and challenges of computer games for learning and teaching in tertiary education.

In Chapter 8, Leon James describes the creation and management of an ongoing course-integrated Web community at a college social science course in Hawaii. Each student enrolled in the course automatically adopts cyber-community membership by reading, processing, and identifying with the reports of prior generation students, and then contributing his or her own reports to the cumulatively expanding "generational curriculum" topics. The benefits of such an approach are discussed in terms of psychological models of acculturation, identification, cyber-citizenship, and the student as scientist model functioning in a Web environment that is increasingly shaped by human social processes. James concludes that the project demonstrates that a course-integrated online learning activity can be effective in producing cybercitizens by managing the students' interactional procedures through the generational community-classroom approach.

Graham Attwell conducts the reader through a journey that examines the social dimensions of personal learning environments in Chapter 9. His chapter examines the social impact of Personal Learning Environments (PLEs). Attwell expects that PLEs will exert a profound influence over established teaching and learning systems and will radically change pedagogic approaches to learning, knowledge development, and sharing. He suggests that the emergence of PLEs and the widespread interest in PLEs are a reaction to the changing ways in which people are using technology for learning. He argues that PLEs result from new societal demands for education and are a response to changing forms of knowledge usage within society.

Part III, titled "Cyber Perspectives," opens up the debate about cyberculture through a number of contrasting views and philosophical positions.

In Chapter 10, titled "Emerging Online Practices," Viv Tucker draws on her experience as an online tutor, to take a poststructural philosophical feminist position as she describes her approach to online postgraduate initial teacher training. She introduces a model that critically resists the limitations of the instrumental approach and argues instead for a teaching and learning model where contemporary poststructural theory can radically inform emerging online practices.

Ken Gale takes a poststructural perspective as he examines cyberculture in the context of online learning. Gale's chapter draws on postmodern philosophies in order to secure a deeper understanding of cybercultures through their use of various deconstructive strategies. He argues that nomadic inquiry can nurture ever-changing structures of multiplicity and interconnectedness in online environments. His chapter explores a number of possible "folds and intersections" between poststructural philosophies and digital learning practices. Gale proposes that new technologies can create many new learning opportunities that bridge the space between the institution and enquiring mind.

Vasi van Deventer's chapter is titled "Cyborg Theory and Learning." In this pivotal chapter, he describes the evolution of the human cyborg. He draws on history, theory, and philosophy to argue that theorists are correct when they assert that we are a lot further down the road to becoming cyborgs than we may think. Van Deventer discusses the implications for education and concludes that human minds have an adaptability and plasticity, enabling students to interface with any technology that is useful to their purpose. He also argues that these students actually become "learning cyborgs," developing a symbiotic relationship with technology that blurs traditional distinctions.

Chapter 13 concludes Part III with a narrative titled "Transfer Through Learning Flexibility and Hypertextuality." Written by Gorg Mallia, this chapter argues that hypertext and hypermedia are causing transformations that reach a long way beyond the well-researched and largely accepted social interaction types. Mallia suggests that technological immersion is causing social and cultural change, and fears that this may contribute toward diminishing personal user participation in society.

In the final section of this volume, Part IV, we present four case studies drawn from contrasting training and learning cultures, examining the cultures of corporate e-learning, cybercriminality, language evolution, and social networking.

David Guralnick and Deb Larson represent the corporate training sector view in chapter 14. They write from the perspective of the company employee and explore the cultural basis of corporate e-learning. Guralnick and Larson describe the current state of employee cyberculture and propose that companies would be far better off using a strategic design approach to e-learning and corporate intranets, one based on helping employees and engaging them in their work. By doing so, companies will be able to integrate technology into employees' work lives in a way that improves their performance and boosts their morale and commitment.

Steven Furnell's chapter, "Cybercrime in Society," presents a disturbing account of the current risks and threats to e-learners and society in general from a number of criminal activities, including malware (viruses), hacking, and identity theft. There is a suggestion throughout that a criminal culture exists alongside other cultures within online life, waiting for the opportunity to transgress by exploiting network weaknesses. Through this chapter, Furnell provides a timely wake-up call for users of the Internet who believe themselves to be safe, and suggests ways in which we can all protect ourselves from the more unsavory elements of the online culture. The penultimate chapter, by Tim Shortis, offers an explanatory framework for the respellings associated with new technology text formats such as e-mail, Internet chat, SMS text messaging, and instant messaging. He considers some of the features and patterns of British adolescents' uses of such writing and technology-enabled semiotics. Shortis argues that technology has encouraged an extended set of orthographies which users draw u on to inflect their purposes and project their identities. He holds that such respelling is not a new phenomenon. Shortis goes on to consider the contextual pressures which act on users' choices and argues that technology has re-regulated what counts as spelling, which challenges the official educational discourses of literacy, particularly where they apply to orthography.

The final chapter in this volume is titled "Imagined Worlds, Emerging Cultures." It was written as a collaborative project with Helen Keegan and we used Google docs to write together across the distance. In this chapter, we present perspectives on cybercultures as "imagined worlds" in education and focus on how emerging online social spaces impact on individual perceptions and practices. We pay particular attention to the social networking and multiuser virtual environment cultures, where imagination is unleashed, but where friendship can be superficial. We focus on old and new media cultures and the shift in perception over issues such as ownership, intellectual property, copyright, personal identity, and privacy. The chapter examines cultural values such as privacy, identity, and ownership and highlights two "digital clan" cultures—Facebookers and Flickrites. We analyze some similarities and differences in an attempt to explore how tribal cultures develop around and through imagined worlds.

Such a spectrum of perspectives on cyberculture must hold something for everyone. It is our hope that readers will find the ideas contained within the book challenging and inspiring. Ultimately, we hope that teachers and lecturers and indeed all those involved in education will be able to take at least some of these ideas and apply them to their own professional practice. The result, we trust, will be a better understanding of the practices and processes that are inherent in online life, and that this better understanding will ultimately encourage better teaching and learn-ing.

REFERENCES

Bell, D. (2001). *An introduction to cybercultures.* London: Routledge.
de Kerckhove, D. (1997). *The skin of culture: Investigating the new electronic reality.* London: Kogan Page.

PART I

DIGITAL SUBCULTURES

CHAPTER 1

LEARNING IN COLLABORATIVE SPACES

Encouraging a Culture of Sharing

Steve Wheeler

THE SOCIAL WEB

There is a sense that the World Wide Web is evolving, and as it does so, it is entering into a new phase of development (Hill, 2008). Most would agree that the Web is in the process of being transformed from a finite and logo-centric space toward an almost infinite space defined by imagery and multitextuality. There are also clear indications that the Web is becoming increasingly interactive and participatory—hence its "social web" tag.

There has been much rhetoric about the pervasiveness of the Internet as a surrogate for friendship, conversation, and entertainment. In essence, this may hold some truth, because a large proportion of real-world experiences and contexts *can* be replicated or at least mediated through online tools and services. Ultimately, it is this open and participatory nature of the present Web that is influencing pedagogy and

Connected Minds, Emerging Cultures: Cybercultures in Online Learning
pp. 3–16
Copyright © 2009 by Information Age Publishing

challenging traditional roles. This "social" Web enables the repurposing of existing content, overlayering and mashing up of content, user generation of content, and social networking, all of which are expanding at an unprecedented rate.

One of the most marked and transformative emergent features of the Web is the transition from the "stickiness" of the early Web (which we shall call "Web 1.0"—where users could do little more than read the content that had been placed on a Web site) toward a socially rich and democratic type of Web that encourages user participation to extend beyond mere guestbook comment boxes. Web 1.0 has been characterized as housing a set of products and commodities that were created at a source and then made available to users (Lankshear & Knobel, 2006). By contrast, the new and emergent features of the social Web are created and maintained by the users themselves, and through iterative use, the artifacts actually improve in quality and gain deeper relevance for the group. This is a key feature of the social online spaces many now refer to collectively as Web 2.0 (O'Reilly, 2005).

The social Web is characterized by the richness of interpersonal experience users enjoy when they use its tools and services. It is this shift in emphasis and a repurposing of the "old" Web spaces into shared environments that is shaping the new digital territories in which the information age is redefining itself. It is this new dynamic that is creating the spaces that the "digital natives," the so-called "net generation," are colonizing. We have noticed a distinct migration from text to hypertext and then toward hypermedia, and we now observe a relentless progression from reading to reading/writing/participation made possible by open architecture tools.

In this chapter, we will explore the concept of one aspect of the social Web known as the wiki. One of the most familiar wiki examples is Wikipedia, an online encyclopedia that contains the accumulated lay-knowledge of many thousands of ordinary people. Such open architecture tools on the social Web are teeming with opportunities for the propagation of new and emerging digital subcultures. Some believe that tools such as wikis are used simply as online repositories in which ideas can be dumped for later use. Others take a narrower view, believing that wikis and other open content tools represent a threat to the integrity of knowledge and contribute toward an undermining of the authority of experts and specialists (Keen, 2006). In truth, wikis can be exactly what their mass of users wishes them to be. Nevertheless, opinions about wikis and other social software tools are divided and opposing camps have taken their stances, some exhibiting almost tribelike attributes. Later in this volume there are chapters that more deeply investigate the idea of digital tribes and clans, emerging practices and protocols, literacies and mores, and other social issues such as criminal activity and language use that are emerging from this relentlessly expanding social web.

This chapter, however, seeks to provide an overview of the cultural topography of the open content Web, by delineating some of the practices that are appearing in educational contexts. The chapter will also evaluate some of the applications of wikis in formal learning and teaching. A study into the integration of this tool into the initial teacher-training curriculum of one British university ($N = 237$) is reviewed and the key findings of the study presented.

First, then, we will examine how wikis can be used to promote collaborative learning and focus in particular on student perceptions of their immersion into a new culture of learning.

CREATING KNOWLEDGE

The idea that knowledge can be created by learners is not a new one, but it is an idea that still sits a little uncomfortably in the minds of some teachers. The notion of "user-generated content" is currently exercising the minds of many in the education profession and generating much debate in the academic press. The wiki is a tool that can be used to create online content, and it has quickly become a favorite across all sectors of education (Horizon, 2007). The word "wiki" was coined by Ward Cunningham, and comes from the Hawaiian *wiki-wiki*, which is translated as "to hurry up." Wikis are well-named because they do enable rapid and easy authoring direct to the Web. Wiki pages can be used by any user to publish new content direct to the Web, including text, images, and hyperlinks, to edit existing content. Moreover, because the wiki is fluid and open to all, and is thus susceptible to vandalism, it is possible to "roll back" to previous versions through a "page history" utility, if necessary. Students can develop their own knowledge repository quite freely using wikis, and then share it with their community of interest. They need rarely study alone because they have an open opportunity to participate in a technologically-mediated social space conducive to the formation of communities of practice (Kamel Boulos, Maramba, & Wheeler, 2006).

Wikis enable students to work collaboratively to generate, mix, edit, and synthesize subject-specific knowledge within a shared and openly accessible digital space. The combined knowledge of the group, dubbed "the wisdom of the crowd," is assumed to be greater than that of the individual, and the group gains ownership; those that read the wiki space are the same group that created it (Owen, Grant, Sayers, & Facer, 2006). While this "architecture of participation" (O'Reilly, 2004) has obvious attractions to the digital generation, what remains contentious is the extent to which the lay-generation of digital knowledge artifacts is appropriate to professional education. Critics point out that user-generated content can be prone to error and can perpetuate errors through self-propagation of its own content through hyperlinks and duplication.

There are, of course, no guarantees for accuracy and veracity on a wiki, although a recent survey conducted through the journal *Nature* found that Wikipedia, one of the most popular wiki-knowledge repositories, is at least as accurate as *Encyclopaedia Britannica* (Terdiman, 2006). Wikis are susceptible to vandalism and malware (virus) attacks (Terdiman, 2006) so those moderating their use need to be vigilant. Although the openness of wikis creates opportunities for the deliberate sabotage, Owen et al. (2006) point out that there is often a critical mass of users who have sufficient ownership of the wiki to quickly intervene and clean up unwanted postings and recover the site. RSS (Really Simple Syndication) feeds alert community members to any changes that have been made to content, so that validation of the entries can be undertaken quickly and effectively (Wheeler, Yeomans, & Wheeler, 2008). "Roll-back" is a common feature of most wikis, and this correction tool can be used to access the entire history of a page so that it can be restored to a previous condition if for any reason the additions need to be removed.

Doubt therefore hangs over the concept of student content creation and whether it will ever be legitimized by the formalized education community. Clearly, there are many issues that influence the use of wiki-based learning activities. One of the most important challenges teachers need to countenance comes from the open, user-centred nature of the wiki and the potential problems that can arise when student content is allowed to be freely generated.

SOME LEARNING BENEFITS

A growing number of teachers and lecturers have discovered the potential of wikis to transform the learning experience through the promotion of a sharing culture. One notable potential is the extent to which student centred learning can be facilitated. Several high-level thinking skills and socially rich activities can be supported by wikis when they serve as repositories for progressive and shared generation of knowledge artifacts. Further, as we have already seen, wiki content can become a focal point of interest for developing communities of practice. It is highly desirable to have quick access to a store of knowledge about specific interests and up-to-date topics, linked to additional online resources, particularly when it has been created in collaboration with one's own specialized community of practice.

Wikis offer appropriate environments where students can develop stronger social ties, even when they are separated geographically from one another. They can be used as tools to enable distributed groups to "draw together" by encouraging each physically dislocated member to create a specific section or "stub" on the wiki. Others are then encouraged to add to the wiki stubs throughout the course of a study program. Individual students could be assigned the task of finding relevant and reliable Web sites they can hyperlink back to the main wiki. Each student might also be assigned a specific time period during which they have responsibility to "patrol" the wiki to ensure it is kept free from sabotage or defacement.

There is a moderator role for teachers in the use of wikis. They will need to encourage all group members to contribute to the knowledge pool, thereby fostering a sense of community, but it is inevitable that some students will contribute more content than others. If work on the wiki is being assessed, there patently needs to be some consideration over how to track who contributed what to the finished piece of work. Teachers should therefore be vigilant for evidence of social loafing. In a wiki context this can be observed where the contribution rate for some students is disproportionately less than others. Social loafing is to an extent inevitable, but in wiki and other online activity, it is sometimes easier to perpetrate. However, providing all members are deemed to have contributed something within a defined period, teachers might be prudent to adopt a laissez-faire attitude. Previous studies have shown that some students learn even when they do not directly contribute toward a message board, in what has been termed "lurking" (Beaudoin, 2002), or legitimate peripheral participation (Lave & Wenger, 1991). Finally, it is important to understand that wikis are group-specific and will likely hold no interest for future groups, who perceive no clear ownership. In one way, then, wikis can be compared to small furry animals—they grow quickly, live a short but busy life, and then they die.

FOLKSONOMIES

Today's students are very good at organizing their own learning. Many now bookmark useful Web sites so that others can benefit later from their sifting and selecting. The more tech-savvy students can now be seen "socially tagging" a particularly useful Web resource using services such as del.icio.us so that it becomes highly visible in a shared space. This process has a democratic basis reflecting the wisdom of crowds. This process can also be taken a step further. Students can vote for those they consider to be the most useful sites or vote against those they consider to be less valuable, using services such as Digg or Reddit. Using these tools, they are able to alert people with similar interests to sites they should visit and sites that are best avoided. Social tagging therefore replaces traditional, externally imposed hierarchies of categorization (the taxonomy) with a more democratic and user-focused process of content organization known as a "folksonomy." Arguably, folksonomies provide a more fluid and accurate representation of the current needs and aspirations of the user group (Owen et al., 2006) which is responsive to change as group interests develop (Kamel Boulos et al., 2006). Further, the social tagging of wiki pages makes their content more visible to a larger audience of readers through search engine listings. Larger audiences often encourage students to be more accurate in their construction of wiki pages when they consider their "hidden audience."

THE STUDY

Two hundred thirty-seven students drawn from the first and second years of the Post-Compulsory Education and Training (PCET) program participated in the study. Most students were mature (i.e., over 25 years old) and the majority were employed by local colleges or training agencies to teach adults, and so were studying on a part-time basis. Some were serving in the military, the prison service, or the police, so often studied within their own institutions. Each participated in this evaluative study voluntarily and all of the contributions were anonymized. The students used their wiki regularly during their classroom sessions and also outside of formal contact time as a place in which they could create and edit work from their learning activities, store useful links to resources, and as a forum for discussion. The wiki was also used in a blended learning approach to optimize classroom contact time and provide an out-of-campus forum for developing discussions and supporting collaborative learning activities. Students were invited via the integrated discussion board to post their views on their use of the wiki. Participants were also invited to complete a postmodule Likert-scale questionnaire.

Joined-Up Thinking

From 2007 to 2008, wikis were fully integrated into the curriculum of initial teacher education at the University of Plymouth. They have the goal of becoming shared repositories of knowledge, where the knowledge base grows over a period of time (Godwin-Jones, 2003). Generally, the wikis are used outside of the main institutional provision of learning management systems, so that students can gain easier access at any time and from any location, and also so that other, nonuniversity Web users are able to view (but not edit or comment on) the work the students are doing. Subsequently, we are with their full knowledge exposing the students' work to public scrutiny. This has the effect of causing the students to think more clearly about the appropriateness and quality of the content they post to their wiki, and encourages them to edit more judiciously and accurately (Wheeler et al., 2008).

Wiki Content Generation

The introduction of the wiki concept into a conservative environment such as the classroom requires all participants to adopt a new culture—one of cooperation and sharing. When faced with the prospect that they can actually generate content and post it to the World Wide Web, or that they can visit a Web site and edit it while they are reading, many students are at first surprised. Some are excited and others daunted by this revelation. We could speculate that those who welcome this experience are already in some way connected to the culture of Web 2.0 and may have accounts with social networking sites such as MySpace or Facebook. They may be familiar with, or regular users of, Flickr or YouTube and be already *au fait* with the protocols that are imposed within these microcultures. Conversely, those who are reluctant or anxious about posting content to the Web may have no conception of the social Web and therefore will need to work a little harder to assimilate the new culture of sharing through content generation. Eventually, as they assimilate into the culture, they begin to feel less reluctant to explore the ways in which they can create content that enables them to learn and recall. It is only later, as they work within shared spaces, that learners understand how they can use wikis to collaborate and join up their ideas. Some never make this transition, and refuse to allow their work to be edited by others, assuming some form of protective ownership over their contributions (Wheeler et al., 2008).

Participating in a culture of sharing in an online space is not just about familiarizing oneself with the concept of being able to contribute to a Web site and collaborate together in the generation of knowledge artifacts. It is also about relinquishing ownership of your contributions. Previously, all Web users could do was read what the Webmaster had determined would be the content on a Web site. This is as alien a concept to some learners as the introduction of videoconferencing was to students in the 1990s. Then, students had to come to terms with the idea that they could "talk to the TV" and it would actually talk back to them. Now the readers become the writers and what they write is instantly placed into a public arena for scrutiny, criticism, and editing.

Wikipedians

What are the expectations of those who are immersed in the open online culture of Wikipedia? It is often the case that Wikipedians acquire more knowledge than they already possess about a given subject through regular visits. Sometimes they find what they want, and then leave. Others may become sidetracked and begin to explore related hyperlinks to their original quest, thereby ending up in tangential activities. Still others become so engaged in the subject that they involve themselves at a deeper level, register as an editor, and then contribute to the page(s) in question as a regular contributor toward the knowledge.

There is a sense that open content wiki-based resources such as Wikipedia are a work in progress that can never reach a point of completion. On the contrary, however, in many cases wiki pages tend over time to achieve a critical mass of content made up of text, hyperlinks, and graphics. It is then that they achieve a point of inertia where little or no new content will be posted. Others, particularly wiki pages with an emotive or controversial nature, can achieve a state of flux in which it becomes necessary to impose a notice tag that warns visitors that content is in dispute and should not be completely trusted for its accuracy or veracity. Such a work in progress may also achieve a state of inertia, but this is often caused by the page being either closed to contributions or rapid and widespread editing that descends into a furious flaming war between two or more opposing groups of contributors.

The WikiLit Project

The introduction of the minimum core curriculum into postcompulsory education and training programs across the United Kingdom has been inevitable. There has long been a discrepancy between the professional standards of compulsory teacher education (Qualified Teacher Status—QTS) and postcompulsory teaching (Qualified Teacher of Learning Support—QTLS). The introduction of the minimum core skills in 2004 as a mandatory requirement in the United Kingdom thus creates some parity of competency across all the education sectors. The minimum core is made up of four components that all teachers training for a qualification to teach post-14 education and achieve QTLS must now demonstrate their competence in. The four core skills are numeracy, literacy, language, and information and communication technology (ICT). The WikiLit project addresses the requirement for students to gather evidence of their skills, by providing an online alternative to deliver activities designed to acquire the skills. Wikis were created for each group housing secure digital environments so that students could collaboratively create content, discuss learning topics, and acquire skills by systematic progression through the wiki-based minimum core activities.

Student Views

Data were collected from students through the use of the discussion boards that were linked to each of the pages in any specific space. All students were also sent a questionnaire to answer. Students were asked a number of questions about their participation in the wiki activities, and those who answered did so in the knowledge that their comments might be selected to be used in research in an anonymized manner. The names of all students in this section are therefore pseudonyms and the contributions below are a small representative sample of the extensive data set.

One student, Jane, recognized a key function of the wiki to provide a meeting place for the group as a surrogate for face-to-face meeting. She saw the site as a useful consolidation tool for learning and that it served as a supportive environment:

> I think the Wiki is a useful tool for consolidating the group—I certainly feel as if I am more in touch with the group than I would do if we did not have the wiki to interact with, particularly as we are only together for two days a week. It feels somehow "supportive."

Over a short period of time using the wiki on a regular basis, some students began to adopt the culture of sharing, and valued the enhanced capability for discussion. Some overcome their initial reticence to contribute once they discovered the conversational nature of the wiki. Julie, for example, recognized the value of dialogue with others and a greater appreciation of the skills of interpersonal communication:

> In using the wiki space, it has enabled me to instigate a form of dialogue with my peers and tutors in reference to the PGCE course. It also highlighted to me the importance of using correct language, grammar in an e-mail and respecting protocol rules of communication.

Andrew believed that the activities on the wiki enabled him to gather evidence to show competence in a number of key skills:

> The extent the wiki has helped my typing skills, has improved my one fingered keyboard typing to a two handed more competent key board specialist. Helpful communications with new wiki users has aided me in my tasks and given me a better understanding of how the internet works and how this powerful tool is helping me expand my knowledge.

Robert, a father of four children and a serving officer in the Royal Navy, leads a very busy life. He appreciated that the wiki provided a supplementary means of learning, seeing it as an opportunity to time-shift his study activities:

> Although initially logging on with my work e-mail address, it has become progressively obvious that Wikis and Work are not compatible. Finding time to navigate around the Wikispace requires thought and consideration away from the stresses of the working environment. I changed my e-mail address to my home system and immediately found the environment peaceful and more conducive to the wiki requirements. As you can see by the time of posting (currently 2330), the use of the Wikispace will be predominately a late evening tool.

Some students experienced anxiety or confusion when they were first confronted with the wiki, but many, such as Cheryl, eventually saw some practical benefits:

> I wasn't keen on joining the wiki, I have little desire to talk electronically. I did however learn about links and down loading objects like photographs from my PC onto the wiki.

Another, Amy, recollected her initial problems using the wiki:

> I did struggle with the wiki initially eg trying to set up links and setting up new pages but I found with a bit of patience and perseverance I was able to do it in the end.

Others found the wiki activities constraining or irrelevant, and resented the imposition of structure onto a supposedly unstructured and open online environment. Sharon, for example, disliked the mandatory elements:

> It feels like a stick to beat us with—it is mandatory to attend these sessions/ do the activities/learn in this way. Whatever happened to autonomy?

The wiki was viewed by Paula as a friendlier, less formal environment than the institutional learning management systems and online discussion boards she had previously experienced. However, she was astute in realizing that a critical mass of student engagement is necessary to ensure the success of the wiki.

> You are relying on everyone to use it regularly to get the full benefit so users have to be engaged with it in some way. Some of the other student communities (University of Plymouth Colleges for example) have set up a discussion forum but this seems to be a far more engaging and user friendly interface. It will be interesting to see how it develops over the year. I think that you need to feel fairly comfortable with ICT to post up here and it might be hard work to get going with some groups.

Limitations were identified by many students during the first few weeks of the wiki activities. Although she welcomed the concept of open and accessible contact and content, Paula, noted that there was a compelling aspect to the wiki that might not be beneficial for some students:

> I enjoy the fact that the wiki space is there although if there are a lot of other things going on, it does seem to have a tyrannical aspect to it. On the whole though I think it is beneficial and I really like the idea that we can use it once we have finished the course to keep in touch, share ideas and resources etc.

A competency element was also deemed necessary for success by some respondents. Neil recognized that both skill and confidence played a part in the success of the wiki as a collaborative online space. He saw that there was a potential for the wiki to be a confusing place, particularly because it quickly expanded in size and content volume:

> The success of how useful it is will be totally dependent on the group members gaining the experience and confidence to be able to make best use of the space. I think at the moment you could quite easily post something onto a wiki page and it be completely missed by the other members of the group. Not because they are not interested but through lack of wiki expertise.

There was evidence throughout the program of study that students began to help each other by sharing information, both in response to pleas for help, and also in the proactive posting of advice to the rest of the group when a fix or answer to a common problem had been found. Several problems and limitations of the wiki were highlighted by the students during this kind of activity. Jenny, for example, pointed out that due to the collaborative nature of the wiki activities, and the loss of immediate feedback or conversation when in an online mode of study, learning was actually slowed down for her. This distance barrier ultimately prompted the group to arrange some face-to-face meetings:

The sets backs in using the wiki space are when you have to work in a collaborative group. You still need to meet up with your peers to undergo the collaborative activities as, via e-mail, it could slow the project down due to peoples' work commitments in relation to writing e-mails and waiting for feedback.

Andrew also reported that due to the asynchronous nature of the wiki, there was a problem with slow feedback from peers, although he thought it was inherently a good tool for communication with the rest of the group:

not as quick as the phone but a good communications device, instant messages sent to multiple personnel (not always a quick answer). Vast amount of people on the wiki sites that can help you find that important information. Limitations: not guaranteed an answer immediately, people can edit your work; people are not always available to use the computer all the time.

Roger, a student at one of the partner colleges, saw collaborative learning as a benefit and experienced no problems waiting for responses from his peer group. It appears that the culture of his group differed to that of Jenny's and Andrew's groups, with Roger's peers taking the responsibility to respond quickly to each other's posts and questions during regular visits to the wiki.

The main benefit is definitely the immediacy and interactivity and the possibility of sharing and solving problems with an online support group.

Finally, David experienced two of the perennial problems of students working in a collaborative online learning environment. He coped with it with good humor:

The main problem I had was logging on, then apparently erasing someone's work accidentally (not proven).

Many students experienced some form of inadvertent deletion of files during the first term of wiki use, but most were reassured when the team intervened to roll back to previous versions of the content. Once students were aware of this facility, they tended to adopt a more relaxed attitude to content generation, and one, Roger, created his own wikis for use at home with his family, and at work as a virtual learning environment (VLE) to support his own students:

I love the Wiki and it has inspired me to set one up for my family to use. I also think it will be a better, more flexible and interactive VLE for me to offer my yoga teacher training students who currently get info and PDFs (documents) off my Web site.

CONCLUSIONS

An examination of the comments from the students above reveals that although there appears to be a differential between the formalized culture of learning most are familiar with and the informalized, democratic (and sometimes chaotic) learning culture that is typical within the social Web, the gap is not too difficult to breach for most. Many students reported that they became more comfortable within a culture of sharing as time goes by, although in concurrence with the author's previous research findings (Kamel Boulos et al., 2006; Wheeler et al., 2008), many students remain reluctant to edit each other work. However, it is apparent from these and other comments that the wiki was successful in achieving its key purpose of providing a supplementary method for students to use to achieved their evidence gathering. It appears that a range of competencies were tacitly acquired, particularly in the areas of ICT and communication skills, through the regular use of the wiki.

The subcultural attributes of any given group appear to have a bearing on the perceptions of the students, with some acutely aware of a stalling effect when their peers do not respond quickly to messages, or fail to engage as fully as might be expected in a group work activity. Others by contrast, experience different problems, many of which derive from the strangeness of the wiki and an initial lack of familiarity in its use. Generally, the culture of sharing tends to emerge on the wiki over a period of time, particularly if the group meet regularly on a face-to-face basis, and where this is blended with the online activities. For future research, it will be essential to identify these factors and to determine to what extent the wiki open spaces can determine the quality of learning outcomes and experiences.

REFERENCES

Beaudoin, M. F. (2002). Learning or lurking? Tracking the invisible student. *Internet and Higher Education, 5*, 147-155.

Godwin-Jones, R. (2003). Blogs and wikis: Environments for online collaboration. *Language, Learning and Technology, 7*(2), 12-16.

Hill, C. (2008) *Teaching with e-learning in the lifelong learning sector.* Exeter, Devon, United Kingdom: Learning Matters.

Horizon Report. (2007). Retrieved September 22, 2008, from http://connect .educause.edu/library/ELI/2007HorizonReport/37041

Kamel Boulos, M. N., Maramba, I., & Wheeler, S. (2006). Wikis, blogs and pod-casts: A new generation of Web-based tools for virtual collaborative clinical practice and education. *BMC Medical Education 2006, 6*(41). Retrieved March 6, 2008 from: http://www.biomedcentral.com/content/pdf/1472-6920-6-41.pdf

Keen, A. (2006). *The cult of the amateur: How today's Internet is killing our culture and assaulting our economy.* London: Nicholas Brealey.

Lankshear, C., & Knobel, M. (2006). *New literacies: Everyday practices and classroom learning* (2nd ed.). Maidenhead, Windsor and Maidenhead, United Kingdom: Open University Press.

Lave, J., & Wenger, E. (1991). *Situated learning: Legitimate peripheral participation.* Cambridge, England: Cambridge University Press.

O'Reilly, T. (2004). *Open source paradigm shift.* Retrieved March 4, 2008 from http://tim.oreilly.com/articles/paradigmshift_0504.html

O'Reilly, T. (2005). *Design patterns and business models for the next generation of soft-ware.* Retrieved February 16, 2008, from http://www.oreillynet.com/pub/a/oreilly/tim/news/2005/09/30/what-is-web-20.html

Owen, M., Grant, L., Sayers, S., & Facer, K. (2006). *Opening education: Social soft-ware and learning.* Bristol, United Kingdom: Futurelab. Retrieved March 6, 2008, from www.futurelab.org.uk/research

Terdiman, D. (2006). Study: Wikipedia as accurate as Britannica. *CNET News.* Retrieved January 15, 2008 from http://news.cnet.com/2100-1038_3-5997332.html

Wheeler, S., Yeomans, P., & Wheeler, D. (2008) The good, the bad and the wiki: Evaluating student-generated content for collaborative learning. *British Journal of Educational Technology, 39*(6), 987-995.

CHAPTER 2

MOBILE SUBCULTURES

John Traxler

INTRODUCTION

Mobile and personal communication devices, systems and technologies are increasingly important in society, providing users with genuinely "any-time, anyplace" sources of contact, information, and entertainment, and access to resources and to each other. The exponential rise in the use of these devices in western industrialized nations—and everywhere else—raises questions about their impact on learners, teachers, communities, and society in general. This chapter offers an evaluation of this impact by exploring their impact on ideas of culture, community, discourse, identity, and their relationships to education, and tries to reconcile one perception that there now exist discrete mobile subcultures with another perception that all cultures are somehow transformed by mobility.

THE OBVIOUS QUANTITATIVE IMPACT

The obvious starting point for any consideration of the impact of mobile communications devices is their quantitative manifestations. On an almost weekly basis we hear about some record broken in terms of the vol-

Connected Minds, Emerging Cultures: Cybercultures in Online Learning
pp. 17–28
Copyright © 2009 by Information Age Publishing

ume of text messaging traffic (apparently 1 billion in a recent week in the United Kingdom in November 2007), we hear of the demise of the landline phone in the face of mobile phone take-up (which in some European countries has reached saturation and continues to rise), the demise of the camera (especially the analog camera) in the face of the camera-phone, and the demise of the music CD (and now the companies that produce them) in the face of music downloads. Equally, objectively and concretely, we see the relentless development and marketing of new handsets, of increased functionality, of greater bandwidth and connectivity, more protocols, new tariff structures, and more powerful and apparently "intuitive" interfaces, all of which testify to the vigor and diversity of mobile communications devices (and the systems, technologies and industries behind them) across many, if not most, of the world's cultures and societies.

It is obvious that mobile communications devices are pervasive and near universal and that in recent years, they have started to transform many aspects of our societies and cultures. Looking first at the more concrete and obvious manifestations, we see economic activity—for example, jobs, commodities, businesses, assets, transactions, and artifacts—that did not exist 5 or 6 years ago (and this is significant to education even if one subscribes to any narrowly utilitarian view of education servicing the economy) and that are growing at the expense of more-established economic sectors.

Most obviously, "m-commerce," the term for transacting business over mobile devices and mobile technologies, adds a new dimension in banking and financial transactions. Wizzit and Globe are two examples in the developing world, but the best documented one is from Kenya (Torma & Williams, 2007). M-Pesa was launched by Safaricom and more than 10,000 people have signed up, with around 8 million Kenyan shillings transferred so far, mostly in tiny denominations. Vodafone developed the service, which holds a 35% share in Safaricom. "We are effectively giving people ATM cards without them ever having to open a real bank account," said the chief executive of Safaricom, who called the money transfer concept the "next big thing" in mobile telephony. The service is simple and users hand over the cash to a registered agent—typically a retailer—who credits users' virtual account. Users can then send between 100 shillings (74p) and 35,000 shillings (£259) via text message to the desired recipient, even someone on a different mobile network, who cashes it at an agent by entering a secret code and showing identification (Rice, 2007). This example is interesting because it shows banking power moving away from the financial sector toward the telecommunications sector, and it shows how mobile devices can empower people and countries often cut off from other forms of technologically driven progress. This perhaps hints that mobile technologies may not merely reinforce or replicate earlier digital divides and could create mobile subcultures based around economic and commercial activity.

As well catalyzing new jobs, new businesses, and new artifacts, mobile technologies are changing the nature of work itself more subtly, especially the work of knowledge workers, including teachers and lecturers (and students). These technologies allow workers to work on the move, to work away from base and to work with "just-in-time" support improving quality, flexibility, and independence (Gayeski, 2002). This may also impose greater supervision and surveillance on previously autonomous workers, and may also de-skill workers. Mobile workers had enjoyed a certain freedom from time and space (e.g., their desk) but now relinquish control when they make themselves constantly visible and available to others. In addition, what were once private places become public territory. Moreover, what were once public places (such as restaurants, airport lounges, railway stations, and hotel lobbies) become private (professional and personal) through e-mail, messaging, text, and voice interaction. Working on the move extends far beyond the home office, or bringing the office home. Mobile technologies are transforming the way people manage their time, offering greater accessibility and flexibility (Perry, O'Hara, Sellen, Brown, & Harper, 2001). Mobile devices allow people to check their e-mail and perform many of their work activities anywhere they may be, known in some circles as the "day extender" syndrome (Sullivan, 2003), producing a mobile "presenteeism." Therefore, we see the erosion of the boundaries between personal and professional time and space and we see implications for learning insofar as it might be seen as work. In relation to work and jobs, there is clearly an emergent mobile culture, but also pockets of more highly mobile subcultures.

ETHICS AND CULTURES

Mobile technologies also have a more pervasive and personal impact on our lives and on the lives of learners, influencing many aspects of culture. In terms of crime and misbehavior, for example, mobile technologies are facilitating existing types of crime such as fraud or identity theft. They are also instrumental in wholly new and original types of crime, such as "happy-slapping" and "bluejacking," from the relatively mild (Haddon, 2007) to the fatally violent (British Broadcasting Corporation [BBC], 2006a). The latter uses Bluetooth technology (Thom-Santelli, Ainslie, & Gay, 2007) to transmit material, sometimes intimidating or offensive, anonymously to nearby devices prior to "pairing." In the words of one exponent, who set up and runs the bluejackQ (Bluejack You) Web site,

I came across the idea of bluejacking at an online discussion forum and it immediately struck me as a fun thing to do.... She said the "priceless" expression on the face of her first victim as he tried to work out what was going on has turned her into a regular bluejacker. "This, mixed with not knowing whether the victim will react in an amused/confused or negative way gives me an adrenaline rush," she said. (BBC, 2006b)

Another subculture defined by its relationship to mobile devices is documented by Rheingold (2002), who describes a group of mobile phone users in Stockholm who exchange SMS (Short Message Service) messages while on the public transport system in order to avoid fines for ticketless riding. These mobile fare jumpers alert each other to spot checks by transport officials by sending out short messages to a distribution list. Jonathon Donner of Microsoft (Donner, 2008) looks at the various ways the "missed call," the mobile call that rings but is not intended to be answered thereby signalling something but costing nothing, is used in different cultures around the world and provides evidence for cultures becoming more mobile as they each exploit the affordances of the mobile phone. Each of these activities, and the expectations and ethics that go with them, are the defining attributes of specific albeit overlapping mobile subcultures.

Mobile devices themselves have also actually defined specific subcultures; pagers, early mobile phones, and the Sony Walkman (du Gay et al., 1997) have each defined a mobile subculture in their time, and each of these subcultures appropriated the technology to say something about their own ethics and expectations. The language(s) of "txt" in its early days denoted the values of specific youth subcultures, but perhaps predictably these languages were co-opted and diluted by commerce and the "establishment." Vodacomm in South Africa, for example, now provides every subscriber with a dictionary of "txt," while the local education authority in Knowsley, Liverpool ran a program called KnowItAll aimed at teenagers and using "txt" to remind school children to revise school exams (www.bbc.co.uk/news).

Mobile devices, specifically mobile phones, have also been instrumental in catalyzing the creation of more transient mobile subcultures. The most obvious, because of press coverage, are "flash mobs," impromptu gatherings organized mainly by SMS for some brief and surreal activity before melting back into the crowd. Alongside this has been the exploitation of mobile technologies, usually SMS, to organize grass-roots or anti-establishment political rallies, demonstrations, and actions; for example, the use of SMS in the antigovernment protests in the Philippines that brought down President Joseph Estrada (Rafael, 2003).

A more unpleasant example occurred on December 11, 2005, in Sydney, Australia's Cronulla beach in the southern suburbs, where there was a race riot. As Goggin (2006) noted,

> At the very heart of this state of siege and the fear, outrage, and sadness that gripped those living in Sydney were the politics of transmission. The spark that set off this conflagration was widely believed to have been caused by the transmission of racist and violent "calls to arms" via mobile text messages. (para. 3)

All of these examples raise questions of technological and social determinism and of culture and affordances beyond the scope of this chapter, but nevertheless it is important to ask about the role and relative significance of mobile technologies in catalyzing and facilitating these various cultures and communities, and perhaps to ask about how our understanding of the relationships between technology, society, and culture are evolving with ubiquitous and pervasive mobile technologies. Ling (2004) provides a review of these issues from an appropriate perspective.

Social networking, the use of network software systems designed and built to increase the sense of community among groups of people, is rapidly becoming a phenomenon on mobile devices. Some systems are native to mobile devices. Twitter is one such system, providing free social networking and microblogging and allowing subscribers to send updates (140-character text-based posts called tweets) to the Twitter Web site by SMS or instant messaging. These updates are displayed on the subscriber's profile page and instantly delivered to users who have signed up to receive them. Subscribers can receive updates from the Twitter Web site, instant messaging, SMS, RSS (Really Simple Syndication), e-mail, or through an application. Twitter is popular in North America, whereas in Europe, Jaiku, another microblogging site, is the comparable phenomenon, this one letting subscribers' friends know not only what the subscribers are doing but also where they are (their "presence") via the mobile component. Jaiku's interface is more polished than Twitter's, but similar.

Until recently, however, the most popular social networking systems or sites have been Web based, not mobile, and have provided ways for subscribers to interact, usually by chat, messaging, e-mail, video, voice chat, file sharing, blogging, and discussion groups. They grow by invitation and trust-based recommender systems, and through social categories such as colleagues and school friends. The most popular sites combine many of these, with Facebook, MySpace, LinkedIn, Bebo, Hi5 and Orkut being the most widely used. However, these services and sites are starting to migrate to mobile devices as the power, speed, connectivity, capacity, functionality, and interfaces of the devices and networks improve and challenge computer-based systems. This is true too of other file-sharing Web sites, Web services suites, and an online community platform such as Flickr or You-Tube.

Facebook and other social software each define their own communities, cultures, and expectations. Facebook, for example, gives subscribers a wealth of tools for engaging with other subscribers, but acculturation is needed for the new subscriber to understand what is intrusive, prying, overfamiliar or inappropriate, and what is acceptable. On the other hand, some people have argued that mobile devices and technologies are leading to the erosion of physical, face-to-face communities. Kenneth Gergen (2002), for example, talks about absent presence, by which he means physically colocated groups, families in a living room, students in a seminar room, for example, all being connected online to other communities.

A recent development from Google on mobiles is an improved "local search experience." It is based on Google's belief that mobile search is often used to find area information such as cinema listings. The service is now available in the United Kingdom, France, Germany, and Canada, and has been available in the United States since March 2007. It is an interesting development, since mobile technologies are documented as instrumental in the creation of virtual communities and cultures at the expenses of physical ones, creating communities with little sense of locatedness (in spite of the ubiquitous "I'm on a train") but here we have mobile technologies introducing locatedness back into virtual communities and providing contextual knowledge.

PLACE, SPACE. AND TIME

Education happens in a variety of spaces and locations. Many of these were historically fixed or dedicated or discrete, but now "developments in mobile communications are leading to changes in the spatial and temporal ordering of social practices as increasingly fragmented 'time-space maps' are disconnected from many of the constraints of 'regionalisation' or 'presence-availability'" (Sheller, 2004a, p. 4).

Mobile technologies are eroding established notions of time as a common structure. We see the "approx-meeting" and the "multi-meeting" (Plant, 2000), "socially negotiated time" (Sørensen, Mathiassen, & Kakihara, 2002), and the "micro-co-ordination of everyday life" alongside the "softening of schedules" (Ling, 2004) afforded by mobile devices. Mobile devices are also eroding physical place as a predominant attribute of space. It is being diluted by "absent presence" (Gergen, 2002), the phenomenon of physically colocated groups all connected online elsewhere, and "simultaneity of place" (Plant, 2000) created by mobile phones, a physical space and a virtual space of conversational interaction, and an extension of physical space, through the creation and juxtaposition of a mobile "social space," whereas Varilio (2000) looks at Gergen's absent presence in a different way, saying "everything arrives without any need to depart" and talks about the instant availability of information leading to a disconnection from the environment, "closer to what is far away than what is beside us, we are becoming progressively detached from ourselves" (p. 83)

Furthermore, the relatively rigid distinctions within spaces, specifically between public and private spaces, are becoming more fluid. As Sheller, (2004b) has noted, they

> are becoming more "mobile" in two ways: first, there is an increasing tendency to slip between private and public modes of interaction, as a result of the new forms of fluid connectivity enabled by mobile communication technologies; and, second, there are opportunities for new kinds of publics to assemble or gel momentarily (and then just as quickly dissolve) as a result of newly emerging places and arenas for communication. (p. 39)

In fact, Geser (2004, p. 34) asks, "how can the stability of social institutions be guaranteed when it can no longer be anchored on the secure basis of immovable physical structures?"

Therefore, there is a relationship between the different spaces and different communities, cultures, and subcultures and each community will occupy them in different ways.

There are also changing relationships between spaces and the type of discourse that occupies them, since

> New degrees and kinds of personal communication or "keeping in touch" are now possible from shifting public locations. Rather than conversation being set aside as something one does at certain moments, for a delimited stretch of time, usually in a private space (or semi-private phone "box" or "booth"), there is now a constant flickering of conversation (Sheller, 2004a, p. 5),

but again differently defined for different subcultures.

Media players such as Apple iPods, as well as mobile phones, are part of these phenomena. As Bull (2005) has noted,

> The use of these mobile sound technologies informs us about how users attempt to "inhabit" the spaces within which they move. The use of these technologies appears to bind the disparate threads of much urban movement together, both "filling" the spaces "in-between" communication or meetings and structuring the spaces thus occupied. (p. 344)

Public spaces are thereby colonized by private activities as an antidote to the day-extender syndrome.

In reviewing literature from around the world, Ling (2007) says,

> The general sense is that mobile communication supports interaction within the small intimate group. It supports and extends our ability to engage in ritual interaction. While there is a strong need for co-present interaction in order to maintain the group, mobile communication extends this possibility beyond the here and now. It allows us to exchange bits of gossip, to banter and to flirt when the opportunity presents itself. (p. 200)

Not Gergen's absent presence, but all these remarks serve to illustrate the extent to mobile technologies are transforming and defining elements of culture and subculture. Accompanying them is a renegotiation of the various relationships and protocols that used to characterize each of these spaces. To take just one example, Murtagh (2002) describes the situation in which a mobile phone rings in public and as it is answered, a couple of responses are observed. First, the called party typically moves their gaze away from the direction of those present, to a neutral place. In some cases, the called party moves their head downward, turns their upper body, or steps away from those that are copresent. Strangers present typically look at the mobile user briefly and then return to what they were doing. If in a social group, others present often display body language to indicate that they are not listening in on the mobile phone conversation (i.e., they would speak among themselves, turn their upper body away from mobile phone user, or simply move away). This shows how we are evolving to manage the intrusion of virtual space into physical space. The converse is almost the coproximity event, where

> conversations in which callers' first topic involves noticing, telling or enquiring about their own location and/or that of others. A particular class of such conversations which blend mobility, technology and sociality into a particular form of social engagement, are those in which the caller frames the way she mentions her location into an assertion about her proximity to the caller's current location, or the caller's likely current location, or to landmarks that are meaningful to both participants and relevant to the ongoing situations. Such talk simultaneously constructs co-proximity as a noticeable fact (on the cognitive side), and an event to be noticed and mentioned (on the normative side). "Co-proximity events" are conversational accomplishments. (Licoppe, 2007, p. 181)

Other examples are the "civil inattention" and "tie-signs" (Goffman, 1971) whereby simultaneous mobile virtual and physical relationships are maintained. These are all examples of emergent mobile subcultures.

IDENTITY

Mobile technologies are also starting to impact on ideas of identity. Geser (2004) points out that "cell phones lend themselves to 'personalization': e.g. by choosing individual colours, ring tones, display images" (p. 6) and suggests that mobile phones are becoming synonymous with individuals as landlines become synonymous with entities such as houses, dormitories, firms and so on.

Anecdotally, within the phone company Nokia, mobile phones are known as "our new private parts" on account of our relationships with them and have become an integral prop to the body language of many users. Katz (2002) describes an archetypical American construction site where the gesture, display, and use of the mobile phone are highly differentiated down the work force's hierarchy.

KNOWLEDGE AND LEARNING

Mobile devices and technologies also have a direct and pervasive impact on knowledge itself, and how it is generated, transmitted, owned, valued, and consumed in our societies. At the most superficial level, they do finally deliver on the "anywhere, anytime" promise and apparently on other slogans too: "just-in-time" and "just-for-me." However, these may be less simple and benign than they seem.

First, knowledge is not an absolute. Certainly, it has been argued that it is socially determined and socially constructed but it has also always been mediated by its container, its medium, its repository. The earliest formats, the book and the lecture, originally constrained knowledge to a linear format, the book having at least usually some facilities of graphics, review, and organization. More recently, computers provided Web-based hyperlinked information. This was delivered with greater multimedia richness than books, but in smaller chunks governed by the heuristics of usability and increased nonlinear navigational complexity.

Handheld mobile devices can now deliver information in far smaller chunks but with a vastly increased navigational overhead. Clearly, these different formats must each affect on information and on knowledge in their different ways, on what is accessible and what is valued. With mobile devices, there is a concern that they serve up vast amounts of information and knowledge in small disconnected and trivial chunks. As T. S. Eliott (1934) said, "Where is the Life we have lost in living? Where is the wisdom we have lost in knowledge? Where is the knowledge we have lost in information?"

Second, search engines and knowledge bases can now serve up information that is uniquely customized to the user and their context, meaning their history, their location, their interests, their preferences and their environment. While this context-aware personalization seems attractive and desirable, there is also concern that knowledge and information become individualized, a fragmented "neoliberal nightmare" in which each user exists in his or her own unique information world.

Third, user-generated content, meaning in user-generated knowledge and user-generated information, is increasingly available on mobile technologies. Google and Wikipedia (originally as Wapedia) are the obvious examples and they both allow learners control over what they learn, unmediated by any formal institutional learning. They also allow learners to participate in creating learning through their contributions. This can take place through such systems as Wikipedia, but most conspicuously with mobile technologies through the activity of citizen-journalism, based on camera-phones, in which members of the public, using (usually) camera-phones, capture images of breaking news and post it straight onto shared file-space such as Flickr or YouTube. Journalism is apparently the first draft of history and is certainly one form of knowledge and here we see it generated without the intervention of professional journalists or centralized and controlling organizations perhaps from the perspectives of a mobile culture or particular mobile subcultures.

Fourthly, language and discourse are defining attributes of cultures and subcultures, including mobile ones, and learning is seen by many as a form of discourse (Pask, 1976). It is defined (or bounded) by perceptions of discourse, perhaps literally by educationalists who espouse the Laurillard conversational framework (2002), so learning must necessarily be redefined by those technologies redefining discourse and culture.

Last, Beetham (personal communication, 2007) has argued that modern computer technology brings in to sharp relief two differing conceptualizations of the relationship between knowledge and experience and the role of education and technology in mediating these relationships. Historically, the role of education has been to present a reductionist and foundationist account of reality within the classroom and now within the computer. Mobile technologies allow learners to learn in vivo instead of in vitro, to go outside the classroom and away from the computer simulation into the mess and noise of the outside world which challenge the order and arrangement of subjects and curricular, to go in Beetham's words from "the-world-in-a-box" to the "box-in-the-world."

These changes influence role of institutions, such as colleges, schools and universities, as the gatekeepers to knowledge and technology. Many otherwise disadvantage subcultures now have their own mobile technologies to access the knowledge of their choice, unconstrained by the "terms and conditions" of the institutions of formal education.

CONCLUSION

This account attempts to document the changes in culture and subculture catalyzed by widespread mobile technologies. It is not possible to identify and unpack all the implications for education, but the changes described—on community, space, or knowledge, for example—are clearly fundamental to any societies' understanding of the role and meaning of education.

REFERENCES

British Broadcasting Corporation. (2006a). Four found guilty of barman's killing. Retrieved October 13, 2008, from http://news.bbc.co.uk/1/hi/england/london/4502662.stm

British Broadcasting Corporation. (2006b). New mobile message craze spreads. Retrieved October 13, 2008, from http://news.bbc.co.uk/1/hi/technology/3237755.stm

Bull, M. (2005). No dead air! The iPod and the culture of mobile listening. *Leisure Studies, 24*, 343-356.

Donner, J. (2008). The rules of beeping: Exchanging messages via intentional "missed calls" on mobile phones. *Journal of Computer-Mediated Communication, 13*, 1-22.

Du Gay, P., Hall, S., Janes, L., & Nequs, K. (1997). *Doing cultural studies: The story of the Sony Walkman.* London: SAGE.

Eliot, T. S. (1934). *The rock.* London: Faber and Faber.

Gayeski, D. (2002). *Learning unplugged: Using mobile technologies for organizational and performance improvement.* New York: AMACON—American Management Association.

Gergen, K. J. (2002). The challenge of absent presence. In J. E Katz & M. A. Aakhus (Eds.), *Perpetual contact. mobile communication, private talk, public performance* (pp. 227-241). Cambridge, United Kingdom: Cambridge University Press.

Geser, H. (2004). *Towards a sociological theory of the mobile phone.* Retrieved September 28, 2008, from http://geser.net

Goffman, E. (1971). *Relations in public.* Harmondsworth, England: Allen Lane

Goggin, G. (2006). SMS riot: Transmitting race on a Sydney beach, December 2005. *M/C Journal, 9*(1). Retrieved October 20, 2008, from http://journal.media-culture.org.au/0603/02-goggin.php

Haddon, L. (2007). More than a phone: Emerging practices in mobile phone use amongst children. In K. Nyiri (Ed.), *Proceedings of Towards a Philosophy of Telecommunications Convergence: Communications in the 21st century* (pp. 123-126). Budapest: T-Mobile Hungary and Hungarian Academy of Sciences.

Katz, J. E (2002). Preface and introduction. In J. E. Katz & M. Aakhus (Eds.), *Perpetual contact: Mobile communications, private talk, public performance* (pp. 000-000). Cambridge, England: Cambridge University Press.

Laurillard, D. (2002). *Rethinking university teaching: A framework for the effective use of learning technologies* (2nd ed.). London: Routledge Falmer.

Licoppe, C. (2007). Co-proximity events: Weaving mobility and technology into social encounters. In K. Nyiri (Ed.) *Proceedings of Towards a Philosophy of Tele-communications Convergence: Communications in the 21st century* (pp. 181-182). Budapest: T-Mobile Hungary and Hungarian Academy of Sciences.

Ling, R. (2004). *The mobile connection: The cell phone's impact on society.* San Francisco: Morgan Kaufmann.

Ling, R. (2007. Mobile communication and generating social cohesion. In K. Nyiri (Ed.), *Proceedings of Towards a Philosophy of Telecommunications Convergence: Communications in the 21st century.* Budapest: T-Mobile Hungary and Hungarian Academy of Sciences.

Murtagh, G. (2002). Seeing the "rules": Preliminary observations of action, inter-action and mobile phone use. In B. Brown, N. Green, & R. Harper (Eds.) *Wireless world: Social and interactional aspects of the mobile world* (pp. 87-91). London: Springer.

Pask, G. (1976). *Conversation theory: Applications in education and epistemology.* New York: Elsevier.

Perry, M., O'Hara, K., Sellen, A., Brown, B., & Harper, R. (2001). Dealing with mobility: Understanding access anytime, anywhere. *ACM Transactions on Human-Computer Interaction, 8*(4), 323-347.

Plant, S. (2000). *On the mobile. The effects of mobile telephones on social and individual life.* Retrieved October 13, 2008, from http://www.motorola.com/mot/documents/0,1028,333,00.pdf

Rafael, V. L. (2003). The cell phone and the crowd: Messianic politics in the contemporary Philippines. *Public Culture, 15*(3), 399-425.

Rheingold, H. (2002). *Smart mobs: The next social revolution.* Cambridge, MA: Perseus.

Rice, X. (2007, March 20). Kenya sets world first with money transfers by mobile. *The Guardian.* Retrieved October 18, 2008, from http://www.guardian.co.uk/money/2007/mar/20/kenya.mobilephones

Sheller, M. (2004a). Mobile publics: Decoupling, contingency, and the local/global gel. Environment and Planning D. *Society and Space, 22*, 39-54.

Sheller, M. (2004b) Mobile publics: Beyond the network perspective. *Environment and Planning D: Society and Space, 22*(1), 39-52.

Sørensen, C., Mathiassen, L., & Kakihara, M. (2002, May). *Mobile services: Functional diversity and overload.* Presented at New Perspectives on 21st Century Communications, Budapest, Hungary.

Sullivan, B. (2003, August 26). *Tethered by a high-tech leash: Computers mean you can (must?) work anywhere, anytime.* Retrieved October 10, 2008, from http://www.msnbc.msn.com/id/3072424/

Thom-Santelli, J., Ainslie, A., & Gay, G. (2007). Location, location, location: A study of bluejacking practices. In *Extended Abstracts of CHI 2007.* New York: ACM Press.

Torma, M., & Williams, H. (2007, May). *Mobile banking: A new way to deliver banking services.* Presented to Mobiles and Development Workshop, University of Manchester.

Varilio, P. (2000). *Polar inertia.* London: SAGE.

CHAPTER 3

PODCASTING AS A LISTENING CULTURE

Implications for Learning

Palitha Edirisingha

INTRODUCTION

Podcasting, with its origins and popularity as a mechanism to create and distribute personal radio shows on the Internet, has gained educators' attention and interest as a tool for teaching and learning. In 2005, the New Oxford American Dictionary recognized "podcasting" as the "word of the year." This is remarkable given that the technology of podcasting began to develop only about 5 years prior to that, around the year 2000.

This chapter looks at the development of podcasting as a culture of listening. In this chapter I want to explore the potential of podcasting for learning. Podcasting both as a technology and as an activity was not developed with learning as its ultimate goal; the major players involved in podcasting are technology enthusiasts and developers, and entertainment and media industries. Their involvement in promoting podcasting has contributed to create a culture and user-genres of listening for entertain-

Connected Minds, Emerging Cultures: Cybercultures in Online Learning
pp. 29–42
Copyright © 2009 by Information Age Publishing

ment. I want to explore this aspect and to examine the implications of these emerging user-genres of podcasting for learning. In doing so I go on to identify a variety factors and trends that have an influence on the development of a listening culture. These include: a mobile listening culture developed through personal stereos such as Sony Walkman, and more recently, digital media players; Internet technologies enabling the lay person to create and deliver podcasts with ease and at a low cost (or free); technology industries actively creating user-genres; and our own relationships with technology through a process of domesticating them. I will then discuss what these complex set of factors mean for learning: how might we "tame" the podcasting technology to support academic learning? In the final part of the chapter, I want to offer some insights into how podcasting can be effectively used for learning, focusing on higher education. This section offers a model of developing and integrating podcasting for learning, based on an empirical study called Informal Mobile Podcasting and Learning Adaptation (IMPALA) (www.impala.ac.uk).

WHAT IS PODCASTING?

Podcasting as an activity of creating, distributing, and listening to audio files (or viewing in the case of video files) has become popular within 4 to 5 years since the concept of distributing audio files on the Internet using feeder and aggregator technologies (RSS or Really Simple Syndication) were proposed and implemented in October 2000. Audio-bloggers and Internet radio broadcasters were quick to embrace the technology and the practice of creating, distributing, and accessing "audioblogs" (as podcasts were commonly identified in the early years of their use). Feeder and aggregator technologies continued to develop while the technological evangelists continued to promote the practice of audioblogging. It was not until the early 2004 when the word "podcasting" was proposed to identify the practice of "portable listening to audioblogs" by Ben Hammersley (2004) in *The Guardian* (a British newspaper) as one of several terms such as "audioblogging" and "GuerillaMedia."

The terms "podcast" and "podcasting," as Salmon, Mobbs, Edirisingha, and Dennett (2008) point out, are new and evolving. For the purpose of this chapter, I use their definition of podcasts. According to Salmon et al., a podcast is a digital media file that plays sound (or sound and vision, in the case of video podcasts); is made available from a Web site; can be opened and/or downloaded and played on a computer, and/or; is downloaded from a Web site to be played on a portable digital player (such as a mobile phone or a dedicated player such as an iPod or other makes).

The above definition differs from the pure technical definitions that aim to distinguish podcasts from other means of delivery and access of digital media files. The main technical characteristic of podcasts are that they are distributed on the Internet using syndication feeds, and they can then be downloaded automatically through a subscription service for playback on a suitable digital media player, such as a dedicated MP3 player of a computer. This process enables the content to be "automatically delivered to [users] computer as soon as [new content] is posted on the web" (British Broadcasting Corporation [BBC], 2005a, para. 12). However, the popularity of the practice of podcasting means that various content producers, including the academic podcasters, have adopted the term to match how they offer their digital audio content. Many academic podcasts are offered as downloadable files (see Nie, 2006, and Ruedel, 2006, for reviews).

DEVELOPING A PODCASTING CULTURE:
SOME CONTRIBUTORY FACTORS

Our awareness of, and engagement with, podcasting are formed by a combination of technological, commercial, and societal drives. The availability of free/low-cost and relatively easy to use software (see Mobbs, Salmon, & Edirisingha, 2008, for a list and Web links) on the Internet for creating and editing media files (sound and video) and for distributing and accessing podcasts, and the widespread ownership of digital media players (dedicated ones such as iPods and other makes and as features of mobile phones, personal digital assistants, laptops, and desktop computers) are key technological developments that are helpful for developing a podcasting culture. Such developments have made podcasting a low-threshold technological activity (Ramsden, 2007). What this means is that software for creating and editing podcasts, and tools and services for hosting them and announcing their availability to the wider world are commonly available on the Internet with many software free to download and easy to use. Podcasting received a further boost in June 2005 when Apple added a podcast directory to its iTunes online music store (BBC, 2005b). With this feature, anyone can use iTunes to publish their podcasts. Guides and advice, written by enthusiastic podcast creators are also widely available on the Internet.

Alongside the development of technologies, the content available as podcasts has been growing, from media, journalism, and entertainment industries. The influence of, and the contributions from, the broadcast media supporting the development of a podcast culture is noteworthy. The BBC has been trialing the use of podcasts since 2004 with its annual Reith Lecture series followed by In Our Times (a radio program exploring the history of ideas), Fighting Talk (Radio Five Live) and TX Unlimited (1Xtra) (BBC, 2005a). (Radio Five Live is a BBC radio station offering live music and sport programs. 1Xtra is a BBC radio station specializing in music.) These programs were made available as MP3 downloads. The Reith Lecturers received about 50,000 downloads over 10 weeks, while In Our Times received 70,000 downloads (Perry, 2004) demonstrating the public's appetite for new ways of listening. The weekly podcast from Chris Moyles, a popular disc jockey on Radio One, was downloaded nearly half a million times in December 2005 (Slocombe, 2006). The trials were extended to 20 more programs made available as podcasts for free download from the BBC Web site (BBC, 2005a). BBC Radio 4's Today program offered a podcast trial of its key 8:10 A.M. interview as downloadable files in MP3 format (Day, 2005), which recorded a total of 413,492 downloads during December 2005.

Text-based media and the journalism industry (both paper and online), through experiments with online publishing of audio content, also contributed to developing a podcast listening culture. The *Guardian* newspaper's trialing of Ricky Gervais' (a U.K.-based comedian) podcasts in early 2005 (Kiss, 2005) was a success. In the second week, the show reached number one in both the U.S. and U.K. iTunes podcast charts, attracting 180,000 downloads. Additional or supplementary content as podcasts is becoming a regular feature of major newspapers and magazines. For example, the *Economist* weekly magazine's Web site features discussions with authoritative figures in the field as podcasts. Similarly, the *Financial Times* newspaper offers podcasts by expert commentators and writers. Offering audio content in addition to the regular text material is helpful to create a new user genre amongst the regular readers as well as to attract audiences who are accustomed to, and perhaps prefer, listening.

Also, we cannot ignore prepodcast technological developments pioneered by the broadcasting industry for creating a culture of listening to audio and viewing video content online. The BBC had been using "listen again," "listen live," and "streaming" services before podcasting came along. Other content creators of music and video files have been doing this for many years. Most of these approaches use a desktop computer or a laptop as the standard set of equipment for accessing and consuming these media files. So, the effect and legacy of the previous technologies have an effect on the use-genre.

DEVELOPING A RELATIONSHIP WITH TECHNOLOGY

The processes involved in how we develop our relationships with technology are key to understanding how cultures of listening to podcasts develop. As Bell (in press) elegantly articulated, people's relationship with technology and the emergence of user-genres can be examined from two perspectives: first, the creation of new user-genres by producers and vendors of new technology and, second, how we, as users of technology, try to domesticate or tame a technology after we acquire it.

Producers of technologies are powerful drivers behind creating a particular user culture around the new technologies they produce (Bell, 2008). Taking mobile phones as an example, and based on research reported by Moisander and Eriksson (2006), Bell points out that corporations such as Nokia are powerful actors in essentially creating a whole range of activities and cultures around their products. Through imagery, symbols, and text in advertisements and corporate documents, these corporations configure the users and create new user cultures such as mobile working, as Moisander and Eriksson's research evidence shows.

A quick foray into the world of the iPod shows how the technology has created or even facilitated new user-genres and created a particular culture around it. According to Bull (2007) the iPod is "the first cultural icon of the twenty-first century, representing a sublime marriage between mobility, aesthetics and functionality, or sound and touch—enabling the users to process their auditory world in the palm of their hand" (p. 1). Sales figures show its impact, with more than 100 million units sold worldwide since its introduction in 2001, and more than 4,000 accessories made specially to accompany its use. Bull's respondents describe, in substantive detail, how the iPod has created new behaviors of listening to music while they traverse the urban spaces on a daily basis. The 3G iPhone, the latest addition to the iPod family, is expected to sell 10 million units in 75 countries by the end of 2008 ("Follow the Leader," 2008). A cross between a media player, a mobile phone, and a handheld computer, this new device no doubt will create new user cultures.

The development of a mobile listening culture has its roots in the postwar period, with the production of home entertainment systems, or Hi-Fis. Bull (2007) reminds us that the Hi-Fis introduced postwar listeners to a deeply private, acoustically intensified, almost entirely nonresonant "fidelity" sound. The invention of miniature transistors and hand-held, battery-powered radios helped this privatized sound to be mobile. In the 1980s, personal stereo players such as the Sony Walkman, with privatizing earphones, helped young people to establish their own personal territory both at home and outside (Morley, 2000). As Bull (2000, p. 1) observes, "each morning millions of urban inhabitants place a pair of headphones over their heads, or place earpieces directly into their ears, and turn the music on as they leave home. They walk down streets, sit on tubes or buses and keep listening till they reach their destination." Personal stereos, Bull considers, are "the first truly mobile consumer technology." Personal stereos offered the user with a tool to be free from listening at a fixed location—to be able to create "manageable sites of habitation," to manage their "space and time," "to create boundaries around the self, and as the site of fantasy and memory" (Bull, 2000, p. 2).

The culture of mobile listening shifted again at the beginning of the twenty-first century, owing to the developments and availability of digital media players at affordable prices. Bull (2007) reminds us that we are "no longer prey to the whims of corporate radio, ... our cathedrals of sound exist in the personal playlist of the iPod" (p. 2). We are now in full control of creating our own and private "mobile auditory worship." Development of digital media technologies had now provided "a technological fix to the management of the contingency of aural desire" (Bull, 2005, p. 344). Unlike personal stereos, digital media players enable the user to "take their whole music collection with them in a machine that is not much larger than a mobile phone" (Bull, 2005, p. 344). No longer is there a "burden of judging what music to take ... on their daily commute" (Bull, 2005, p. 344). Even though there were miniature versions of personal stereos available (Du Gay, Hall, Janes, Mackay, & Negus, 1997), they were limited in terms of choice and portability of sound tracks for the mobile listener. Digital media players such as iPods, through the exponentially increased storage capacity and new ways of arranging music tracks such as "playlists," offer the user "an intoxicating mixture of music, proximity and privacy whilst on the move" (Bull, 2004, p. 344). Being able to listen to music through a home sound system, through the radio in the car, through the home/work computer all give the user "unprecedented ability to weave the disparate threads of the day into one uniform soundtrack" (Bull, 2005, p. 344).

One of Bull's (2007) interviewees paints a picture of how the technology can have a profound impact on the user's experience, clearly showing how the various features of a technology influences its use:

> Technology, precisely in its miniaturisation—the whole digital world in your hand—acquires a magical quality ... the design is flawless. It feels good to hold it in your hand, to rub your thumbs over the navigation wheel and the touch the smooth white surface. It looks nice, I'm proud of owning such a device. (p. 3)

Clearly, the user (and Bull himself) talks about an iPod that predates the later editions, such as iPod Touch, with its touch sensitive and innovative user interface and variety of applications. What might a user of an iPod Touch (or a 3G iPhone released in 2008) have to say about the design and feel, and therefore the overall personal experience?

Digital media players have contributed to the development of a culture of listening to recorded sound on the move; devices such as iPods have created new user-genres of listening, similar to how corporations such as

Nokia contributed to developing a mobile working culture. New cultures and user-genres no doubt emerge with more recent additions to the iPod family, such as the iPhone and 3G iPhone that provide access to the Internet, as opposed to the general iPod, which was a stand-alone device.

The iPhone with its customized buttons are directly linked to Apple's recommended online worlds (through a Web browser) such as the iTunes store (to access and buy music and other content), to YouTube, among a few others. The images and text that are included in advertising material for these devices, including more simple versions of MP3 and MP4 players, all contribute to what Bell (2008) considers as creating new discourses and user-genres related to entertainment, recreation, and mobile working. iPods and other media players have created a listening culture, creating an "auditory territory" for the user through a specific form of "sensory gating"; to "screen out unwanted sounds," a sort of "soundscape" (Bull, 2007, p. 8). So what chances do we have getting the users of these devices for learning?

DOMESTICATING AN IPOD

Our relationship with technology is not solely dependent on how the manufacturers of these technologies create new user cultures and practices. We do not completely passively react to what is presented to us. As Bell (2008) reminds us, we are active agents in shaping our relationship with technologies: we are engaged in a "messy learning process" in getting used to new machines/technologies; in this process, the technology and the human being are "reciprocally influence each other," giving rise to new user-genres and cultures of use.

Such a process of people learning to live with and making use of new technologies is referred to as "domestication," a concept developed by Silverstone and his collaborators in the 1980s to explain how we accept, use, and reject media and technology in a household (Haddon, 2007). According to Haddon, the metaphor of domestication came from the taming of wild animals. In a traditional sense, domestication is what happens when we tame a wild animal. As with a wild animal, a new technology can be considered as something "strange" and "wild," that have to be "house-trained"; that need to be "integrated into the structures, daily routines and values of users and their environments." Domestication also implies that, just like pets, technologies "can become part of the family" (p. 2). "When the domestication of technologies have been 'successful', the technologies are not regarded as cold, lifeless, problematic and challenging consumer goods" (p. 3).

Silverstone and his colleagues applied the concept of domestication to illustrate the processes of how electronic technologies such as TVs, VCRs, and computers are tamed and obtain a physical and functional space in the household. The domestication process involves four stages: appropriation, objectification, incorporation, and conversion (Silverstone, 2006). These stages describe the process of gaining entry into the household from its original location of the shop floor, arrangements and rearrangements made to the physical and social space within the household to accommodate it, and eventual fitting into the household routines. As Haddon (2007) point out, the concept of domestication offers a perspective of examining and understanding how we develop use cultures around particular technologies.

Haddon's (1992) study on home computers illustrates the domestication process. The technology is resisted and accommodated in the household, family negotiations before acquisition of the technology, the process through which individual identities and the collective family identify are formed in relation to the family itself and the outside world.

The concept of domestication challenged the conventional view of technology adoption as a linear process. The widely cited technology adoption approach developed by Rogers (2003) holds the view that people accept or reject new technologies—be they computers or new crop production techniques—following a rational process, leading to an S-shaped curve depicting the cumulative adoption of the technology. The concept of domestication represents a shift away from such models, which assume the adoption of new innovations to be monocausal, linear, and technologically determined (Berker, Hartmann, Punie, & Ward, 2006, p. 1). Domestication considers the "complexity of everyday life and technology's place within its dynamics, rituals, rules, routines and patterns." The concept helps "understand what happens with media and technology when they are acquired and used" (p. 1).

Although we can think of parallels, an iPod is, to use Bull's words, a personal, and privatizing, technology. So how does the taming process occur with an iPod? Is it the same as that with a TV or a VCR?

While the domestication approach provides a way of thinking about how we develop a relationship with electronic technologies, there are two limitations of the concept that I see as problematic in describing our relationships with digital communication and entertainment devices such as MP3/MP4 players and mobile phones. First is the way of looking at media and technology as "untamed animals." Unlike VCRs and computers that were made in the 1980s and 1990s, when the concept of domestication was developed, digital gadgets such as iPods and modern laptops cannot be categorized as "untamed"; they are ready for use without much technical configurations and/or know-how. Unlike a 1980s/1990s VCR, new digital devices are ready to be operated once they are out of the box. There is still a process of domestication, not entirely in the conventional sense of "taming," but as a process of getting to know—just like a pet brought into the household—and understanding its behavior and learning how to take care of it and enjoy its company.

The second point of limitation of the concept of domestication to explain our relationships with a device such as an iPod is that MP3 devices are personal and not an item used mostly collectively in the household, such as a TV. Haddon cites research by Norwegian researchers who argued for the case of looking beyond the home (Lie & Sørensen, 1996, cited by Haddon, 2007) and mobile telephones and mobile computing—how the domestication framework can be applied to consider interactions with wider networks outside. However, these studies do not provide insight into the process of developing a personal and intimate relationship between the user and personal digital devices such as MP3 players. We need to take into account the fact that listening to music on an iPod is a very different experience from using a mobile phone for communication and a laptop for work, however mobile they are. They have a broader social impact as well as a personal aspect to it. The personal dimension of iPod (or any one of the preferred make of MP3/MP4 player) use is much more profound, as Bull's interviews so graphically illustrate.

We need to consider how the domestication/taming occurs at a more personal and emotional level, and how individual users develop a relationship with their digital media player once it leaves the shop floor and arrive at the door from a mail order company or received as a gift.

PODCASTING FOR LEARNING

As Bell (2008) elegantly reminds us in a critique of podcasting for learning in universities, we need to move away from looking at our use of technologies from a purely technological determinist point of view. A technological determinist view holds that people chose to use a technology based on the new and good features added to it. Bell warns us the dangers of such a view of digital media players and assumptions made on their use for learning. As educators, we need to realize that we are "shepherding learning" into "already-stable and the still-emerging use genres" that are associated with entertainment, recreation, personal communication and business. We should not assume a seamless transplant. "Just because a device has learning affordances does not mean that learning can (or *should*) be made part of the repertoires of its use" (Bell, 2008).

If we want our students to use their digital media players for learning, we need to be aware of the listening culture associated with these devices, for recreation and entertainment. We also need to be aware of how corporations develop new user-genres and user cultures around these technologies that are not generally associated with academic learning. There is also a process in which we domesticate or tame a technology. Perhaps this is a process where academic community can proactively engage and help our students to tame their iPods and other digital media players for learning. This process can be enhanced if we develop our podcasts to address specific teaching and learning challenges and demonstrate to students how they can in fact use their media players for learning, in addition to using for entertainment. This kind of dual purpose is indeed possible, as pointed out by David Noble (1984) as a "double life" of a technology, and Bell (2006) as "an important unofficial second function" of a technology.

IMPALA APPROACHES FOR PODCASTING

There are a number of positive and encouraging examples of how students are able to give their iPods and other media players a "double life." I want to offer some insights from the Informal Mobile Podcasting and Learning Adaptation (IMPALA, impala.ac.uk) project based in the United Kingdom, and a 10-factor design model as a helpful way of developing pedagogically sound podcasts to support student learning.

IMPALA was a collaborative research and development project between five U.K. universities: Leicester, Kingston, Gloucestershire, Royal Veterinary College, and Nottingham. IMPALA also drew from its friends at other universities: Edinburgh, Chester, Charles Sturt University and University of New South Wales (Australia), and University of Cape Town (South Africa).

The IMPALA podcast development involving the first five universities was initiated with a pilot study leading to guidelines for pedagogical design and the development of podcast applications addressing specific teaching and learning challenges. Students' perceived benefits of podcasting for learning and staff experience of developing podcasts were evaluated over two academic years, within an action research framework. The pilot study was based at the University of Leicester in an undergraduate engineering module (Fothergill, 2008) that integrated podcasting and e-tivities based on Salmon's (2004) five-stage model. The pilot study was helpful to develop a set of guidelines for developing and integrating podcasting with other learning activities and promoting their use amongst students. Using these guidelines and a preliminary pedagogical model for developing podcasts, IMPALA partners developed their own podcasts to address specific teaching and learning challenges and to explore the potential of the technology for learning. More than 500 students and 20 academic staff took part in IMPALA during academic years 2006 and 2007. The impact on the students' learning of podcasting was studied through qualitative and quantitative data collection and analysis. Salmon and Edirisingha (2008) provide a comprehensive overview of the findings and specific podcast applications.

A 10-Factor Design Model

IMPALA project developed a 10-factor design model for developing podcasts that can be tried out in different teaching and learning contexts (Edirisingha, Salmon, & Nie, in press). The empirical data collected confirm that the model offers an effective and logical approach to developing podcasts that students find useful to support their learning. The 10 factors are:

1. the purpose or pedagogical rationale;
2. the medium used (audio only or audio and visual);
3. the convergence (how much the podcasts are integrated with other e-learning);
4. the authors and contributors of content;
5. the structure of podcasting (frequency and timing);
6. the reusability of content;
7. the length;
8. the style (presentation, interview, dialogue);
9. the framework of content organization; and
10. the access system (via virtual learning environment [VLE] or Internet-based feeder service such as RSS).

Each factor in the model helps the teachers to focus on their teaching and learning context leading to a design step.

This chapter can only provide a summary of the 10-factor model. An interactive version of the model is available at www.podcastingforlearning. com for you to try out. Salmon and Edirisingha (2008) provides a comprehensive coverage of the 10-factor design model with real cases illustrating each point. Examples of pedagogical rationale for using podcasts include limitations of lectures in teaching complex and often difficult to understand topics, limitation of conventional approaches to teaching software tools, improving feedback offered to students' assessed work, supporting online and independent learning of campus-based students, supporting distance learners, and developing students' learning and study skills. The model provides guidance on selecting the medium for your podcasts (audio or video) and the access system (VLE-hosted or via an Internet feeder service) that will encourage your students to make use of your podcasts.

The model can be used in different ways depending on the level of expertise that you have on podcasting. A novice podcaster is advised to start with the first factor and follow the model step by step, considering each factor and design step in detail. Podcast design process in practice, however, might require you to backtrack and reconsider some of the earlier design steps. Experienced podcasters and competent technologists can review the model to compare their own practice with the one presented in the model. The model will in any case will be useful in providing academics with new perspectives on podcasting for supporting students' academic learning.

CONCLUDING REMARKS

In this chapter I wanted to examine podcasting as a listening culture formed alongside the developments of technologies of recorded sound and voice and the progress of digital technologies. I also wanted to look at processes through which we develop relationships with technologies, especially more personal, mobile, communication and entertainment devices that have not been originally designed for learning. These are technologies bought for purposes other than learning, for personal uses such as recreation; they also are tools through which we express our identities. Many students, from all levels and contexts of education, own digital media players (Trinder, Guiller, Margaryan, Littlejohn, & Nicol, 2008), providing academics a potential new learning technology. As I pointed out in the chapter, however, we should not make assumptions that students will use their personal devices for learning just because they are used to listening to recordings. A podcasting culture developed for listening to music might not transfer easily into a similar culture for learning. Corporations who develop and market new digital technologies construct particular user-genres and cultures that have nothing to do with learning. We also develop a relationship with technologies where we domesticate the technology, and learn to live with it in particular ways.

How might we develop a podcasting culture for learning and tap into the culture of listening (for entertainment)? The cultural habit of listening to enjoy (for example, music) will not transfer across to learning. The 10-factor model, based on research carried out over 2 years, offers a useful tool for academics to try out for developing podcasts that a support their students' learning.

REFERENCES

British Broadcasting Corporation. (2005a). *BBC to podcast up to 20 more programmes including Today and Radio 1 speech highlights* (Press release). Retrieved January 14, 2008, from http://www.bbc.co.uk/pressoffice/pressreleases/stories/2005/04_april/14/pod.shtml

British Broadcasting Corporation. (2005b) *Wordsmiths hail podcast success.* Retrieved January 14, 2008, from http://news.bbc.co.uk/1/hi/technology/4504256.stm

Berker, T., Hartmann, M., Punie, Y., & Ward, K. J. (Eds.). (2006). Introduction. In *Domestication of media and technology* (pp. 1-17). Maidenhead, England: Open University Press.

Bell, D. (2006). *Science, technology and culture.* Maidenhead, England: Open University Press.

Bell, D. (in press). The university in your pocket. In G. Salmon & P. Edirisingha (Eds.), *Podcasting for learning in universities.* London: McGraw-Hill and Open University Press.

Bull, M. (2000). *Sounding out the city: Personal stereos and the management of everyday life.* Oxford, England: Berg.

Bull, M. (2005). No dead air! The iPod and the culture of mobile listening. *Leisure Studies, 24*(4), 343-55.

Bull, M. (2007). *Sound moves: iPod culture and urban experience.* London: Routledge.

Day, J. (2005). Today tunes into the iPod generation. *The Guardian.* Retrieved February 18, 2008, from: www.guardian.co.uk/media/2005/apr/14/radio.newmedia

Du Gay, P., Hall, S., Janes, L., Mackay, H., & Negus, K. (1997). *Doing cultural studies: The story of the Sony Walkman.* London: SAGE.

Edirisingha, P., Salmon, G., & Nie, M. (2008). Developing pedagogical podcasts. In G. Salmon & P. Edirisingha (Eds.), *Podcasting for learning in universities.* London: McGraw-Hill and Open University Press.

Follow the leader: Apple ditches its unusual business model to boost handset sales. (2008, June 12). *The Economist.* Retrieved November 1, 2008, from http://www.economist.com/business/displaystory.cfm?story_id=11543761

Fothergill, J. (2008). Podcasts and online learning. In G. Salmon & P. Edirisingha (Eds.), *Podcasting for learning in universities.* London: McGraw-Hill and Open University Press.

Haddon, L. (2007). Roger Silverstone's legacies: Domestication. *New Media and Society, 9*(1), 25-32.

Haddon, L. (1992). Explaining ICT consumption: The case of the home computer. In R. Silverstone & E. Hirsch (Eds.) *Consuming technologies: Media and information in domestic spaces* (pp. 82-96). London: Routledge.

Hammersley, B. (2004). Audible revolution. *The Guardian Unlimited.* Retrieved January 14, 2008, from www.arts.guardian.co.uk/features/story/0,,1145758,00.html

Kiss, J. (2005). Guardian's *Gervais podcast tops US and UK charts.* Retrieved February 18, 2008, from www.journalism.co.uk/2/articles/51639.php

Lie, M., & Sørensen, K. (Eds.) (2006). *Making technologies our own? Domesticating technology into everyday life.* Oslo, Norway: Scandinavian University Press.

Mobbs, M., Salmon, G., & Edirisingha, P. (2008). Appendix: How to create pod-casts—practitioner's guide. In G. Salmon & P. Edirisingha (Eds.), *Podcasting for learning in universities*. London: McGraw-Hill and Open University Press.

Moisander, J., & Eriksson, P. (2006). Corporate narratives of information society: Making up the mobile consumer subject. *Consumption, Markets and Culture, 9*(3), 257-75.

Morley, D. (2000). *Home territories. Media, mobility and identity.* London: Routledge.

Nie, M. (2006). *The pedagogical perspectives of mobile learning.* Retrieved January 22, 2008, from www2.le.ac.uk/ projects/impala/documents

Noble, D. (1984). *Forces of production.* New York: Alfred Knopf.

Perry, S. (2004). Podcasting primed, BBC Radio MP3 download success. *Digital Lifestyles*, blog entry posted on December 17,2004. Retrieved January 14, 2008, from http://digital-lifestyles.info/2004/12/17/podcasting-primed-bbc-radio-mp3-download-success

Ramsden, A. (2007, September). Podcasting as a social network tool: Is it a student reality? *Programme and abstracts of ALT-C 2007*, 117-18, 115-16. Nottingham, United Kingdom.

Rogers, E. (2003). *Diffusion of innovations* (5th ed.). New York: Free Press.

Ruedel, C. (2006). *A draft literature review of mobile learning and podcasting.* Retrieved May 15, 2007, from http://www2.le.ac.uk/projects/impala/documents

Slocombe, M. (2006). BBC release first podcast chart. *Digital Lifestyles*, a blog entry posted on January 23, 2006. Retrieved January 18, 2008, from http:// digital-lifestyles.info/2006/01/23/bbc-release-first-podcast-chart/

Salmon, G., Mobbs, R., Edirisingha, P., & Dennett, C. (2008). Podcasting technol-ogy. In G. Salmon & P. Edirisingha (Eds.), *Podcasting for learning in universities*. London: McGraw-Hill and Open University Press.

Salmon, G. (2004). *E-moderating: The key to teaching and learning online* (2nd ed.). London: Routledge.

Salmon, G., & Edirisingha, P. (Eds.) (in press). *Podcasting for learning in universities*. London: McGraw-Hill and Open University Press.

Silverstone, R. (2006). Domesticating domestication. Reflections on the life of a concept. In T. Berker, M. Hartmann, Y. Punie, & K. J. Ward (Eds.), *Domestica-tion of media and technology*. Maidenhead, England: Open University Press.

Trinder, K., Guiller, J., Margaryan, A., Littlejohn, A., & Nicol, D. (2008). Learning from digital natives: Bridging formal and informal learning. *The Higher Edu-cation Academy*. Retrieved June 8, 2008, from http://www.heacademy.ac.uk/ assets/York/documents/LDN%20Final%20Report.pdf

CHAPTER 4

THE EMERGENCE OF UBIQUITOUS AND PERVASIVE LEARNING CULTURES

Mark A. M. Kramer

"The world's new global cell phone culture is giving us the power to communicate with anyone, anywhere at anytime."

—Wang Jianzhou
Chairman and CEO, China Mobile Ltd.

INTRODUCTION

A new learning culture seems to be emerging in our universities. A culture that is increasingly more collaborative and takes place anytime and anywhere. This culture can be observed as a pervasive and ubiquitous learning culture that is being made possible through wireless communication infrastructure, which allows for this culture to emerge.

It can be observed almost universally that societies place a tremendous emphasis on the use of wireless-communication infrastructure. Regardless of the level of development, societies throughout the globe are moving

Connected Minds, Emerging Cultures: Cybercultures in Online Learning
pp. 43–50
43

toward a more mobilized, networked infrastructure. This infrastructure, coupled with the associated mobile information and communication technologies, allows for many qualities of mobile communication and interaction. As a result, new forms and modalities of learning and collaboration are emerging because of this infrastructure and the ways individuals choose to use the associated tools that use this infrastructure. This emergence can be observed in the establishment of pervasive and ubiquitous learning environments and communities that harness the power of various network-enabled technologies to shape a new quality of learning that is independent of constraints of time and location. We stand at a juncture of new possibilities.

The purpose of this chapter is to explore how students are beginning to harness mobile networked-enabled technologies to create a new culture of learning and collaboration. This new culture of learning and collaboration can be understood as a ubiquitous and pervasive learning culture in which anyone can engage in a form of learning that takes place anytime, anywhere.

A NEW CULTURE OF LEARNING

It is 7:00, and Walanda is waking from her slumber and begins to prepare herself for a busy day at her university. While performing her daily morning routine, Walanda glances at the display of her Internet-enabled multimedia device (mobile) to see if there are any changes to her academic schedule that day and to see whether there are any messages or updates for the courses she is taking. As Walanda walks into her kitchen to prepare a cup of tea for breakfast, she receives a message from one of her classmates inviting her to meet at a local café so that they can (physically) meet to discuss a seminar paper that is due today. Walanda responds to her classmate (through a voice-texting service) that she cannot meet that morning, but offers her the possibility to read the revisions of their paper on her way to campus. Her classmate sends a revised version of their seminar paper to Walanda's mobile, and it is simultaneously printed-out on Walanda's networked-enabled printer. Walanda finishes her breakfast and grabs the printout of her paper and makes her way to her university campus.

On Walanda's commute, she reads the seminar paper she is working on with her colleague and comes across some concepts she is not completely familiar with and consults some academic resources on the Internet through her mobile. Upon arrival to campus she glances at her mobile and informs herself as to whereabouts of her colleague on a map that indicates the presence and global positioning of her friend. She knows that her friend is waiting for her in the main library and proceeds there to meet-up and finish their paper.

As Walanda and her friend busily work on their paper on a student terminal at the library, they both realize they will be late for one of the morning lectures they are required to attend. They save their work and send a back-up copy of their paper to a student server on the network for later retrieval if needed. While they make their way across campus to their lecture, they connect to the live audio stream of the lecture and listen with their wireless headsets. When they enter the lecture hall, their attendance (physical presence) and apparent lateness is automatically logged into the lecturer's attendance logbook. While taking their seats they receive the lecture notes and presentation slides via Bluetooth for their personal reference. While half-listening to the lecture, Walanda and her colleague continue to work on their paper on their mobiles, because they know they will be able to review the lecture again at a later time on video or audio-cast.

Summary of a New Culture of Learning

The scenario illustrated above demonstrates the application of existing mobile services and technologies to create a form of blended-technology enhanced learning. Walanda and her friend tapped into networks through their mobiles to coordinate meetings with each other, acquire learning resources such as streamed-audio lectures, and generally engage in what can be referred to as a flexible learning environment. As we observed, Walanda and her colleague harnessed mobile technologies to allow themselves to accomplish their academic obligations and learning requirements. They used the tools available to them to work within their existing educational system and were also helping shape a "new quality of learning" this chapter refers to as "pervasive" and "ubiquitous learning."

OVERVIEW

The adoption and utilization of mobile information and communication technologies within formalized, informal, and nonformal learning contexts is fundamentally transforming the ways in which society views and engages in educational practices. It is commonly accepted that mobile information and communication technologies have tremendous potential to make an immense impact on education, which is observed by M. Castells (1996, 2007) and researched by B. C. Bruce (see references). This impact can be observed within the context of individual and collaborative learning practices. Students, individually and collectively, are using mobile technologies to augment and enhance existing learning scenarios, but are also creating a "new quality of learning" which is born out of the use of mobile technologies and associated services. This new quality of learning can be observed in how students harness mobile technologies and wireless networks to create a culture of ubiquitous and pervasive learning, which can be observed on many university campuses today.

The purpose of this chapter is to briefly explore the concepts of ubiquitous and pervasive learning as demonstrated in the possible learning scenario illustrated above. The central questions behind this chapter are the following:

1. What is ubiquitous and pervasive learning?
2. Are ubiquitous and pervasive learning practices feasible and will they bring about a positive impact on education?

The research conducted to address these questions is based mostly on personal observations and practice supplemented with a partial review of existing literature on topics related to the subject discussed in this chapter. It is important to stress that this chapter is exploratory in nature, and thus will not be able to cover in depth many of the concepts and topics surveyed. It is helpful to view this work as a medium to encourage thoughtful discourse and to inspire dialogue regarding how the emergence of ubiquitous computing practices are affecting individual and collaborative learning and education in general.

UBIQUITOUS AND PERVASIVE LEARNING

Mark Weiser's vision of ubiquitous computing has had an enormous impact on the formation of the field of ubiquitous computing (UbiComp) in which Weiser's central thesis was that while computers for personal use have focused on the excitement of interaction ... the most potentially interesting, challenging and profound change implied by the ubiquitous computing era is a focus on calm computing (Wieser, 1993). The "calm technology" Wieser refers to is the technology that recedes into the background of our lives (Wieser & Brown, 1996) which, according to Yvonne Rogers "make our lives convenient, comfortable and informed" (Rogers, 2006). While following in the footsteps of Weiser's "calm computing" vision, this chapter draws on Weiser's vision and attempts to define ubiquitous learning in relation to ubiquitous computing's vision to make the lives of the students "convenient," "comfortable," and more "informed."

At present, we are beginning to see the first glimpses of ubiquitous "calm" technologies saturating our societies and therefore setting the foundation for a ubiquitous and pervasive learning culture to emerge. These first signs are manifesting themselves through the presence of a mobile Internet and associated wireless infrastructure (WiFi-hotspots) that have already permeated most Western societies. Users of these mobile networks find themselves checking their e-mail, logging onto Web portals from home, within their automobiles, at work, cafés, airports, train stations, on ski lifts, and within washrooms. This new trend of using the Internet anytime, anywhere, is an emerging sign that demonstrates individual desire to stay informed, keep in touch, and be up-to-date with colleagues, friends, family, and other daily activities. In doing so, individuals are inadvertently creating a culture which, when applied to learning and education, sets the foundation for ubiquitous and pervasive learning cultures to emerge.

Ubiquitous Learning

According to Weiser, ubiquitous computing enhances computer use by making many computers available throughout the physical environment, while making them effectively invisible to the user (Weiser, 1993). If such a scenario could be duplicated and applied to educational institutions a new quality of learning could (and should) emerge. This new quality of ubiquitous learning can help make the lives of students and faculty alike more convenient, comfortable, and informed by providing an "invisible" infrastructure that would support and allow for enhanced collaboration and communication. In the learning scenario described above with Walanda, we observed that ubiquitous learning can enable a more flexible way of learning and has the ability to enhance and potentially bolster an individual student's ability to achieve his or her own personal learning goals. This can be done, essentially, by making networked-enabled computers available throughout a physical environment (university campus) while making them effectively invisible. By having the infrastructure in the background and invisible, it would allow individuals to go about their activities without needing to worry about the associated networked technologies. Essentially, students would be tapping into and using ubiquitous networks and related infrastructure through mobile multimedia devices, freed from sitting behind a desktop computer in a crowded computer lab, and engaged in more dynamic and flexible learning scenarios. The invisibility of the technology (computational power) is one of the main characteristics of ubiquitous learning and is an enabler or what is called pervasive learning.

Pervasive Learning

Pervasiveness of learning refers to the aspects of learning that are more visible and tangible to the learner. That is to say the practices that the learner engages in to access learning resources and digitized artifacts (such as PDFs and audio/video files) to augment and supplement individualized or group learning scenarios under almost any condition. Bearing this is mind, pervasive learning gives students the ability, and more importantly the flexibility, to learn anytime and anywhere. These anytime, anywhere characteristics can be understood as *the* main enablers of pervasive learning practices.

Summary of Ubiquitous and Pervasive Learning

In summary, ubiquitous learning can help make the lives of students and faculty more convenient, comfortable, and informed by provide an "invisible" infrastructure that supports and allows for enhanced collaboration and communication. The ubiquity of the technologies allows for pervasive learning to occur. The anytime, anywhere characteristics of pervasive learning are understood as the key enablers of pervasive learning practices, and refer to the social practices involved in learning.

IS UBIQUITOUS AND PERVASIVE LEARNING FEASIBLE?

In order to answer the question whether ubiquitous and pervasive learning practices are feasible, one must also ponder the question of why would anyone want to do this. Rogers asserts that "humans are very resourceful at exploiting their [own] environment and [are adept at] extending their capabilities using existing strategies and tools" (Rogers, 2006). We are beginning to see the first glimpses of ubiquitous learning unfolding because individuals see a value in making the process of learning more flexible and learner-centered. According to Glotz (2005), Keegan (2002), Rheingold (2002), and Alexander (2004), students are already harnessing the power and potential of mobile information and communications technologies in order to augment their own personal and collaborative learning.

It can be argued that our educational systems have changed very little in relation to the changes and advances in mobile technologies and services. Individuals, (students especially) are beginning to witness the potential mobile technologies have in shaping a more flexible, dynamic environment for learning. They may not be calling the learning practices they are engaged in "ubiquitous" or "pervasive" learning. Moreover, students are acutely aware of the benefits of having a more flexible and dynamic learning experience, and this is beginning to make an impact on formal educational systems.

Impact on Education

As with any learning scenario involving technology, there will always be disruptions to the prevailing ways and methods of accomplishing things. Educational systems, regardless of their maturity, are experiencing incredible stresses on their institutions as many societies are being called upon to equip their students (citizens) with new skills for the present and emerging knowledge economies. Many schools are constrained by budgetary limitations while experiencing a surge in student enrolment. Technology is one tool to help find creative solutions to overcome challenges and obstacles for individuals to obtain a quality education.

As to whether ubiquitous and pervasive learning practices will bring about a positive impact on education, it is too early to give a definitive answer. However, it can be argued that ubiquitous and pervasive learning practices can theoretically be a catalyst to positive change within educational systems and equip individuals with the capacity to pursue and complete their own personal education goals. Let us encourage this, and help further the development of this new culture of learning within our educational establishments.

CONCLUSION

The purpose of this chapter has been to briefly explore the concepts of ubiquitous and pervasive learning and to make an attempt to determine whether ubiquitous and pervasive learning practices are feasible. With regards to whether ubiquitous and pervasive learning practices are able to make a positive impact on education, it has been determined that it is too early to speculate on these developments, but there are many promising signs that ubiquitous and pervasive learning practices can and will make a tremendous contribution to bringing about positive change within educational systems and allow individuals and collaborative learning communities to achieve the desired education goals.

This new culture of learning and collaboration that we have defined as a culture of ubiquitous and pervasive learning is inevitable, although it may take time for individuals to adopt these practices. Lang (2004) reminds us that the adoption of technology is a process that takes time, our social embedding of technologies lags necessarily behind their introduction. In addition, the ways in which they are adopted and the uses to which we put them are not necessarily the same as what prompted their development. (p. 171)

Students and faculty will help shape and adopt ubiquitous and pervasive learning scenarios if they find a benefit in doing so. In the meantime, we need to reflect on how we want to shape learning in the future. Do we want to follow the vision that ubiquitous and pervasive learning can make our lives "convenient," "comfortable," and more "informed" while learning "anytime, anywhere"? Or, do we envision a different quality in ubiquitous and pervasive learning, which is less technologically fixated and more socially oriented. It is the wish of this author that this chapter adds to the discourse on technology enhanced education and brings to the surface crucial questions to address the future of education within ubiquitous and pervasive learning contexts.

REFERENCES

Alexander, B. (2004). Going nomadic: Mobile learning in higher education. *Educause Review, 39*(5), 28-35.

Bruce, B. C. (in press). Ubiquitous learning, ubiquitous computing, and lived experience. In W. Cope (Ed.), *Ubiquitous learning*. Champaign, IL: University of Illinois Press.

Castells, M. (1996). *The rise of the network society: Vol. 1. The information age: Economy, society, and culture*. London: Blackwell.

Castells, M., Fernández-Ardèvol, M., Linchuan Qiu, J., & Araba, S. (2007). *Mobile communication and society: Global perspective*. Cambridge, MA: MIT Press.

Glotz, P., Bertschi, S., & Locke, C. (Eds.). (2005). *Thumb culture: The meaning of mobile phones for society*. Bielefeld, Germany: Transcript.

Keegan, D. (2002). *The future of learning: From eLearning to mLearning*. Hagen, Germany: Institute for Research into Distance Education.

Rheingold, H. (2002). *Smart mobs: The next social revolution*. Cambridge, MA: Perseus.

Rogers, Y. (2006). Moving on from Weiser's vision of calm computing. In P. Dourish & A. Friday (Eds.), *Ubicomp 2006, LNCS 4206* (pp. 404-421). Berlin, Germany: Springer-Verlag.

Lang, R. (2004). *The mobile connection: The cell phone's impact on society*. San Francisco: Elsevier.

Weiser, M. (1993). Some computer science issues in ubiquitous computing. *Communications of the ACM, 36*(7), 75-84.

Weiser, M., & Brown, J. S. (1996). *The coming age of calm technology*. Retrieved September 1, 2007, from: www.ubiq.com/hypertext/weiser/acmfuture2endnote.htm

PART II

ROLES AND IDENTITIES

CHAPTER 5

IDENTITY IN CYBERSPACE

Hugh Miller and Jill Arnold

The study of electronic selves shows how the social rules employed to manage a presence in virtual environments are as important as those in embodied life. People construct and reconstruct themselves in cyberspace in ways that are subject to cultural restrictions on both sides of the screen, as well as being influenced by the affordances offered by new media. To learn is to come to a new understanding of the world, but it also requires a re-adjustment of one's *self*. The complexities of the relationship between the engagement of students with their work and the sense of themselves as learners are increased as the systems they are working with offer more opportunities for presence. To be present is to foreground one's identity in some way, if only as a named member of a group, or by minimal contribution. Given that identity is both individual (reflexive and subjective) and social (depending on relationships and context), in the e-learning environment it is important to consider how individuals and groups of learners are extending and adapting "ways of being" and interacting with others in the new spaces.

A short discussion of what we mean by identity is necessary. Identity can best be understood in terms of performance (Gergen, 1991), as the way people establish difference from others (their individual style) as well as similarity to others (the social context within which that individuality is

Connected Minds, Emerging Cultures: Cybercultures in Online Learning
pp. 53–64

located). Identity in this context is primarily a social matter and can be part of group involvement and might even involve a demonstration of group conformity (Tajfel, 1981). Identity is something that is claimed by an individual and it is necessary that it be accepted and recognized by others for that claim to succeed.

Representation in this way then becomes not so much a matter of a portrayal of a "true self," but a demonstration of who you are and by what persona you wish to be understood. The context of this demonstration provides both possibilities and restrictions in the management of identity and limits how far the presentation of self is manipulable, but it also challenges people to use their knowledge of self and of others in that context to create or identify credible self-presentations. Identity is therefore a *product* (produced out of our social interactions) that is both multilayered and multifunctional, but it is as much about what we feel/understand about ourselves as it is about what we do and the roles we play. The self and identity can also be seen as *active* and fluidly constructed from the surrounding cultural narratives; we interpret things for ourselves, and our subjective experiences are generally understood in terms of the dominant narratives.

We have found Goffman's (1959) account of the presentation of self in everyday life useful in understanding the presentation of self online (Miller, 1995). He suggests that social interactions can usefully be analyzed as though they were theatrical performances, in which those present collude to maintain smooth and believable *performances* of self. Those performances in public areas are supported by preparatory work done in back regions, spaces where things can be tried out, checked over, and generally prepared for public consumption. The distinction between back and front regions works well for an analysis of the online self, where being offline can be seen as a back region for an online enactment of who we are. In fact, even the time spent revising and considering a text message before clicking "send" can be seen as an online back region. Older technologies like e-mail and discussion groups provide more of these online back regions than more immediate, higher bandwidth technologies, and might be less threatening for the novice learner as a result. Goffman also stresses the importance of the embarrassment caused by a failed attempt to claim a certain kind of self as an important motivator for limiting our claims, but also for others to collaborate with us (since they feel embarrassment, too) in mending the breaches caused by unwarranted claims. Although this kind of analysis seems appropriate for the online presentation of the self as learner, it is also the case that face-to-face teaching and learning encounters raise many of the same issues of prepared, performed, and validated self. The ideas that "bodies are text" and could be used to game-play in a cyberspace conceptualized as virtual theater seems to imply that this metaphor would allow new freedoms of characterization and allow a mask of difference. Theories of identity maintenance and reconstructions (Gergen, 1996; Wetherell & Maybin, 1996) can explain how some people are at pains to maintain consistency of character while others feel free to exploit opportunities for difference.

The psychology of dealing with threat (we mean everything from feeling slightly uncomfortable, embarrassed, needing more time to prepare, feeling bound by class, language, gender or cultural unfamiliarity, through to outright discriminatory or excluding situations) is part of identity work; it is what psychologists mean by talking about people "doing" gender or actively managing their identity involving renegotiations and reformulations of self narratives. Social constructions of self and identity are "work in progress" or the working self (Markus & Wurf, 1987) and this is seen as an active matter rather than explanations in terms of people passively influenced by situations and others. If people are involved in the situation, they are contributing and creating a sense of self out of what it means to be (for instance) a student working on a project. This means that the sense of self available depends on the meanings the participants put on what is going on. This possibility could be exploited so that learners could be encouraged to try out writing or interacting in more critical or creative ways (e.g., as if they were researchers, or scientists out exploring new worlds). Hayes (2004) has pointed out the e-learning possibilities of constructing a "practice self" in a game environment.

An important aspect of considering identity as performance is that we require props and costumes to enable us to play our roles convincingly and acceptably according to gender, status, et cetera, and these are the objects in the material world, including functional things such as glasses, computers, phones, and cars so that our sense of self is bound up with enabling cultural artefacts (Dittmar, 1992). Developing technology has enabled us increasingly to present ourselves at a distance (phone, letters, and, over the last 15 years, e-mails and interactive Internet access, Web home pages, blogs, etc.). So the boundaries of self are changed as self-construction takes account of the new opportunities to understand "what things mean," and the way distance and time can be restructured by new technologies.

In the cyber environment, the learner is restructuring or creating themselves using technology to link to others, but will be doing so according to those principles well understood by recent social psychological notions of the multifaceted self, the presented self, the managed self, the self in relationship, and socially constructed identity. Research from role-play and gender swapping (Turkle, 1995) shows that identity management fulfils other psychological requirements including dealing with role conflict (student as fun-loving with peers or as serious scholar with academic staff), self-esteem (online confidence to be witty or talk of problems compared to real world shyness), or relationship (going beyond expectations of skills or interests or showing aspects of character or sexuality).

The *geographies* of cyberspace also have an effect. The organization of the new spaces is important for the management and maintenance of identity, in the same way that the objects we carry, the décor of the home we live in, the style of clothes we wear, and even the things we might have around our desks at work are important. The culture of the space is going to allow some to feel "at home" and others repulsed or repelled in a place where perhaps they "wouldn't be seen dead." We are sensitive to the influence of place in self-presentation offline, and we use "acting with style" to manage the performance of self in our interactions with others, so it matters how much a place allows people to be themselves as they talk or learn about the things online. So, for instance, a possible issue is that for the most part women see cyberspace as a *place* or a *community*, not a space for individual occupation. Just to be "there" is not enough in itself: there is concern for the function or purpose of the communal activity. This is a reflection of the long-established idea that women will use communications to "do" other identity work compared to men. There are many aspects of gendered identity and the psychology of social interactions, which are relevant to understanding learning environments, but a few examples should give some idea of what might be significant.

Starting with the space itself: to propose that many people are now so at home with the common format and "house style" of discussion groups, VLEs, Wikis, and social networking sites that there are no barriers to the presentation of self, and that these are an open and approachable inviting space for both men and women, is to overlook an obvious point that much of the world is designed by men for men. When entering any such space, women have learnt from an early age that spaces need to be negotiated. Use of equipment and resources may have been equally managed under the controlled circumstances of school, but in the outside world of design and technology this is not the case.

We might assume that it is important to recognize that the gender of the learner needs to be acknowledged because there are differences in the way men and women present themselves and their work: for men, what they do is what they are and for women it is who they are and how they are to be understood by others (Miller & Arnold, 2000). The sexual politics of gendered identity has changed over the years, but cultural representations continue to offer male oriented narratives and stereotypical notions of women, assumptions of character from status, and the restrictions of bodily presentation (Gergen & Davis, 1997; Haraway, 1991; Henwood, Kennedy, & Miller, 2001).

Cyberspace as a territory is claimed, without question, as "rightfully theirs" by both men and women, but our point is that how the self and identity are presented will follow the same psychological requirements as in real life performance (because of course it is real life performance). So we argue that the performance and management of identity for everyone in first-life depends on the context and the place as well as role requirements, but women are rightly cautious to treat cyberspace with the circumspection required when entering any space dominated in form and structure by men. Personal social skills are developed as part of identity work as we manage the transition from one place and from being one kind of a person to another. However, the vulnerability, which we identified in our research (Arnold & Miller, 2001) that women experienced when some particularly significant aspect of themselves (for example, their work, or reputation in the academic community), even when their authority and status was well established, was presented with constraint. The same kinds of issues are likely to arise with students in spaces constructed and owned by academics. For instance, we have found that students are more comfortable posting comments in discussion threads on course wiki pages than in daring to alter the pages themselves, even though the point of the wiki is that anyone is free to alter the pages.

The representations that people construct to take part in role-playing games or environments like Second Life are usually called avatars, and might be taken to be independent of the embodied self. For instance, Meadows (2008), in an interesting discussion of the relationship between "self" and "avatar," consistently talks about people "driving" avatars. We would prefer to talk of people "animating" avatars, because we propose that avatar, although it might be of a different gender or even species from the person who animates it, is still an aspect of self. Although it is quantitatively different from all the other aspects of self that are animated, validated, and lived out in real life, it is not qualitatively different from those other aspects of the multifaceted self. Some may even feel that their avatars are more solidly themselves than other ways they exist. Just as you cannot choose your family, but you can choose your friends, you may feel that you have lost the chance to choose your workplace self, but you can choose who and how to be in Second Life. However, the rest of your self may leak through: the ideology, imagination, and vocabulary of the lifelong bank customer support assistant may color both the deeper nature and the surface performance of the hermaphrodite bounty hunter, try as we may. (Cohen & Taylor, 1992, discuss the difficulty of escaping the mundane with earlier technologies).

Just as it seems that full-blown avatars are not intrinsically separate from those who drive or animate them, we suggest that all expressions of self online are avatars of one kind or another. Even picking a name for your discussion group contributions, and deciding not to have a humorous quote in your signature, amounts to a self-presentation statement. In populating a Facebook page, picking a photo, deciding what to reveal and what to lie about, picking your "friends"—and failing to reject others who want to be your friend—you are involved in the same kind of mundane self-presentation and facework that is involved in going to a party, and simultaneously in some of the possibilities for openness and self-construction available in Second Life. Different kinds of online presence afford and support different opportunities. It is easier to appear intellectual and widely read on a blog than on Second Life, more difficult to show visual flair in a discussion group than in either of those, and so on, but the same variety of opportunities and affordances augment and limit our real-life animations. Shelf-stackers who demonstrate their visual flair too expansively may get warnings, and grandparents are not supposed to be reckless risk-takers when taking care of grandchildren, though they may find opportunities to show a generosity and playfulness which is restricted elsewhere.

We need to explain how someone's attempts at virtual presence may start with a "personal" effort but then respond to others and to feedback. This notion of "performance" and "exchange" is an important starting point for understanding working and learning in virtual spaces, which provide a theater or context for the reconstruction of identity. The boundaries of self are open to changes from the characteristics of the new "space" itself, as well as from the possible new roles or performances it affords. The learner in this case is both responding to the situation and possibilities for being themselves in a different way, as well as "acquiring" knowledge that enables them to present different aspects of who they are. Learning to do things differently and to be different as a consequence, is a feature of cyberspace and as the avatar or personal textual representation takes part in learning it can be seen as part of self-change, but also change in relation to others in the group.

Our own research has shown that the psychology of identity and self presentation on the Web is best understood in terms of how people draw on those same signifiers of who and what we are as are used elsewhere: use of photos, claims made of achievements, hobbies, geographical origins, etc. We argued that when people enter cyberspace they bring with them expectations, challenges, and vulnerabilities from everyday life experience and the experience of managing an identity in various circumstances, and here was just another mode (or exciting new theater) to explore and to play out being oneself. So, ways to represent ourselves were those obvious from our existing available repertoire. These ideas concur with Haraway's (1991) ideas about the possibilities for cyborg identity, as she argued that people respond to cyberspace in ways that are familiar from people's long-standing readiness to interact with technology (tools, clothes, language, etc.) as extensions of self at a distance. In social psychological terms, we recognize the efforts people make to converse, exchange goods or information, or send greetings for the credible management of self (Miller, 1995). There is little here that does not also happen face-to-face, and it is surprisingly difficult to lose all traces of your "real-world" self. Miller's early paper on the presentation of life in Web home pages assumed that cyborgian activity could be seen, therefore, as a reflection of already-existing ways of representing the self (Miller, 1995). In our joint work (Arnold & Miller, 2001; Miller & Arnold, 2001) we discussed the cyberpsychology of some of the problems of presenting and representing ourselves in the virtual world of the Web homepage, and many of the same issues still remain as people now use many more (and more technically advanced) spaces. For example, there are still issues for the learner concerning the public/private identity divide as they negotiate their place in discussions, or chat rooms, or decide what to reveal and what groups to join in Facebook, but most will not necessarily be aware of what is happening to their identities as they engage in this way.

The overall point, therefore, is that people entering cyberspace draw on all the same psychological knowledge and strategies for successful acceptance and credibility as they do in embodied identity.

In earlier literature on identity in cyberspace, notions about the theatrical quality of cyberspace (Laurel, 1993) where people might find or create social and cultural commonalities (Danet, 1998; Donath, 1998; Turkle, 1995) provided a justifiably exciting prospect. The psychology of people learning to exploit the medium first focussed on the use of language (Herring, Johnson, & Di Benedetto, 1995; Lawley, 1993) then to studying a number of aspects of identity "play" (for example, gender changing (Braidotti, 1996; Erikson, 1996; Stone, 1991) and then to realizing the complexities of identity in action as discussed by social constructionists (Gergen, 1996; Harré, 1989) and others. That the Internet as theatrical space was rapidly being used in a more interesting and interactive ways gave rise to theoretical positions on the way people were using the Internet drawn from many disciplines, including sociology and psychology (Chandler, 1998). The realization that cyberspace was a frame for action meant that those interested in how we use language to claim identities (Shotter, 1993; Shotter & Gergen, 1989) could also offer theoretical models for understanding the process of both creating and maintaining a cyber identity presence (Arnold & Miller, 2001; Haraway, 1991).

The resources for constructing identity online are still mainly text and still images, but increasingly voice and video and animated avatars are available. Social networking sites also offer a way of constructing a collage or hypertext representation of self, which can incorporate material from others (friends, links, music) as well as multiple representations of the person themselves. The learner may not be skilled at maintaining a sense of identity that is so multifaceted, but in the end we all manage to deal with roles that juxtapose, overlap, or conflict in more or less adequate ways. So when people are faced with a new "presentation of self" problem, how they cope will depend in part how familiar identity shift in this new context seems to them. To many, it will be second nature if not second life.

The locus of control for the frame and modus operandi of the application or site is usually not with the contributor and, like any public space, it will both excite and inhibit. The rules for privacy and anonymity are often there, but some open forums can quickly change character and attitude and communicating by text alone can facilitate flaming as the pre-signals are not noticed or looked for until the change in mood has happened.

Another difficulty can be the seemingly private nature of the spaces; some are labeled as part of a project, a chat "room," as though it were a finite space with closed doors, when clearly it is not. The possibility of anonymity and dissembling in cyberspace is powerful and discussed at length in other contexts (Braidotti, 1996; Donath, 1998), but is for the most part illusory (in discussion group exchanges, students forget we can often track "anonymous" postings). But once the interactions are taken at face value and people's directly made claims to be who they say they are accepted, the images available and the operations permitted will allow interactions of increasingly sophisticated exchange to take place. But meanwhile we need as teachers in higher education to find ways to use these same technical possibilities to encourage engagement that is productive of scholastic work and outcome.

The technologies afford management of a multifaceted, dynamic self, but that is not of course enough in itself. It takes no less time and energy to make the learning relationships happen online than it does in real life, and the real value of presence, online and offline, is in the possibility of generating contacts and building trusting, sharing relationships, as well as through the activities engaged in production of a shared product. There is no doubt that exchange of information and ideas and discussing them freely and without loss of face with people of similar interests and ideas is an ideal. We would suggest that unless there is acknowledgement of the socialness of online activities, then the possibilities of online scholarship will be reduced. For example, Grenfell (2007) shows the importance of family, friends, and the wider social milieu in how adult learners construct their learning identities.

Further issues concerning online identity may relate to status and legitimacy. If identity is performance, and a way of managing roles and relations as well as the individual's personal narrative and autobiography, then the visible actions (e.g., taking certain lines, showing off about knowledge of reading beyond set texts) are more quickly seen than in offline circumstances. The relatively loose affiliation of an ad hoc group project can result in people being willing to work cooperatively, but they might also construct a different understanding of their identity as a result of such interactions with others. This could be a shift in someone's self narrative (for example, personal qualities: supportive; technical skills: speedy reference finder; Gergen & Gergen, 1988; Polkinghorne, 1991). So it is this aspect, along with the possibility of creativity through safe critical exchange and the sense of building something together, that some of the new technologies are intended to develop.

The "acting" metaphor has possibilities online, as much as it has in the primary school play room, for learning through activity and social interaction. In this case we are arguing that it is not just social roles that are important in dealing with the threat of change or with demands to work in different ways, but to understand more about what it means to be a student, what is required over and above the production of certain scholastic outputs. This understanding of cyber-identity is an extension of our position that the activities of people to animate a virtual self happen through mediated interactions with the others on *both* sides of the screen (i.e., virtual and real peers working on screen, sometimes side by side in the computer room, and sometimes collaborating in real space). This post-traditional social psychology of identity would also argue that the motives or rewards (cultural understandings) for creating cyber-relationships remain those that afford or challenge us in offline interactions. However, the implication would be that we need to encourage offline relationships and social interactions that are directed towards learning. Students would in this way learn to complement each other's different strengths, attitudes, and ways of working.

The advantages of working in cyber-learning environments may be to offer students a way to interact in short bursts of activity, at times and places to suit a complex student life. This is a way of maintaining a social identity as an involved student when the opportunities for face-to-face student group work may be limited. The online identity can operate without many high-maintenance social requirements (going for coffee, chatting about other things, personal hygiene). However, the presumed group identity may not necessarily be very well developed and for such identification to play its psychological part (Tajfel, 1981) in working with purpose it has to be established even if only in a contrived way. In traditional social psychology, group conformity enables people to feel confident about how to maximize trust and use the motivation for productivity. Some students (usually male) will use group situations to distance themselves from the role of good student and instead use the opportunity (and audience) to do identity work to develop "joker" characters, use sarcasm and/or nit-picking to establish a role distinction for themselves. Students are often willing to work cooperatively without much prior affiliation, but the idea that they might construct a different understanding of their identity might not occur to them until they are engaged in the task. Social constructs of identity and identity change (Gergen, 1994; Potter, 1996) rely on reflexivity of self and others, so it is this aspect along with the possibility of creativity through safe critical exchange and the sense of building something together that some of the new technologies are intended to develop.

Salmon (2004) gives a model of the processes involved in supporting others' online learning (e-moderating): the moderator should be a confident, constructive, developmental, facilitating, knowledge-sharing, and creative person, and she points out that a range of social and communication skills are essential in presenting that kind of self online. There will be a similar, and partly complementary, list of characteristics of the effective online learner, which students may be presenting. But, beyond the need for effective (and pleasant-seeming) communication, more personal aspects of the selves involved may be significant. For instance, Bennett, Hupert, Tsikalas, Meade, and Honey (1998), in a study of science professionals e-mentoring girls in high school, found that mentoring was likely to be more successful if students knew about interests and hobbies, and if mentors gave personal information about themselves in their e-mails, and gave attention to the students' personal details. Mentors who used humor and light-heartedness were more likely to establish satisfactory online relationships. Such findings are not surprising, but they underline the point that working with people online still involves much the same kind of social issues and processes as working face to face.

The aim for Internet social interactions in education is usually to encourage open debate, honest critical review, and positive contribution. Time offline can be used to support work online, and being offline can be the back-region for preparation of presentation of self online, but the most efficacious benefit may still be to develop good offline group, peer, and colleague relations—in situations that enable the teacher to be involved and be daring in using all the technical facilities but socially constructive in respecting the vulnerabilities of online identity.

REFERENCES

Arnold, J., & Miller, H. (2001). Academic masters, mistresses and apprentices: gender and power in the real world of the Web. *Mots Pluriels, 19*. Retrieved

January 31, 2008, from http://www.arts.uwa.edu.au/MotsPluriels /MP1901jahm.html

Bennet, D., Hupert, N., Tsikalas, K., Meade, T., & Honey, M. (1998). *Critical issues in the design and implementation of telementoring environments*. Retrieved January 31, 2008, from http://www2.edc.org/CCT/publications_report.asp

Braidotti, R. (1996). *Cyberfeminism with a difference*. Retrieved January 31, 2008, from http://www.let.uu.nl/womens_studies/rosi/cyberfem.htm

Chandler, D. (1998). *Writing oneself in cyberspace*. Retrieved January 31, 2008, from http://www.aber.ac.uk/media/Documents/short/homepgid.html

Cohen, S., & Taylor, L. (1992). *Escape attempts: The theory and practice of resistance to everyday life*. London: Routledge.

Danet, B. (1998). Text as mask: Gender, play and performance on the Internet. In S. G. Jones (Ed.), *Cybersociety 2.0: Revisiting computer-mediated communication and community* (pp. 129-158). London: SAGE.

Dittmar, H. (1992). *The social psychology of material possessions (to have is to be)*. Hemel Hempstead, Hertfordshire, United Kingdom: Harvester Wheatsheaf.

Donath, J. (1988). Identity and deception in the virtual community. In P. Kollack & M. Smith (Eds.), *Communities in cyberspace* (pp. 29-59). Berkeley: University of California Press.

Erikson, T. (1996) *The World Wide Web as social hypertext*. Retrieved January 31, 2008, from http://www.pliant.org/personal/Tom_Erickson/SocialHypertext .html

Gergen, K. (1991). *The saturated self: Dilemmas of identity in contemporary life*. New York: Basic Books.

Gergen, K. (1994). *Realities and relationships: Soundings in construction*. Cambridge, MA: Harvard University Press.

Gergen, K. (1996). Technology and the self: From the essential to the sublime. In D. Grodin & T. R. Lindlof (Eds.), *Constructing the self in a mediated world*. London: SAGE. Retrieved January 31, 2008, from http://www.swarthmore.edu/ SocSci/kgergen1/web/page.phtml?id=manu11&st=manuscripts&hf=1

Gergen, K., & Gergen, M. (1988). Narratives and the self as relationship. *Advances in Experimental Social Psychology, 21*, 17-56.

Gergen, M., & Davis, S. (Eds.). (1997). *Toward a new psychology of gender*. New York: Routledge.

Grenfell, M. (2007, November). *Emotionality and social presence: Stories of learning online*. Presented at the annual conference of the AARE, Freemantle, Australia. Retrieved January 31, 2008, from http://www.aare.edu.au/07pap/ gre07204.pdf

Goffman, E. (1959). *The presentation of self in everyday life*. New York: Doubleday Anchor.

Haraway, D. (1991). *Simians, cyborgs, and women: The reinvention of nature*. London: Free Association.

Harré, R. (1989). Language games and the texts of identity. In J. Shotter & K. Gergen (Eds.), *Texts of identity* (pp. 20-35). London: SAGE.

Hayes, E. (2004). *Becoming a (virtual) skateboarder: Communities of practice and the design of e-learning*. Retrieved January 31, 2008, from http://www

.academiccolab.org/resources/documents/Becoming%20a%
20_Virtual_%20Skateboarder.pdf

Henwood, F., Kennedy, H., & Miller, N. (Eds.) (2001). *Cyborg lives? Women's techno-biographies*. York: Raw Nerve.

Herring, S., Johnson, D., & Di Benedetto, T. (1995). This is going too far! Male resistance to female participation on the Internet. In K. Hall & M. Bucholtz (Eds.), *Gender articulated language and the socially constructed self* (pp. 67-96). New York: Routledge.

Laurel, B. (1993). *Computers as theatre*. Reading, MA: Addison-Wesley.

Lawley, E. (1993. *Computers and the communication of gender*. Retrieved January 31, 2008, from http://www.itcs.com/elawley/gender.html

Markus, H., & Wurf, E. (1987). The dynamic self concept: A social psychological perspective. *Annual Review of Psychology, 38*, 299-333.

Meadows, M. (2008). *I, avatar*. Berkeley, CA: New Riders.

Miller, H. (1995). *The presentation of self in electronic life: Goffman on the Internet*. Retrieved June 22, 2008, from: http://ess.ntu.ak.uk/miller/cyberpsych/goffman.htm

Miller, H., & Arnold, J. (2000). Gender and Web home pages. *Computers and Education, 34*, 335-339.

Miller, H., & Arnold, J. (2001). Breaking away from grounded identity? Women academics on the Web. *Cyberpsychology and Behaviour, 4*(1), 95-108.

Polkinghorne, D. E. (1991). Narrative and the self concept. *Journal of Narrative & Life History, 1*(2-3).

Potter, J. (1996) *Representing reality: Discourse, rhetoric and social construction*. London: SAGE.

Salmon, G. (2004). *E-moderating: The key to teaching and learning online*. London: Kogan Page.

Shotter, J. (1993). *Conversational realities: Construction of life through language*. London: SAGE.

Shotter, J., & Gergen, K. (Eds.) (1989). *Texts of identity*. London: SAGE.

Stone, A. R. (1991). Will the real body please stand up? Boundary stories about virtual cultures. In M. Benedikt (Ed.) *Cyberspace: First steps* (pp. 81-118). Cambridge, MA: MIT Press.

Tajfel, H. (1981). *Human groups and social categories*. Cambridge, England: Cambridge University Press.

Turkle, S. (1995). *Life on the screen: Identity in the age of the Internet*. New York: Simon & Schuster.

Wetherell, M., & Maybin, J. (1996). The distributed self: A social constructionist perspective. In R. Stevens (Ed.) *Understanding the self* (pp. 219-279). London: SAGE/OUP.

CHAPTER 6

DIGITAL TRIBES, VIRTUAL CLANS

Steve Wheeler

THE TRIBE

Anthropologists ascribe a variety of definitions to the word "tribe." Most are agreed, however, that a tribe is a small society that has its own customs and culture and that these define it. Tribes are different to clans in that tribes consider themselves totally separate, whereas clans are large kin groups that are retain their distinctiveness, while remaining a part of the larger tribe. Tribes make up an entire society and clans in turn make up the tribe. In this chapter we examine the culture of the virtual learner, and to serve its purposes, I shall use the terms clan and kin group more or less interchangeably to represent subcultural groups. These constitute the larger societal groups that I shall refer to as tribes.

A WEB OF SIGNIFICANCE

Throughout human history, tribal identity has been a pervasive feature of human experience. The need to belong to a homogenous group of indi-

Connected Minds, Emerging Cultures: Cybercultures in Online Learning
pp. 65–75
Copyright © 2009 by Information Age Publishing
All rights of reproduction in any form reserved.

viduals seems to be deeply seated in the human psyche (Maslow, 1954). Individuals identify with those they recognize as their "own kind"—their kin group—through a variety of ways. They can be distinguished through the wearing of a specific dress code or style of jewelry, modification of appearance through skin markings or body piercings, particular styles of talking and language dialect, the performance of specific rites and rituals, or the consumption of specific kinds of food and drink at particular times of the year.

The internalization of identification with own kind groups is generally established at quite a young age. The school environment can act as a catalyst for children. School is the melting pot in which individuals learn to adhere to a particular kin group of their own kind. At the time of writing, in British schools there are several clearly defined groups of young people, sporting strange and exotic names as Art Freaks, Emos, Goths, Jocks, Geeks, Plastics, and Chavs. Similar groups are present in schools in other countries. Each group has a clearly marked dress code, hairstyles, and set of rehearsed behaviors, and can often be identified by the particular styles of music they listen to. All of these serve to identify the individual as a member of their "clan." Art Freaks, for example, are young people whose life revolves around music, the arts, and so on. They dress in original or highly individualized "makeshift" clothing and jewelry, often designed and made or repurposed through their own handicraft. Emos, by contrast (the name is short for Emotional), are darker in the manner they represent themselves. They tend to dye their hair black to match their tight, dark clothes, and they adorn themselves with studded belts and wristbands. Their hair is grown long at the fringe to obscure their faces and they dwell on melancholy themes, enjoying the angst-filled lyrics of cult bands such as My Chemical Romance. They even have their own Valhalla—it is called the Black Parade.

The details of these youth kin groups were obtained through conversation with my two teenage daughters who should know, as they each proudly claim membership in one of these distinct kin groups.

Each individual has made a conscious decision to join his or her specific kin group and is eager to conform to its norms—the modus operandi of that specific group. A visit to one of the largest evolving digital tribal artefacts currently available—namely Wikipedia—reveals that there is general agreement that commonality is a significant feature of tribal membership: "In common modern understanding the word tribe is a social division within a traditional society consisting of a group of interlinked families or communities sharing a common culture and dialect" (Wikipedia, 2006).

TRIBAL IDENTITY

Tribes use common culture to construct group identity and will employ dialects as a shared but often exclusive form of communication. The dialect of the London East End, for example, is peppered with a continually evolving rhyming slang, whereas just a few hundred miles away, the Geordie dialect of the northeast of England is heavy with accent and vocabulary that have survived from the incursions of the Norsemen several centuries before. Such linguistic devices, although deriving from different roots, serve to exclude outsiders who may attempt to enter into the circle. Thus, the shared symbolism of the slang or dialect tacitly protects the tribal culture and secures its social exclusivity for its members. Communication, including speech, clothing, and actions all serve to signal our cultural identities and group membership (Pahl & Rowsell, 2006). Cultural transmission is the communication of ideas. According to Dawkins (1976), key actions and thinking patterns of members of a culture are influenced by contagious patterns of information known as "memes." Memes carry no specific rules, but in effect are adopted and shared around by the tribe as a means of perpetuating that culture.

The smaller elements with the tribe, which can be called "clans," also employ shared symbolism. Each clan, for example, has its totem, a symbol that represents it and distinguishes it from other, possibly rival, clans. In primitive clans, the totem was often a representation of an animal or tree. Durkheim suggests it is easier for clan members to project their feelings of awe toward a totem than toward something that is as complex as the clan itself (Haralambos & Holborn, 1995). For digital tribes and virtual clans, their totems—the traditional rallying points for all tribal activity— are patently the social networking tools within the World Wide Web. Not only are these digital spaces objects of intense interest and rallying points for the clans, they also act as transmitters of units of cultural knowledge. Several authors have argued that digital technologies and electronic networks provide perhaps the best environment for the transmission of memes (Blackmore 1999; Adar, Zhang, Adamic, & Lukose, 2004). Such new literary practices of communication (Lankshear & Knobel, 2006) rely heavily on shared spaces, shared symbolism, and the viral nature of the social Web.

Weber originally suggested that culture per se should be construed as a "web of significance" that was spun by the individuals who comprised the culture (Weber, 1947). Significantly, the increasing role the World Wide Web plays in the shaping of modern tribal culture causes Weber's notion to resonate. Web artifacts are indeed woven into textures of rhizomatic quality. They are created by adherents to serve a number of purposes, but perhaps ultimately to "mark their territories." Until recent technological innovation, people with common tribal identity lived in geographically specific locations, and considered areas of land to be their sole territory. Such territories are now being eroded due to the emergence of new digital tribes who occupy spaces located within cyberspace—a virtual space that transgresses all traditional, social, and political boundaries.

THE DIGITAL TRIBE AND THE "NETWORK NATION"

I will argue here that within the present information age, where digital communication technologies have fractured the tyranny of distance beyond repair, and where computers have become pervasive and ubiquitous, identification through digital mediation has become the new cultural capital (Bordieu & Passeron, 1990). Cultural capital is the set of "invisible bonds that tie a community together" (Curtis, 2004, p. 72), without which societal cohesiveness begins to unravel. It is this "social glue"—such mutual understandings and exchanges that occur on a daily basis—that holds together the basic building blocks of social life in which people simply look out for each other. In a real-world community, people work hard to sustain such mutual exchange, and its value is instilled in them from an early age. This results in the transmission of the culture from generation to generation, through verbal traditions, role modelling, and via created artefacts. For the digital community, such tribal identification operates at least within the social and individual levels, but may be inherently more complex, transcending age, ethnicity, gender, and other social divisions such as disability. Paradoxically, it is largely the individual figures within this equation who act in concert to perpetuate the social cohesion of the tribe. Even stranger in the digital age, such vital exchanges are conducted regularly between people who rarely or never meet face to face, through one or more mediating technologies.

The anthropologist Erving Goffman suggested that the performance of the self is a social act designed to regulate the impression one presents to others. Goffman's notion of impression management in public spaces evokes the construction of the self simultaneously in the mind of the individual and in the collective mind of the audience (Goffman, 1959). We see ourselves reflected in the eyes of the other, and adjust our behavior to conform and remain accepted by those with whom we choose to identify (Cooley, 1902). Rheingold (2002) applies this "theory of being" to the use of short message service (SMS) texting by young people—who they send texts to, and receive them from, defines an element of their social identity, as constructed by themselves in relation to the others in their SMS circle of communication. Such small friendship circles may be physical, or virtual, or a combination of both, and for the individual, this may matter little, but the friendship circle remains very much an essence of his or her identity as a tribal member. The content of the text message may also be secondary to the fact that the message has been sent, and the perception that the sender has simply been "thinking about you." Such management of impression is projected through the technology to show the sender in a best light to others.

SMART MOBS

Rheingold (2002) coined the term "smart mobs" (a play on the word *mobile*) to describe individuals who work collectively toward a particular goal without necessarily having met. Unlike their more feral counterparts, smart mobs tend to act intelligently and with a purpose. They are distributed beings (Curtis, 2004), carrying devices that have immense computing power and telecommunication capability, enabling them to collaborate in ways which were previously inconceivable. The immediacy of their communicative ability and the ubiquity and persistence of their engagement (they are always connected) within the smart mob enable them to perform collective feats of imagination, cooperation, trading, and the exploitation of aggregative mind power, beyond anything humankind has ever achieved. This may appear to read as a eulogy but, in reality, smart mobs are the vanguard of an influential social movement that will gather pace over the next few years and will ultimately radically change the face of education.

INTELLIGENT SWARMING

Smart mobs can act for the public good, for example when drivers use their mobile phones to inform a local radio station of a road traffic accident. They can also act concertedly for more nefarious purposes, such as tram or bus passengers who text their ticketless friends to warn them of the location of ticket inspectors. Some smart mob activities may be pointless to all but those who participate in the action. In recent years, a new social phenomenon has been observed, particularly in urban areas. Known as "flash mobs," they are large groups of people who suddenly gather in a public place, perform some meaningless activity for a period of time, and then just as quickly disappear. Flash mobs are almost always coordinated by one or more individuals through mass SMS texting, e-mails, or other electronic message transmission methods. Technology-directed flash mobs have occasionally gathered for political purposes at times of civil unrest in Romania and China, but generally their purpose is ill defined. Flash mobs have been hailed as a classic example of the innate need for people to belong to a group, be privy to inside knowledge, and be able to participate in what is "happening." What is more, they reflect the immediacy and social richness that are redolent of contemporary digital cultures.

"ALWAYS CONNECTED"

Rheingold also identifies the "thumb tribe," which consists predominantly of those younger members of society who appear to be constantly connected to the rest of their tribe and who communicate principally through "one thumb signaling" via mobile phone texting. They belong to the larger tribe of the "always connected" who are identifiable by their apparent dependency on mobile telecommunication technologies. They are clearly identified not only by the means through which they communicate, but also by the manner in which this communication is constructed (i.e., their vocabulary). SMS text is constrained by a single message limit of 160 characters. To save money, texters have developed a reduced form of language made up of letters, numbers and symbols. Known as "squeeze text" or simply "txt" (Carrington, 2005), this clannish form of language alters the morphology of the language being used, with little or no loss of its semantics for those who are members of the clan. For those outside the clan however, txting can present a bewildering conundrum. Tim Shortis' chapter in this volume delves into this phenomenon more deeply.

DIGITAL PERVASION

Mark Kramer and John Traxler have both already articulated in their chapters that digital technologies are in the process of pervading every aspect of our lives. "We are all digital now," claimed Paul Longley of University College London, in a research report (British Broadcasting Corporation News, 2006). In so doing, he identified a global digital tribe. Taking into account the fact that much of the world's population is more than a day's walking distance from a fixed line telephone, and even allowing for the growing trend toward mobile phone usage in developing countries, or the paucity of computers in the third world, Longley's claim could be considered contentious. However, where applied to Western industrialized nations, it musters some credibility. There is nonetheless a need to acknowledge the digital divides that are perpetuated wherever technology is applied. Interestingly, Longley's claim may hold some truth when contextualized in a world where cable and satellite television channels proliferate, digital mobile communication becomes ever more pervasive, surveillance of civil movement and activity is automated, and where digital identification of individuals, commodities, and services is becoming commonplace. The location of a global digital tribe within this landscape is a feature of interest for this chapter.

Longley's research team identified digital tribes by their socioeconomic activities and by the manner in which they used information and communication technologies. Yet there are more subtle distinctions that can be made, particularly at the perceptual and motivational levels of analysis.

LOSS OF IDENTITY?

There is an argument that due to the process of globalization, national boundaries (and therefore tribal boundaries) have been eroded to the point that we are amalgamating into a homogenous mass of humanity, and where the last vestiges of tribal identity are vanishing. In essence, the forces of globalization have amalgamated us all into one tribe. We are living in a "corporate age," runs the argument, in which all of our decisions are being dictated by "those who have the real power." Thus, wherever I travel, I can find the same fast food outlets and the same familiar chain stores where I can purchase clothing and footwear I will be comfortable wearing. I can blend into the background because I am wearing a similar style of clothing to the hundreds of other people milling around in the high street, and I will not be conspicuous, because I am eating the same food and drinking from an identical soft drink can as the natives. Have I therefore blended in to such an extent into the local culture that I lose my identity? No, my individual identity remains intact, while my individualism is subsumed into the social *melange* within which I am located. Identity and individualism are not synonymous, even though there are obvious commonalities. The identity argument may break down when it is applied to the formation of a single "digital tribe," but clearly there are many personal identities represented within the tribe. It is quite possible, then, that there is in fact one digital tribe in the broadest sense of its meaning, but there are many subsets of this large digital tribe—what we can term "virtual clans."

VIRTUAL CLANS

Virtual clannish behavior can be observed in a number of ways, but probably most overtly in the subtly distinctive ways in which people use their mobile phones. Members of the mobile tribe can be divided into at least two clans. One clan can be observed holding their mobile phones to their ears, while another group tends to stare down at their devices. This is the audio message clan and the text message clan. The former continue to conceive of the mobile phone as having the same functionality of the fixed line telephone—"that's why it's called a phone." The latter have made the conceptual leap of seeing the mobile phone as a multifunctional communication tool, and as we have already seen, have developed their own reduced or slang version of common language.

Another example is the social networking tribe which boasts many clans, such as the MySpace clan, the Bebo clan, the YouTube clan, and so on. One particularly interesting comparison can be made between the users of Flickr and Facebook. The Flickrite kin group generally trades in images (photographs), and members rarely identify themselves using their real names. By contrast, Facebookers identify themselves using real names and photographs, and coalesce around groups with common interests that are wider than photography. Facebookers also have a reputation for being frivolous, and engage in virtual food-fights, "poking" each other and sending inane notes, much akin to the naughty school children who fool around in the back row of the classroom. Flickrites are more likely to trade in affirmative comments, the "favoriting" of attractive images and the awarding of prizes in mutual celebration of each other's photographic skills. Facebookers, on the other hand, are more intent on gathering together as many "friends" as possible—some with strong social ties, the majority with weaker ties, as "friends of friends" (or simply random acquaintances) begin to outnumber close friends. For a fuller analysis of Flickrite and Facebooker subcultures, see Steve Wheeler and Helen Keegan's chapter in this volume.

One virtual tribe will behave in a manner that can be distinguished from other tribes. Clans, on the other hand, tend to be large "kin groups" that generally involve themselves in an identifiably common practice, but are subtly distinct in some way within this practice. They yet remain a part of the larger social mass of the tribe. Whereas clans represent a part of society, tribes may constitute the entire society. Virtual clans are defined more by the technology they subscribe to, and ultimately, the software they use. Although we are bombarded on all sides by advertisements and corporate images prompting us to subscribe, buy into, and involve ourselves in commodities of all shapes and sizes, many of us also have infinitely more choice in what we do, the alliances we make, and how we spend our money. As a result of this plethora of choice there are many virtual clans; the distinctions are often minute, but the clans are different, inspired by different motives, identified by different artefacts and activities and, ultimately, distinguished by different aims and destinations.

Virtual youth clans spend much of their time texting each other on their mobile phones. They may identify their clan members more readily through the kind of mobile phone they use, its features and capabilities. They may identify as a part of a clan through the use of specific language and other symbolism. Tim Shortis' chapter in this volume deals with this "txting" phenomenon in more depth. Some virtual clanships are emerging through the choice of social networking service; Bebo users are distinctly different in many small ways from their counterpart clans who subscribe to Facebook, who are again different from those who use MySpace.

EN MASSE, ONLINE

Still other virtual clans are emerging from the cultures surrounding online leisure activities, such as massively multiplayer online role-playing games (MMORPGs), strategy games and transnational special interest groups that meet en masse, online. In massively multiplayer online gaming, the clan (sometimes referred to as "guild") is the name used to describe a group of individuals who play competitively against other clan groups. One very popular online role-playing game, World of Warcraft, has millions of adherents who compete seriously on a regular basis in guilds with strangers they become very familiar with but never meet face to face. MMORPG clans who engage with war games sometimes name their virtual clans after real or fictitious military divisions or armies. They may further identify themselves as members of their clan by creating uniformly themed avatars (their digital altar egos) to represent themselves within cyberspace. World of Warcraft even introduced digital tabards that could be adjusted electronically to show unique features that identify a particular guild. Members then purchase their own for their avatar to wear, thereby identifying more closely with their virtual kin group.

Furthermore, virtual clans often develop their own closed newsgroups and e-mail listings to keep their geographically distributed members informed. In MMORPGs, clans can identify themselves further by developing their own virtual territories, building businesses, and earning virtual currency (Childress & Brasswell, 2006). They can be fiercely competitive and often take immense pride in their achievements at the expense of rival clans. As virtual clans become larger and more organized, they also tend to become more hierarchical, even electing their own leaders—clan chieftains—and developing their own unique "tags" that can be used to visually identify themselves as clan members during text communication.

In the 3-D multiuser virtual environment (MUVE) Second Life, which at the time of writing has attracted in excess of 8 million subscribers, there is a distinct differential between those SLifers who own land and commodities, and those who are simply "visiting" and making use of these commodities. The traders and the consumers are a reflection of real life, so in effect, in-world experience mirrors our observations of real, embodied life. The use of avatars is a departure from embodied life, with many SLifers participating in the practice of gender swapping or in some cases, create both male and female versions of themselves so they may act as a "couple." Even more significantly, some SLifers employ avatars that represent themselves as animals—some common, some exotic—or as human characters with "perfect" dimensions. Still others choose to represent themselves as fantasy figures, such as characters with anime cartoon features, or as aliens, wizards, pixies, or fairies. Yet the clear cultural distinction in Second Life is between those who trade and those who purchase. The SLife tribe thus has at least two distinct clans based on the notion of commodity, and it is highly likely that others will emerge as Second Life and other MUVEs become better established.

CONCLUSION

This chapter has explored the notion of tribes and clans and has applied these concepts to those who use digital technologies. Digital communication technologies and electronic networks provide ideal environments within which new cultural transmission can propagate and it has been argued here that new tribes and clans are emerging as a direct result of sustained interaction with technology. Furthermore, clans tend to emerge within tribes as cultural definitions and the generation of artefacts become more pronounced. There may be one single "digital tribe" in the broadest sense of its meaning, but analysis of the many social activities found on the Web indicates that there are many subsets of this large digital tribe—the "virtual clans."

REFERENCES

Adar, E., Zhang, L., Adamic, L., & Lukose, R. (2004). Implicit structure and dynamics of blogspace. Cited in C. Lankshear & M. Knobel (Eds.), *New literacies: Everyday practices and classroom learning* (chapter 7, pp. 221). Maidenhead, England: Open University Press.

British Broadcasting Corporation News. (2006, August 8). *Britain's digital tribes revealed*. Retrieved September 14, 2006, from http://news.bbc.co.uk/1/hi/technology/5256552.stm

Blackmore, S. (1999). The meme machine. Cited in C. Lankshear & M. Knobel. (2006). *New literacies: Everyday practices and classroom learning* (chapter 7, p. 221). Maidenhead, England: Open University Press.

Bordieu, P., & Passeron, J. -C. (1990). *Reproduction in education, society and culture.* London: SAGE.

Carrington, V. (2005). Txting: The end of civilisation (again?) *Cambridge Journal of Education, 35*(2), 161-175.

Childress, M. D., & Brasswell, R. (2006). Using massively multiplayer online role-playing games for online learning. *Distance Education, 27*(2), 187-196.

Cooley, C. H. (1902). *Human nature and the social order.* New York: Scribner.

Curtis, M. (2004). *Distraction: Being human in a digital world.* London: Futuretext.

Dawkins, R. (1976). *The selfish gene.* Oxford, England: Oxford University Press.

Goffman, E. (1959). *The presentation of self in everyday life.* New York: Doubleday Anchor.

Haralambos, M., & Holborn, M. (1995). *Sociology: Themes and perspectives* (4th ed.). London: HarperCollins.

Lankshear, C., & Knobel, M. (2006). *New literacies: Everyday practices and classroom learning.* Maidenhead, England: Open University Press.

Maslow, A. H. (1954). *Motivation and personality.* New York: Harper.

Pahl, K., & Rowsell, J. (2006). *Literacy and education: Understanding the new literacy studies in the classroom.* London: Paul Chapman.

Rheingold, H. (2002). *Smart mobs: The next social revolution.* Cambridge, MA: Basic Books.

Weber, M. (1947). *The theory of social and economic organisation.* New York: The Free Press.

Wikipedia. (2006). *Tribe.* Retrieved September 15, 2006, from http://en.wikipedia.org/wiki/Tribe

CHAPTER 7

GAMING AND THE NETWORK GENERATION

Nicola Whitton

INTRODUCTION

There is a conception of the modern student, brought up on computers and interactive media, as part of a cognitively different generation, who learns in ways that are significantly different from previous generations of learners. It has been argued that computer games, through the provision of immersive interactive environments, have the potential to motivate and engage this new breed of learner (Oblinger, 2004; Prensky, 2001).

This perceived change in the learning needs of the "games generation" (Prensky, 2001) or "Net generation" (Oblinger, 2004), coupled with the ongoing growth in use and acceptability of a range of communications technology, has precipitated a growing interest in the potential of computer games for learning. In a recent survey, 36% of primary school teachers and 27% of secondary school teachers said that they had used games to teach (Sandford, Ulicsak, Facer, & Rudd, 2006). It is not clear, however, the extent of use of games-based learning in postschool education, or the appropriateness of this method with older learners.

Connected Minds, Emerging Cultures: Cybercultures in Online Learning
pp. 77–89

This chapter considers the acceptability of computer game-based learning in the context of university students. It discusses the potential of computer games in relation to theories of learning, examines the conceptions of a cognitively different type of learner, and explores the notion that these learners find computer games the ideal environment in which to learn. The chapter then goes on to discuss student game preferences in terms of genre and the types of computer game that may be more appropriate for learning, and aspects of computer game design that may influence student use. The chapter concludes by considering the benefits and challenges of computer games for learning and teaching in tertiary education.

COMPUTER GAMES AS
CONSTRUCTIVIST LEARNING ENVIRONMENTS

This section will argue that certain types of computer game, designed for educational purposes, can provide authentic situated learning experience. The constructivist perspective hypothesis is that people learn by constructing their own perspectives about the world, by problem-solving and personal discovery. The design of student-centered online learning environments and interactive, exploratory learning objects has been very much influenced by the constructivist perspective (e.g., Grabinger, Dunlap, & Duffield, 1997; Land & Hannafin, 2000). However, students do not always use learning environments in the manner expected (Beasley & Smyth, 2004) and it is the activities that are carried out in a learning environment that support autonomous learning and higher-level thinking skills. By the provision of problem-based contexts with authentic tasks, computer games have the potential to be truly engaging constructivist learning environments.

A constructivist learning environment provides real tasks with just-in-time information and resources to support the completion of activities in an authentic and transferable context. Wilson (1996) describes a constructivist learning environment as:

> a place where learners may work together and support each other as they use a variety of tools and information resources in their guided pursuit of learning goals and problem-solving activities. (p. 5.)

Honebein (1996) describes the pedagogic goals of the design of constructivist learning environments: they should support students to take responsibility for their learning, including the topics they pursue, methods of learning, and strategies for problem-solving; provide experience of multiple perspectives and viewpoints; encourage ownership and self-awareness of the learning process; make learning realistic and relevant, based on authentic, real-life activities; make learning a social experience, supported by collaboration and interaction; use multiple modes of representation; and use rich media.

Computer games can provide the opportunity for learners to explore and navigate immersive virtual worlds using rich media, they can create authentic contexts for practising skills that can be transferred to the real world, and they can present a forum and context for problem solving. Researchers have highlighted that computer games have the facility to create real-life problem-solving experiences. Kiili (2005) argues that "games provide a meaningful framework for offering problems to students. In fact, a game itself is a big problem that is composed of smaller causally linked problems" (p. 17), and in a survey of 25 educational experts using game-based learning, de Freitas (2006) found that "broadly the experts interviewed seemed to advocate the use of simulations and games for problem-based learning" (p. 349). Gee (2003) argues that playing video games has key learning principles built in and involves learning a new literacy and, although games are not necessarily appropriate for teaching content, they do teach people how to interact in a new domain and learn transferable skills. He says that when we learn new domains we learn to experience things in new ways, gain the potential to join new social groups, and prepare for future learning in related domains.

Collaboration and learning from others is fundamental to the constructivist perspective, and multiuser games or collaborative game playing in the same physical space are two ways that facilitate this. Central to the notion of constructivist learning is the idea of students working together, sharing and clarifying ideas and opinions, developing communication skills, and learning from one another. Working collaboratively enables students to work to their strengths, develop critical thinking skills and creativity, validate their ideas, and appreciate a range of individual learning styles, skills, preferences, and perspectives (McConnell, 2000; Palloff & Pratt, 2005).

Vygotsky's (1978) work in the field of social constructivism is particularly concerned with the collaborative aspects of learning, theorising that learning takes place at a social level first and then at an individual level. His theory of Zones of Proximal Development contends that the zone of proximal development is the difference between what a student can learn working alone, and what he or she can achieve when being supported and guided by a teacher or some other expert. In collaborative gaming, this apprenticeship role is provided by more experienced players supporting and initiating "newbie's" (Steinkulher, 2004). Participating in communities of practice provides a legitimate and ongoing way of learning from others as part of a group through apprenticeship and education in the context of the group norms, processes, and identity (Lave & Wenger, 1991). Wenger (2000) describes these communities of practice as "the basic building blocks of a social learning system" (p. 229). Multiuser computer gaming communities provide a platform for collaboration, support, and learning through in-game interactions, out-of-game support sites, observation, and provision of just-in-time information (Ducheneaut & Moore, 2005).

The constructivist perspective also puts forward the idea that students learn better by exploring and experiencing authentic contexts for themselves and discovering their own meaning from the experience. The experiential learning cycle (Kolb, 1984) emphasizes the importance of active learning, with planning, reflecting, and theoretical underpinning. According to this cycle, learning takes place as part of a sequence of steps. Computer game-based learning provides the interaction and feedback that is crucial to the experiential learning cycle. Computers can facilitate a whole range of types of interaction—from basic items that can be clicked, moving backwards or forwards through a linear sequence—to the use of hyperlinked environments and virtual interactive worlds (Sims, 1997). Computer games have the potential to offer sophisticated interaction systems and intrinsic feedback mechanisms. Gee (2003) argues that computer games reflect the experiential learning cycle in that students must examine the virtual environment, reflect on the situation and form a hypothesis about what something in the situation might mean, and re-probe the virtual world to see what effect it has. While it is true that this cycle maps onto learning within the game world, it does not necessarily provide students with scope for the metacognitive processes that are required for them to truly engage with and take responsibility for their own learning when applying their learned knowledge and skills to the real world. It is important to recognize that game-based learning is necessarily part of a larger learning process and should be considered in terms of the other activities and reflection that surround the game and not as a stand-alone activity.

Adult learning theory, or andragogy (Knowles, 1998), argues that the key characteristics of adult learners, as related to their motivations and learning needs, are that: adults need to know why they need to know something before they are willing to invest time and energy in learning it; they have a deep psychological need to be self-directing and to take responsibility for their own learning; they have a wide variety of backgrounds and experience and it cannot be assumed that all adult learners come from the same starting point; they become ready to learn something when they need to know it to be able to cope effectively with real-life situations; and they are task oriented in their learning. They learn things best in the context of using them to do things they want to do. It is important to note, however, that pressure of life and work commitments and limited time to devote to study is becoming more true of younger students also. Adult learning theory has much in common with the constructivist approach in that it advocates learners taking responsibility for their learning, and learning through experience in an authentic context, so it can be argued it is actually of relevance to all learners to varying degrees.

Adult learning theory highlights the fact that motivation to learn is paramount and that learning activities must be purposeful. This brings into question the acceptability of game-based learning with adult learners, who may perceive games as frivolous and a waste of time. Play is perceived by many as only for young children, as not being a respectable thing to do, and as activity that is easy (Rieber, 1996). It is important to ensure that any gaming experience in an educational context is appropriately designed so that it not only meets an educational need in the most effective manner, but is perceived as doing so by the students. The next section discusses student attitudes and perceptions toward computer games in more detail.

ATTITUDES TO GAMES-BASED LEARNING IN HIGHER EDUCATION

Prensky (2001) describes the definite distinction between "games generation" learners, or "digital natives" who have grown up with computer games, television, and other media, and use them to learn instinctively; and older learners, for whom interacting with these types of technology has to be done through conscious effort and who exhibit more traditional learning strategies. He argues that the generation of people brought up in a world of computers are cognitively different from previous generations and that this immersion in technology has fundamentally changed the way in which people acquire and assimilate information. He describes ten cognitive changes in people of the Games Generation associated with a fast pace of learning and ability to process information from multiple channels at a greater speed, but with a need for quick rewards and feedback. He also describes a preference for visual materials and working collaboratively, actively seeking and evaluating information with no distinction between play and learning, and a greater acceptance of games and fantasy contexts for learning, change, and new technologies in general.

Two recent U.K. studies have provided evidence that students may not be as comfortable with technology for learning and new ways of working as may be assumed. In a study into student expectations of higher education, Ipsos MORI (2007) investigated information and communication technology provision and found that while the group of potential students were classed as digital natives (e.g., have grown up with technology, see it as a core part of their engagement, see ubiquitous Internet as the norm) they do not value the use of technology for its own sake, but instead put a high value on face-to-face teaching and traditional teacher-student interaction. CIBER (2008) found that the assumption that young people who are brought up in the information age are more Web-literate than older people is false and, although they demonstrate an apparent ease with computers, they rely heavily on search engines and lack critical and analytic skills. In fact, the study claims, character traits that are often associated with young Web users, such as lack of tolerance of delay in search and navigation, are actually true of all age groups of Web users.

Throughout the literature on game-based learning, it is sometimes assumed that a primary reason for using computer games for learning is that they are intrinsically motivating to students (e.g., Alessi & Trollip, 2001; Becker, 2001; Oblinger, 2004). A study was carried out at Napier University in Edinburgh to examine student perceptions of game-based learning, in particular the motivational aspects (Whitton, 2007). This study consisted initially of 12 in-depth interviews with current or exstudents to draw out themes and opinions relating to the potential of game-based learning in higher education. There were an equal number of male and female participants, ranging in age from 20–29 to 60+ and containing a mix of game-players and people who did not play games recreationally. These interviews were used to identify areas of interest and a survey was carried out with a larger population ($n = 200$) to examine student attitudes to computer games for learning. The population used for this study was a group of third-year undergraduate, and master's-level postgraduate computing students. It was hypothesized that, out of any population of students in higher education, the demographics of computing students matched those most likely to engage with computer games recreationally (i.e., men aged between 20 and 29 [Entertainment Software Association, 2007]), so could be argued to be a group for whom this mode of teaching may be perceived most positively.

The vast majority (98.5%) of this population had played a computer game at some point previously, while 48.5% still played regularly and 38.5% occasionally: this is a group that engages with games in their leisure time and, if the assumptions in the gaming literature are to be believed, would be expected to be motivated by educational games. The two primary motivations cited for playing computer games were to be able to play with others (social benefits) and for the mental challenge. This provides some evidence that games as constructivist learning environments that support problem solving may match the types of game that students prefer to play in their leisure time.

In order to consider whether game-based learning would be seen as an acceptable, or even motivational, way to learn in the student group under study, they were asked if they would be positively motivated to learn something with a game, whether they would not be motivated either way, or whether they would find using a game to learn demotivating. Only 62.5% said that they would find computer games for learning positively motivational and previous experience of playing educational games did not significantly affect the level of positive perception. It is interesting to note that even in a group of predominantly male, predominantly young, game playing students, who it might be expected to be more motivated than other groups to learn with computer games, fewer than two thirds of the students said that using a game to learn would be positively motivating.

This research provides evidence that fewer students find learning games motivational than might be expected of "net generation" learners. However, from the initial interviews (many of the participants of which were considerably older) there was a universal feeling that while computer games for learning may not be motivational for their own sake as *games*, they would be motivational as *learning experiences* if they were perceived as being an appropriate and effective way to learn and not merely as a gimmick.

While this is clearly a small study, it provides evidence that the reasons for using computer games for learning should not be based on the supposed cognitive needs of one generation, but because they can be effective tools for learning, for all learners. Despite the potential motivational aspects of games not providing a compelling rationale for their use educationally, there are other pedagogic reasons for considering computer game-based learning. A more persuasive argument for using games to learn is based on the changing profile of university students. Changes have taken place in the needs of learners, but this is due to changes in the student population leading to greater diversity of age, background, and ability coupled with changes in students' attitudes toward their education, increasingly seeing themselves as customers in the education system, and having greater expectations. Computer games will not suit every learner, or every learning context, but when effectively designed can provide authentic collaborative learning environments which, while not intrinsically motivational to all students, will be seen as an appropriate way to learn if they are the best tool for the job.

GAME GENRE AND DESIGN CHARACTERISTICS

Two other important aspects that influence the effectiveness of computer games for learning as constructivist environments are the genre of game and the design. Certain types of game may be more appropriate for learning than others, but these may not be those that are typically played by students in their leisure time.

In the Napier University study described in the previous section, students were asked about their gaming habits. There was a wide range of types of games played within this group, including adventures, multi-player games, puzzles, role plays, shooters, simulations, sports, and strategy games. The most favoured genre overall was first-person shooters, which, because of their fast-pace and violent content may be inappropriate for education. So, while the group who took part in the study may show a greater propensity to play games, the types of games favored are not always suitable for learning in a formal context.

However, adventure games and strategy games were the next two most popular genres. These game types exhibit many of the characteristics of constructivist learning environments, such as an authentic experiential context, cognitive puzzlement, and problem-based situations. The use of multiplayer games among this group was also high, indicating acceptability of a collaborative environment.

A second issue to that of genre is the types of virtual gaming world that are most appropriate for learning. This can be in terms of the number of players (single to multiplayer to massively multiplayer), the fidelity of the environment (textual to graphical to immersive), and the playing medium (desktop, console, mobile device, real world). A second study was carried out at Napier University to compare the effect of interface design on engagement (Whitton, 2007). Two collaborative online game-based activities with the same learning outcomes were compared: the Time Capsule, a direct online translation of a face-to-face collaborative activity; and the Pharaoh's Tomb, a graphical multiplayer adventure game. Both game-based activities were designed to take the same time to complete and with the same set of learning outcomes and supporting materials. Each of the sessions was designed to fit into a one-hour time slot, because this fitted with the timing of lessons at the universities where the trials were undertaken.

The Time Capsule is an interactive group negotiation activity with an explicit goal to agree on items to be placed in a time capsule and clear rules regarding the number of items and their total cost. There are no measured outcomes or scoring; therefore, beyond achieving the goal or not, it is not possible for teams to compare themselves with others, removing the element of competition. The Time Capsule provides a fantasy scenario for the participants. It does not present an immersive world that can be explored as part of that scenario, although it does provide interactivity and feedback to actions.

The Pharaoh's Tomb is a three-dimensional collaborative graphical adventure game that offers a range of challenges based on group problem solving and has explicit group goals of returning an object to a certain place within the tomb and enabling the whole team to escape, and implicit rules as to what the team members can do (e.g., each player can carry only one object at a time). The Pharaoh's Tomb game is scored, which means that there are measured outcomes (as opposed to simply achieving the goal or not), and teams can compare themselves with other teams, introducing an element of competition. The game is not designed to support intergroup competition because this would be at odds with the collaborative nature of the exercise. It provides a fantasy environment of an Egyptian Pharaoh's tomb that can be navigated and explored; characters can interact with objects and gain feedback from the environment as well as from other players.

The comparative study was undertaken with undergraduate computing and marketing students ($n = 112$) such that each student was allocated to one of the activities. When a student logged in to the multiuser software engine, he or she was automatically allocated to the next available game, which effectively meant that players were allocated to teams at random. Students were asked to complete three questionnaires: background information before the session, engagement after the online element, and self-perceived learning after the debriefing and discussion. This chapter only considers the analysis of the engagement questionnaire (although there was also no significant difference in self-perceived learning).

The responses to each question in the engagement questionnaire were summed to produce an overall engagement score for each individual. To see whether there is a significant difference between the levels of engagement of those students using the Pharaoh's Tomb game and those using the Time Capsule learning activity, the nonparametric Mann-Whitney statistical test was considered to be appropriate (Greene & D'Oliveria, 1993).

There was found to be no significant difference in engagement between the two conditions. However, engagement was hypothesized to be made up of five factors: challenge, control, interest, immersion, and purpose, and the questionnaire was developed so that specific questions mapped to each of these factors. It was therefore also possible to use the Mann-Whitney statistical analysis to examine whether there was a significant difference in any of the factors between the two experimental conditions.

There was no significant difference between the level of challenge, interest, immersion, and purpose between the two activities. However, there was a significant difference, at the 0.01 level of significance, in perceived control between the two activities, with the Time Capsule activity being rated more highly for control. This is a particularly interesting finding as it provides evidence that, while the Pharaoh's Tomb was designed to provide an environment with many options and objects that could be manipulated, students actually felt a significantly higher level of control using the Time Capsule application. This could be due to the greater complexity in the interface of the Pharaoh's Tomb, or the fact that the Pharaoh's Tomb required three-dimensional spatial navigation skills, which left a small number of students unable to move around in the environment, whereas the Time Capsule did not require the players to master navigation or interact with objects in a virtual environment.

In considering the type of game-based environment that is appropriate for student learning, it is important to think about the needs of the teaching situation to ensure that they are met without adding additional cognitive elements (e.g., steep learning curve, complex interface, navigation) that are unnecessary to the learning process.

CHALLENGES OF GAME-BASED LEARNING IN VIRTUAL WORLDS

It is important that educators do not make assumptions about the current generation of students, or take for granted that tools used for entertainment will transfer into appropriate tools for learning. There are several challenges for computer game-based learning in education.

The rationale for using games must be clear to both teacher and students. While some games may support learning, educators must be clear that they are using them for their pedagogic benefits and not simply because of an assumed motivational effect. If this is the case, then students will be more likely to perceive the game as being an appropriate and effective way in which to learn. There needs to be an explicit pedagogic rationale and a strong match between gaming outcomes and learning outcomes so that engagement in the game is linked directly to learning from the game. Learning from games needs to be scaffolded to ensure that all aspects of the experiential learning cycle are catered for, and that all student learning styles are taken into account, with activities to encourage reflection, collaboration, and application outside of the gaming environment; computer games need to be seen as an element in a learning package rather than a stand-alone activity.

Problems associated with the design of bespoke education software often involve the amount of money spent on producing it compared to entertainment software, and how this affects the expectations of learners. Jenkins (2002) argues that most educational software is of poor quality, badly edited, and unprofessional. It will never be the case, however, that the amounts of money spent on commercial software will be available for education, and it is more important that resources be used to ensure that educational games are well-designed in terms of playability and learning. The growing trend towards modifying existing games software for use in education (de Freitas, 2007) may provide one way to address this issue. Whatever method for development is adopted, creation of a complete learning package is timely and expensive, and requires specialist expertise.

It is also important that the use of games does not lead to accidental exclusion, particularly on the basis of extra cognitive load caused by the game design or interface. In particular, spatial ability may limit navigation in three-dimensional environments. While the studies described in this chapter were carried out with a predominantly male sample, it is also important to consider the perceptions of females as relates to game playing, as these may be very different to those of males. The act of learning to play a game itself is often considered to be part of the experience in entertainment software; however, this needs to be kept to a minimum in an educational context (when it does not relate to the learning outcomes). There is also a danger with the use of computer games for learning, as with any educational innovation, that motivation to engage by students is partly due to a novelty effect and, as it becomes over-used, students cease to be motivated.

A number of researchers believe that students can learn by developing or creating games, as well as by simply playing them. Rieber, Smith, and Noah (1998) argue that learning by building games can be an at least, if not more, effective way to learn than traditional methods, while Shubik (1989) says that "possibly at least as important as playing a game is constructing one" (p. 186). Gee (2003) argues that active, critical learning should lead to learners becoming designers, either by physically designing extensions to the game or by cognitively extending the game design and using that to inform their play.

A final issue to highlight is the lack of robust empirical studies into the effectiveness of computer games for learning, particularly in postschool education. Much of the research into game-based learning is anecdotal and small scale, or does not address issues of educational effectiveness. There is an identified need among policy makers for more robust empirical work to provide a baseline of evidence on how educational games can be used most effectively to teach (de Freitas, 2007). Mitchell and Savill-Smith (2005) conclude that

> the literature base is relatively sparse, findings often conflict in their outcomes, there is a lack of studies regarding educational games use by adolescents, some studies have methodological problems, and longitudinal studies are needed. (p. 61.)

The author strongly believes that there is a place for computer game-based learning in tertiary education, but that it is certainly not suited to every teacher, student, or learning context. It is key to see games as simply another option available to teachers to effectively integrate with other traditional and electronic pedagogic practices. However, when used for its pedagogic aptness, with appropriate scaffolding for learning and reflection, computer game-based learning environments have the potential to provide truly useful, engaging, and collaborative educational experiences.

REFERENCES

Alessi, S. M., & Trollip, S. R. (2001). *Multimedia for learning*. Boston: Allyn & Bacon.

Beasley, N., & Smyth, K. (2004). Expected and actual student use of an online learning environment: A critical analysis. *The Electronic Journal of E-learning*, *2*(1), 34-50.

Becker, K. (2001). Teaching with games: The minesweeper and asteroids experience. *Journal of Computing in Small Colleges*, *17*(2), 23-33.

CIBER. (2008). *Information behaviour of the researcher of the future*. Bristol, England: JISC.

de Freitas, S. I. (2006). Using games and simulations for supporting learning. *Learning, Media and Technology*, *31*(4), 343-358.

de Freitas, S. (2007) *Learning in immersive worlds: A review of game-based learning*. Retrieved September 19, 2008, from http://www.jisc.ac.uk/whatwedo /programmes/elearning_innovation/eli_outcomes/GamingReport.aspx

Ducheneaut, N., & Moore, R. J. (2005). More than just "XP": Learning social skills in massively multiplayer online games. *Interactive Technology & Smart Education*, *2*, 89-100.

Entertainment Software Association. (2007). *Facts and research: Game player data*. Retrieved from: http://www.theesa.com/facts/gamer_data.php

Gee, J. P. (2003). *What video games have to teach us about learning and literacy*. New York: Palgrave MacMillan.

Grabinger, S., Dunlap, J., & Duffield, J. (1997). Rich environments for active learning. *ALT-J: Research in Learning Technology*, *5*(2), 5-17.

Greene, J., & D'Oliveria, M. (1993) *Learning to use statistical tests in psychology*. Buckingham, England: Open University Press.

Honebein, P. C. (1996). Seven goals for the design of constructivist learning environments. In B. G. Wilson (Ed.), *Constructivist learning environments: Case studies in instructional design* (pp. 11-24). Englewood Cliffs, NJ: Educational Technology Publications.

Ipsos MORI (2007) *Student expectations study*. Bristol, England: JISC.

Jenkins, H. (2002, March 29). Game theory. *Technology Review*. Retrieved September 19, 2008, from http://www.technologyreview.com/Energy/12784/

Kiili, K. (2005) Digital game-based learning: Towards an experiential gaming model. *The Internet and Higher Education*, *8*, 13-24.

Kolb, D. A. (1984). *Experiential learning: Experience as the source of learning and development*. Upper Saddle River, NJ: Prentice Hall.

Knowles, M. (1998). *The adult learner* (5th ed.). Houston, TX: Butterworth-Heinemann.

Land, S. M., & Hannafin, M. J. (2000) Student-centered learning environments. In D. H. Jonassen & S. M. Land (Eds.), *Theoretical foundations of learning environments*. Mahwah, NJ: Erlbaum.

Lave, J., & Wenger, E. (1991). *Situated learning. Legitimate peripheral participation*. Cambridge, England: University of Cambridge.

McConnell, D. (2000). *Implementing computer supported cooperative learning* (2nd ed.). London: Kogan Page.

Mitchell, A., & Savill-Smith, C. (2005). *The use of computer and video games for learning: A review of the literature*. London: Learning and Skills Development Agency.

Oblinger, D. (2004). The next generation of educational engagement. *Journal of Interactive Media in Education, 8*, 1-18.

Palloff, R. M., & Pratt, K. (2005). *Collaborating online: Learning together in community*. San Francisco: Jossey-Bass.

Prensky, M. (2001). *Digital game-based learning*. New York: McGraw Hill.

Rieber, L. (1996). Seriously considering play: Designing interactive learning environments based on the blending of microworlds, simulations and games. *ETR&D, 44*, 42-58.

Rieber, L. P., Smith, L., & Noah, D. (1998). The value of serious play. *Educational Technology, 38*(6), 29-37.

Sandford, R., Ulicsak, M., Facer, K., & Rudd, T. (2006). *Teaching with games: Using commercial off-the-shelf computer games in formal education*. Bristol, UK: Futurelab.

Shubik, M. (1989). Gaming: Theory and practice, past and future. *Simulation and Games, 20*(2), 184-189.

Sims, R. (1997). Interactivity: A forgotten art? *Computers in Human Behavior, 13*(2), 157-180.

Steinkuehler, C. A. (2004, June). Learning in massively multiplayer online games. In Y. B. Kafai, W. A. Sandoval, N. Enyedy, A. S. Nixon, & F. Herrerapp (Eds.), *Proceedings of the 6th International Conference on Learning Sciences* (pp. 521-528). Santa Monica, CA: International Society of the Learning Sciences.

Vygotsky, L. (1978). *Mind in society: The development of higher psychological functions*. Cambridge, MA: Harvard University Press.

Wenger, E. (2000) Communities of practice and social learning systems. *Organization, 7*(2), 225–256.

Wilson, B. G. (Ed.). (1996). What is a constructivist learning environment? In *Constructivist learning environments: Case studies in instructional design*. Englewood Cliffs, NJ: Educational Technology Publications.

Whitton, N. (2007). *An investigation into the potential of collaborative computer game-based learning in higher education*. Unpublished doctoral thesis, Napier University, School of Computing. Retrieved March 10, 2008, from: www.playthinklearn.net

CHAPTER 8

CREATING AN ONLINE, COURSE-INTEGRATED GENERATIONAL LEARNING COMMUNITY

Leon James

This chapter describes the creation and management of an ongoing course-integrated Web community that spans the semesters of a college social science course in Hawaii. Every student enrolled in the course automatically becomes a cyber-community member by reading, processing, and identifying with the reports of prior-generation students, and then contributing their own reports to the cumulatively expanding "generational curriculum" topics. The benefits of such an approach are discussed in terms of psychological models of acculturation, identification, cyber-citizenship, and the student as scientist model functioning in a Web environment that is increasingly shaped by human social processes.

INTRODUCTION

User empowerment is strengthening and spreading as the social-biological technology (Nahl, 2007a, 2007b) transforms personal knowledge and

Connected Minds, Emerging Cultures: Cybercultures in Online Learning
pp. 91–117

individual situation to group information and social practice that are cumulative, collaborative, archived, and accessible to the public. For example, at the beta version of Askville by Amazon (2007), visitors "can ask a question, get real answers from real people." Anyone can join the online community and provide answers to the questions. Often one question gets answers from several people within hours or a few days. According to the site's FAQ,

> Askville is a place where you can share and discuss knowledge with other people by asking and answering questions on any topic. It's a fun place to meet others with similar interests to you and a place where you can share what you know. You can learn something new every day or help and meet others using your knowledge.

Accessing information and finding answers is transformed into a community practice in which socializing and information searching are fused through the online environment that supports the collaborative construction of information and knowledge. Users have an online profile where people can also read the comments that were posted by others. "Experience points" are accumulated when writing answers, which determine a user's "level" or knowledgeableness in the community. Those who posted the questions can also vote on each answer as to its quality or helpfulness.

The read/write Web invites collaborative editing and project writing. Authors whose subject is too narrow or specialized by traditional publishing standards are able to attract readers specifically interested in that narrow subject from the immense Web audience. According to Habib (2006) "The Long Tail is a term introduced by Chris Anderson to describe how the web makes it possible to provide services to small niche groups" (see also, Anderson, 2004). An important feature of the multiplication and diversity of information niches in Web 2.0 is the birth of what has been called "collective intelligence" or group intersubjectivity. The results of a query delivered by search engines like Google are shown by some form of "PageRank algorithm" that is determined by the number of links that point to a site and the type of sites they are, thus integrating content with centrality and popularity of use. In participatory culture, user contributions determine the content of collective intelligence or group mind. Joining, logging in, clicking, browsing, voting, contributing, sharing, inviting, organizing, tagging, responding, initiating, and cocreating are the new user activities that give value to a site, both commercially and socially.

Internet2, which was formed in 1996, is a network consortium of the research and higher education community. Its goals are to provide new network capabilities and to facilitate the development of interactive technologies. Starting with 34 universities, Internet2 has grown to more than

300 members, including more than 200 U.S. universities working in cooperation with corporations, government agencies, and research institutions (Werle & Fox, 2007). Internet2 was designed to handle much larger than the usual amounts of data transfer in the regular ("commodity") Internet, using "interactive, media-rich applications, such as real-time streaming events, access to remote instrumentation, high-definition videoconferencing, online gaming, and interactive immersive worlds and simulations" (para. 10). A DVD-quality movie that takes several hours of download time using DSL or cable modem, takes only 3 seconds on the fiber-optic cables of Internet2. "This has clear implications for those embracing the principles of a user-centered, multimedia-rich, socially engaged, and community-innovative library embodied by Library 2.0" (Werle & Fox, 2007, para. 11).

The next-generation Internet is built on a philosophy of user-centeredness that does not seek merely to accommodate user needs, but wants users to play the central role in determining its features and innovations. It is an academic and educationally focused initiative, extending its connectivity to all schools, colleges, universities, and libraries. Next-generation online courses can use the faster technology for remote-instrumentation, virtual laboratories and simulations, as well as real-time collaboration. Advanced videoconferencing services allow workshops to be offered simultaneously in several locations or to individuals regardless of geographic location. The Information Literacy Competency Standards for Higher Education (Association of College and Research Libraries, 2000) distinguishes between "computer literacy," "information literacy," and "information technology skills," which illustrates how complex the user's information life has become. Hence, "developing lifelong learners is central to the mission of higher education institutions" (para. 6). To function adequately in the digital world today, users must become lifelong learners. In the new media culture, a participation gap is developing (Jenkins, Purushotma, Clinton, Weigel, & Robison, 2006) for those who are not engaged in the participatory culture of the digital world, and who see the Internet as an occasional information resource. The "divide" is not access to technology, but insufficiency of or contrarian to social and affective skills that drive technological interactivity. Without information literacy and technology skills, people are not only cut off from information, but also excluded from participation and contribution, and thus, to some extent, also from community, opportunity, leadership and, ultimately, citizenship. Those who choose not to participate in online intersubjectivity on philosophical grounds also cannot interact and cocreate in that domain.

The following project describes the creation and management of an online generational community made up of college students enrolled in a one-semester course. The Web component of the project started in 1993, the first year that the World Wide Web became operational. Each semester students published their reports on the Web using the College of Social Sciences server and facilities on the Manoa campus of the University of Hawaii. Currently, the online archives contain 27 generations, each successive semester contributing the records of one generation of students.

Right from the first class, the instructional environment and method is described to the students as a "generational community classroom" in which students in each semester, or generation, read the reports of prior generations, analyze them, and write their reports for future generations. The reports include various topics in psychology that the students write about, do research on, and gather social psychological data on themselves, their friends, and specified activities they engage in (e.g., driving cars and mopeds, being in relationships, involvement with songs, music, the World Wide Web, etc.). All generational student reports (G1 to G27) are available on the Web and show up on search engines (James, 2008). The online generational approach is suitable for any subject field in any instructional setting.

This project began in 1975 using typed student papers that were written, read, collected, bound, and referenced by each succeeding generation of students in each of several college courses that I taught at the University of Hawaii (social psychology; statistics; personality theory; history of psychology as a science). In the 1980s, the collection of student reports was augmented by electronic course-integrated activities on the PLATO system (discussion groups by topics across classes) (Jakobovits-James, 1991). Starting in 1993, all required course activities were conducted on the Web through the facilities of the College of Social Sciences on the Manoa campus.

I have been calling this approach "the generational curriculum" (James, 1997a, 1997b; James & Bogan, 1995; James, 1995; Nahl & James, 1992) because it has these two components. First, there is the creation of a social learning community through the metaphor of "generations." Each semester a new crop of students start from scratch in terms of the target skills that are presented by the instructor in a generational context. They look back on the finished work of prior generations and see their own work as serving the future generations. Second, the generational reports of all prior students are read, processed, and augmented by each succeeding generation. Thus, a significant portion of the student's work and grade come from these generational curriculum activities.

The Spring 2008 semester marked the 27th generation of the online generational curriculum in three Internet-integrated courses that I teach every semester: driving psychology, social psychology, and general psychology.

During the first few generations (starting in 1993), students were computer novices and unfamiliar with the Internet or the Web. On day 1, they found out what was expected of them and they were given weekly exercises designed to help them acquire basic online skills such as using a Web browser and search engine, learning basic HTML code, using UNIX commands, uploading/downloading, and home page architecture.

During those early years, word processors did not yet allow people to "save as a Web page," requiring students to learn HTML code, as well as how to operate within a UNIX environment for creating, saving, and uploading files. As a result, half of each class was devoted to group discussions and lectures about the course topics in psychology, and half to computer lab sessions where each student sat at an online workstation. At the end of the 16-week semester, all students who had not quit by midterm (about 80%) were successful in this pragmatic respect: each student left behind a self-produced generational Web site containing various assigned reports and integrated by hyperlink to specific content in the reports of prior generations.

There is no theoretical limit to the generations. In terms of cultural and instructional resources, the longer a particular online generational project goes on, the richer is its content and the educational opportunities it can provide. I believe that the approach can be replicated in all subject fields in any online learning setting, and is equally suitable for college, high school, or elementary school. Other institutional settings that may benefit from an online generational approach include semester courses, social clubs and networking, work teams, and correctional retraining facilities. The rationale for this expectation is outlined below.

In order to allow me to understand the process of how an online community evolves psychologically and educationally, I instruct students to write self-reports on various aspects of their experience as member of a generational online community. Content analysis of these reports helps identify various dimensions of learning in an online environment. Results indicate (Nahl, 1997, 2001) that students go through three phases during the 16-week semester:

Phase 1: Becoming computer adequate and information literate
Phase 2: Becoming self-directed autonomous learners (problem solvers)
Phase 3: Exercising leadership and inventiveness

Within each of these phases, evidence focuses on student learning in three behavioral areas (Nahl, 2001):

- *affective* (e.g., improving self-confidence, feeling connected);
- *cognitive* (e.g., acquiring new knowledge of content, vocabulary, reasoning process); and
- *sensorimotor* (e.g., acting as a generational participant, practicing new information habits integrated into one's life).

A classified inventory of online student behaviors was prepared with samples of text from the student reports (James & Nahl, 1997a, 1997b). The taxonomy of online educational objectives and skills is usable for planning and assessing online instruction. Several principles of online instruction are identified, including how to help students to think creatively and use group socializing forces as a learning resource.

EDUCATIONAL PRINCIPLES OF THE
ONLINE GENERATIONAL COMMUNITY-CLASSROOM

An issue of the *Journal of the American Society for Information Science* (November 1996) was devoted entirely to the "Perspectives on … Distance Independent Education." Among the important issues raised is the instructional challenge of transforming passive classroom students into active, self-directed learners capable of benefiting from the special advantages of the new online technology that is now becoming available in traditional instructional settings. In an article focusing on "cognition and distance learning," Linn (1996) described passive learners as expecting to "absorb information," failing to "identify connections between ideas," and "frequently forget what they learn" (p. 827). In contrast, "autonomous learners" use books, electronic media, networked communication, even computer manuals to gain a linked, connected, integrated and cohesive understanding of a topic.

Linn (1996) identified some features of an online environment that would support the development of autonomous lifelong learners:

1. Helping students make effective decisions and creating new ideas;
2. Helping learners recognize when, how, and why they learn new material;
3. Helping students diagnose personal goals, strengths, and limitations, and select activities compatible with their goals;
4. Providing opportunities for independent projects tailored to personal goals within an academic discipline;
5. Encouraging students to take responsibility for their own learning—setting realistic goals for themselves, monitoring their own

progress, reflect on their understanding, and seek guidance from peers as well as instructors;

6. Creating activities that permit students to practice these skills;

7. Making disciplinary knowledge, practice, and culture visible to students through autonomous learning activities that include linking ideas, comparing alternatives, reflecting on progress, critiquing ideas with guidance and support; and

8. Structuring courses so as to take advantage of the social nature of learning and social contributions to learning by engaging students in collaborative practices and providing for their mutual support as a helping community.

These eight characteristics are, according to Linn, essential for creating autonomous lifelong learners in an online instructional setting. I believe that the online generational project I am describing here meets many of these desirable objectives. The following instructional principles describe the approach used in the creation and management of the online course-integrated generational curriculum.

Principle 1: Mining the Infosphere as a Collaborative Learning Resource

The World Wide Web allows the creation of knowledge by interlinking ideas that are generated by millions of people focusing on a particular topic. This record of this collective intersubjectivity is enriching and helpful to individuals who were not part of the construction but make use of it as information consumers. This is fundamentally what motivates the creation of archives or digital databases. Powerful and instantaneous online search engines make it possible to navigate effectively across trillions of files on our desktops or on the Web. This hypertext information sphere provides consumers of information a nearly endless panorama of knowledge, information, opinion, and human-to-human-contact, both instant and delayed.

In 1 decade the online social environment has taken on new world significance for culture, education, and commerce. It is now instructionally feasible as a routine activity to build learning communities in an online learning setting. Course-integrated use of the Internet has opened up new educational possibilities for augmenting classroom learning. Students can now produce Web documents with links to other students and to whatever the instructor's assignments direct them, such as research, opinion, illustrations, applications, variations, et cetera. The electronic hypertext environment, accessed through search engines, provides the medium in which students can practice authorship, critical analysis, and social development through integration within a learning community.

This course-integrated telecommunications activity has several valuable instructional features:

1. engaging students in the reading and processing of each other's work and commentaries;

2. creating a generational student contributed cumulative digital library usable by fellow students specifically, and the Web generally;

3. providing a virtual learning community that spans across generations of students from which they derive an identity as an author and publisher of information on scientific and educational topics of interest to the general public;

4. encouraging the acquisition of broader information and writing skills, including creating an integrated home page with hypertext reports on assigned scientific topics linked to related Web sites and online journal articles in library databases;

5. practicing social interactions in the online environment, including e-mail, online discussion groups, shared Web research, comparison shopping for particular items, file sharing, joint authoring and publishing, online surveys, and collaborative research.

These instructional features transform the students' work into an intellectual contribution through their participation in a generational cyberspace learning community for one semester. Each semester, students of the new generation contribute their series of home pages to the digital library, and integrate their writing into its hypertext fabric through commentaries they create that are linked backwards to earlier student reports. This process of *meaningful backward linking*, analogous to tradition, simulates the growth and evolution of a virtual learning community in cyberspace. At any time in the future, former students may revisit their home page architecture through search engines and see how it has been weaved or integrated into the evolving and living fabric of the continuously evolving generational virtual superdocument (James & Bogan, 1995).

The power of hypertext to create new knowledge lies in meaningfully linking text to text. For instance, scientific reports contain references to prior reports by the author and others. Each reference is a link that integrates the current work to earlier work. Making a link is equivalent to creating a new context. Two ideas may exist independently, but when someone makes a meaningful link between them, new knowledge has been created; thus, new solutions to existing problems. With each new crop of students, the generational superdocument (or digital library) is enriched in two ways. First, students add their home pages and reports, thus enlarging the generational hypertext collection. Second, students add links between their own work and specific prior reports. Note that *the links are not merely to each other's reports globally but to each other's paragraphs.* These paragraph-to-paragraph links make a creative association between one of their ideas or claims, and the idea or claim of one or more prior students. The assignment structure insures that each student will add several dozens of pages or screen full of materials, and hundreds of annotated hypertext links.

The generational curriculum thus grows at an exponential rate. It not only serves as a constantly growing educational and cultural resource, but also as a useful ethnographic record of the development and evolution of a cyber-community classroom. This record can be analyzed and studied from the perspective of educational anthropology and instructional psychology, since the virtual super-document (now containing hundreds of reports) contains the feelings, thoughts, and actions of succeeding generations of students learning from each other over time and space.

Questions of interest include how the growth of knowledge takes place in an online community and the type of community-building forces that encourage successful learning and the acquisition of excellence. For instance, the first four generations brought out the effectiveness of encouraging generational identification, modeling, and loyalty. In addition, the hypertext superdocument is a cumulatively growing database or repository of student behaviors in an online social context from which researchers can build inventories and taxonomies useful for instructional design, planning, evaluation, and measurement.

Principle 2: Creating Community-Building Forces Among Online Learners

A critical factor in the success of a cyberspace learning community is the ability of the instructor to create community-building forces within the class; that is, within the students who form the current generation. A group of people who are given a collaborative task to accomplish can find motivation in group solidarity as well as in competitiveness. Because few can accomplish complex tasks on their own, a socially organized framework of mutual assistance needs to be put in place so that no one is left behind in failure and embarrassment. A visible communal product to which all contribute, and with which all can identify, needs to be developed and perceived as the outcome of their labor and effort. In short, the cyber-community created within an instructional context needs to be *real, believable, and authentic*. To the extent that it has these properties, to that extent the generational virtual learning community will be effective and evolving developmentally to higher and higher achievement.

The educational project described here will be examined to see how these community-building forces were built up to maintain effective cyber-socialization practices, and what instructional management mechanisms need to be maintained in order to foster the growth of a cyberspace learning community. The social and educational context for the online generations has been a continuation of the community-classroom techniques I developed through 40 generations of students in the pre-computer era. In 1979 I attempted to formulate some of the principles that were evolving in my instructional practice, which I came to call the "generational community-classroom approach" (James & Nahl, 1979). In terms of educational philosophy, I identified three properties of this naturally evolving approach in my teaching. They were (a) intentionality, (b) being cumulative and generational, and (c) organicity.

Intentionality

I found that I can promote intentionality in learners through assignments that required an objective self-focus. For instance, when the course topic is social psychology, the student reports have to do with social psychology concepts applied to one's experience or *self-witnessing* on the daily round of social exchanges. In other words, learning about "social forces" in a group or community meant studying how "my" feelings, thoughts, and acts are influenced by the presence of others.

Or, when the subject matter is a course on driving psychology, the student reports have to do with "my threefold self" as a driver—"my" feelings, thoughts, and acts behind the wheel and how these are influenced by other drivers and the surrounding conditions. Again, when the course is on marriage relationships, the students write reports about how "my" feelings, thoughts, and acts in my current relationships are influenced by the other person and the daily routines. Topics of student reports from the past generations include pet psychology, health and fitness, theistic psychology, dream analysis, conversational analysis, cyberpsychology, observing myself learning the Internet, information literacy skills, history of psychology, statistics and research design, and others. The instructions to students for writing and Web publishing their reports, as well as the student home pages and reports, can be accessed for the 27 online generations through the directory of links available at http://www.soc.hawaii.edu/leonj/leonj/leonpsy/gc/generations.html (James, 2008).

The objectified focus on the self through the various course subjects helps create the positive condition of intentionality within the online learning community. In the present project this focus on self is objectified through the scientific rationale of data collection and analysis. The approach was presented to students as the method of "self-witnessing," which was defined as the systematic monitoring of my feelings, thoughts, and acts when engaged in a specific activity. The objectified data collection focused on the self in community contexts and in social interactions. This objectified focus on the threefold self was embedded in a relevant theory or principle of psychology that was being studied, so that the self-reports were informal mini-experiments designed to reveal how the psychological principle applied to self in an empirical or live context.

Interestingly, the approach of creating intentionality through the objective focus on self worked equally well with the statistics course as with the driving psychology course, thus allowing me to confirm the appropriateness of the generational community-classroom approach in a diversity of subjects. Even in the study of statistics the objective focus on self helps create intentionality in learners. The issue students had to handle in their reports was not, for example, "What's the difference between correlated and independent treatment conditions?" but rather, "How do I explain to myself the difference between correlated and independent treatment conditions?" and, additionally, "How do my friends respond when I try to explain to them this difference"? Intentionality in the acquisition of statistics concepts was fostered by allowing the group topic to focus on one's actual reasoning behaviors while engaged in the effort of learning formal or abstract formulations. As a supplement to this objectified focus on self, students were assigned the task of teaching a friend or family member some statistical piece of reasoning they acquired (e.g., the difference between median and mean). It was not enough for them to teach; they also had to report on how the teaching went, and it is here that intentionality was greatly strengthened. The relationship between intentionality and objectified self-focus is discussed explicitly as a method in ethnomethodology (James & Nahl, 1995).

Various provisions were made for protection of privacy that included these procedures and options:

1. Students were allowed to use a pseudonym on their home pages and reports.
2. They were allowed to present data by averages or selected samples, or to exclude anything they chose to.
3. They were allowed to modify the instructions and apply them to unspecified others instead of to self.
4. They were allowed to privately hand in typed reports to the instructor that were returned to them after grading.

5. They were allowed to modify or remove their reports from the Web at any time during the semester, or thereafter by email request to the instructor.
6. They were allowed to do alternative reports that did not focus on self.

Over the 27 generations involving hundreds of students, about 15% chose one or more of these modified privacy procedures, while about 85% chose to perform the unmodified instructions. I attribute this large ratio to the intentionality created through the instructional setting as a generational online learning community. This intentionality is constructed by the participants' desire to be an authentic link in the generational culture. The objective focus on self allowed each participant to write and contribute from a position of knowledge and believability, of empirical reporting in the field of life.

Grohol (2006) argues that anonymity or "pseudonymity" can sometimes be detrimental to the purpose and function of an online community, calling it a "double-edged sword" that "can wreak havoc on a community" through the "disinhibition" that anonymous interactions facilitate (para. 2). According to Suler (2000)

> When people have the opportunity to separate their actions from their real world and identity, they feel less vulnerable about opening up. Whatever they say or do can't be directly linked to the rest of their lives. They don't have to own their behavior by acknowledging it within the full context of who they "really" are. (para. 3)

In the current context of a course-integrated online community there is an emphasis and tradition for being a published author on the Internet with worldwide access through search engines. Self-expression and identity evolve within the context of practicing being a contributing member with a social and academic reputation to protect and maintain. I have noted that online discussions and Web blogs are almost never anonymous in professional contexts and interactions.

Being Cumulative and Generational

The generational approach started in 1971 with my search for methods that help students write authentically (James, 1973). I was trying to go beyond skills of imitation that students display when they write about an assigned topic in a style that imitates the journal articles and books from which they obtain the information. Paraphrasing and referencing—that's about as far as it used to go. I refer to this type of student writing as "inauthentic," even if they add a section at the end titled "My Own Views." I realized that inauthentic writing inhibits independent, autonomous, and self-directed learning of any subject.

One symptom of inauthentic writing is that students have little or nothing to say about the concepts they write about in an assignment, and they can only repeat in paraphrase what others have written or said. I noticed that when class breaks up into small work groups, the room is filled with talk and students are eager to get their views aired with each other. What, then, is the environmental difference between having little to say and being eager to say things? The answer came to me eventually: *get them to write and say things for each other, not for the instructor.* From then on, all assignments were directed to be written by students for other students and by extension, for the general public. Now they had to come up with an authentic point of view; they had to find something of value to say to other students about the assigned concept. Instead of mimicking the statistics textbook, for instance, now students had to write "for next semester's class" on various subjects that would help out the future generations (e.g., "Tell them how to remember which is the dependent and which is the independent variable" or "Make up study questions that will help them find the median of an uneven distribution," etc.). Each semester, students began by studying prior semester reports as a way of preparing themselves for their own reports, and that's how the generational approach came into existence. In the precomputer days this cumulative collection was, of course, in print, consisting of the typed reports handed in by students and voluntarily contributed by them for the generational curriculum. Starting in 1994, the students published their reports on the Web.

In addition to authentic writing assignments (or writing for each other and the public), other methods that I have used to help strengthen the benefits of generational community forces include:

1. making up indexes and annotations of prior student reports (to help information retrieval);

2. forming volunteer work teams that leave behind some legacy or service (e.g., class pictures, audio tapes, handouts, access lists, scanning or digitizing, updating files, helpful instructions);

3. allowing for prior generation "alumni" contacts and activities (e.g., coaching, advice);

4. fostering the growth of generational lore and tradition (e.g., comparisons between generations in appearance of home pages, content of instructions and reports);

5. featuring the work of certain individuals from prior generations (e.g., everyone reads the same designated reports for analysis and discussion);

6. taking and displaying class photos or videos, and making up songs with lyrics based on class topics;
7. Publishing Web directories that list "award winning" reports and home pages; and
8. maintaining live contact with the past (e.g., allowing students from prior generations to email the instructor an attached modified file of any of their old reports, and substituting the updated version.

Organicity

This aspect of the generational community-classroom evolved from my involvement with Lewin's (1935) field-dynamic concepts in social psychology. His lifetime work was dedicated to show the ways in which new social forces are created when you form a group of individuals and give them a joint task to accomplish. The interactivity under a joint purpose creates an organic social entity capable of releasing and fostering social forces that strongly influence activities and outcomes. I tried to apply this principle in the classroom by fostering the idea among students that "this is a community classroom" and "you are one of the generations" and "this is a community of learners in which each person is essential," and so on. Along with this declared philosophy, came assignments that put it into practice. In addition to individual reports and quizzes, part of the grade was determined by collaborative efforts, teams sharing authorship, team quizzes, collective assignments, a newsletter, committee reports, mini-conferences and poster sessions; awards and certificates, etc. The community-building forces of organicity, along with generational writing and intentionality coalesced into a new approach to teaching that I called "community classroom" (James & Nahl, 1979).

Principle 3: Maintaining a Focus on Learning Skills

The skills students acquire through this course-integrated cyber-community can be usefully categorized into three phases of acquisition and practice:

Phase I: Information literacy skills
Phase II: Scientific or scholarly skills
Phase III: Leadership and citizenship skills

Phase I: Information Literacy Skills

In terms of information literacy skills, students achieve the following significant steps by the end of the semester consisting of 16 weekly 3-hour meetings in class and computer lab:

1. Students stop feeling panicky or depressed about technology and start feeling enthusiastic and self-confident.
2. Students become familiar with the use of the electronic medium of communication (e-mail attachments, FTP, home page architecture, online discussion groups, file sharing, Web search engines and library databases, social networking, collaborative software, etc.)
3. Each student creates a Web site consisting of integrated files and links that include text-to-text connections to the work of prior students online. The reports have a scientific or informational purpose and include the author's research and opinions.

Phase II: Scientific and Scholarly Skills

In terms of scientific and scholarly skills, students are engaged in the following performative practices:

(a) learning to write in a public arena and for an interactive purpose;
(b) learning to perform critical analyses of other people's writings;
(c) making individual contributions to the building of a generational virtual superdocument or collection, and thus learning to perform the responsibilities of being a published author;
(d) learning to express one's public intellectual position on pre-assigned topics; and
(e) modeling scholarly activities through special assignments, such as the maintenance of a Web database, or the design of Web facilities (e.g., a way of collecting opinion data from visitors to their Web page).

Phase 3: Leadership and Citizenship Skills

In terms of leadership and citizenship skills, students are given opportunity and encouragement to acquire a service orientation within the generational membership role. For example:

(a) maintaining an intellectual presence or voice within a generational learning community through citizenship activities in cyber-community, such as, maintaining a home page on the Web and acting as host to visitors from both inside and outside the learning community;
(b) encouraging volunteer projects for the sake of community benefit (e.g., tour guides and indexes to facilitate retrieval of information by students and visitors);
(c) introducing innovations that are pleasing or useful to current and future students (e.g., gadgets, clocks, counters, ticker tapes, applets,

special effects, frames, embedded videos, annotated links to Web sites, etc.);

(d) going beyond what's required and expected for the sake of loyalty and service to the community, and thereby achieving excellence in appearance, content, and use; and

(e) encouraging the practice of maintaining and improving ongoing community projects so that they never end (e.g., scanning precomputer generational reports and creating a home page for them that is integrated with the online curriculum reports).

Principle 4: Students as a Cyberspace Learning Community

I foster an informal discussion atmosphere in class and I openly rely on the group's solidarity with each other to get an individual unstuck when in trouble. The faster learners help the slower, and within 6 to 7 weeks 80% of the class is on board, surfing the Internet and creating Web documents. Yes, you can hear them complaining a lot, very excitedly but also very happily. The written student comments reveal that many experience a changed self-image that no longer is tainted with depressive technophobia. This relief is visible in their heartfelt and genuine appreciation for the course expressed in their published reports. In this new electronic collaborative experience students feel challenged to find their own voices, and prompted to express their own thoughts and feelings in a public and informational context. Students see their own writing on the Web, impressed by the fact that their writings are, in a real sense, "published" and available to millions of browsers. Students are, in effect, modeling the role of author, scholar, and scientist. They are thus awakened and introduced to intellectual citizenship.

Principle 5: Creating Ethnographic Instructions

I found through much experience that besides providing a community-classroom atmosphere, a second essential component is the creation of what I call "ethnographic instructions." To prepare these, I go over every single activity students must go through, and witness myself executing the microsteps. I record these steps in their sequence and exactitude, and instruct students to step through them in this identical way. I indicate the steps by number so they can keep track of each one in its own right. A report may have as many as 50 steps specified, and each must be addressed by the student. This is an effective learning procedure insuring a positive outcome even with the least prepared students. Part of the participants' generational role is to prepare such instructions for each other across the generations. The newer generations can read the instructions of the prior generations prepared for them.

Analysis of Generation 4 Student Reports

Using prior research on an empirical taxonomy for Generation 2 reports, I set up the Generational Curriculum Taxonomy of Instructional Objectives (see the Appendix). Since this taxonomy is based on the reports of Generation 2 students, the question arises whether it is accurate or general enough to describe the reports of Generation 4 students. Thus, the taxonomy in this current form represents the prediction that Generation 4 reports will contain evidence for student behaviors within each of the nine zones of the taxonomy. In other words, if I inspect the Generation 4 student reports, will I be able to find student behaviors that fit within each of the nine zones of the taxonomy? If the answer is yes, it would suggest that the taxonomy may be used by other researchers or instructors in different online settings. The taxonomy provides an explicit map for what specific online skills one wishes to target for. It also provides a guide for constructing comprehensive assessment measures of learner skills.

The taxonomy shown in the Appendix and Tables 8.1 and 8.2, will be used to define or categorize segments of text taken from the students' self-witnessing reports. There are nine zones or classification categories, and I was interested in finding statements by students that illustrated each of these zones. I systematically read all the online reports of the 35 students who made up Generation 4 in the fall of 1996 and copied segments that illustrated one of the nine zones of the taxonomy. I thus obtained 95 statements that describe some feature of the student's self-witnessing of the threefold self during the three learning phases. The statements may be viewed in this file: www.soc.hawaii.edu/leonj/leonj/leonpsy/instructor/kcc/g4inventory.html_

This classified inventory of student statements corresponds to the taxonomy in the Appendix and Tables 8.1 and 8.2. Each student statement is a small segment of the report and is taken as an index that a certain skill has been acquired. For example, here is a report segment that I take as evidence for phase I affective (A1) and cognitive skills (C1):

> I benefited greatly from being able to read others failures and successes (A1) and I learned a lot about what it takes to be successful with computers (C1). At first I was overwhelmed (A1) by the topics and all the different commands that you need to know (C1)" said CA from Generation 4b—quoted by LV from Generation 4b.

**Table 8.1.   Chart of the Nine Zones of
Instructional Objectives for the Online Generational Curriculum**

Phases (Levels)	Instructional Domain		
	Affective	Cognitive	Sensorimotor
Phase 3: Acquiring democratic leadership skills (through generational *loyalty*)	A3: Acquiring balance between inventiveness and service orientation	C3: Showing creativity and integration within a disciplinary context	S3: Achieving user-centered excellence
Phase 2: Acting as self-directed autonomous learners (through generational *modeling*)	A2: Exercising sustained effort and acquiring project orientation	C2: Gaining critical thinking skills and professional assessment criteria	S2: Achieving self-paced monitoring and acting as a lifelong learner
Phase 1: Gaining information literacy (through generational *identification*)	A1: Overcoming technophobia and low self-confidence	C1: Acquiring disciplinary content and culture	S1: Behaving as an active learner and transmitter of knowledge and culture

Note: Read table from bottom up.

**Table 8.2.   Internalization of Instructional Objectives
Through the Community-Classroom Approach of the
Online Generational Curriculum**

Phases of Internalization	Instructional Objectives	Community-Classroom Methods
Phase 3 (internal)	Becoming leaders and inventors	through generational loyalty
Phase 2 (intermediate)	Becoming self-directed autonomous learners	through generational modeling
Phase 1 (external)	Becoming information literate	through generational identification

Here the student shows evidence of learning to overcome his initial feeling of being overwhelmed and of acquiring new online skills. The fact that I was able to obtain one or more student statements for each of the nine zones of the taxonomy indicates that the classified inventory is sufficiently general to apply to different generations of students. To me, this means that instructors in different settings might benefit from adopting it as a working hypothesis.

The Three Phases of Internalizing Learned Online Skills

The three predicted phases (or levels) of student learnings represent a continuum of internalization of skills from external (phase 1) to internal (phase 3). "Internal" refers to the top-down hierarchical organization of a system so that what is higher is more internal or central to the control function. The more internal or central areas of a motivational hierarchy exert control over the lower or more external items. For instance, the skill of perseverance (sustaining a project effort rather than quitting) is a level 2 skill. Prior to learning that, one needs to learn better self-efficacy expectations and to overcome technophobia (level 1 skills). Generally, the development of expertise proceeds from the acquisition of lower, external items and continues with higher, more internal items. For example, in the educational taxonomies (Bloom, 1956), lower objectives and learnings in, say the cognitive domain, consist of "memorizing items" in coherent clusters called "knowledge." Somewhat higher or more internal learnings consist of "analyzing and interpreting" knowledge structures. The most internalized cognitive skills, and also the highest, consist of "restructuring, evaluating, and synthesizing" new principles of knowledge. The number of steps, levels, or phases may vary from theory to theory in education, but the idea of a progression is universal. For the sake of convenience, all continuums for internalization will be assumed to have three phases or levels, corresponding to the popular and non-technical subdivisions of *Beginner* (or Novice), *Intermediate*, and *Advanced*.

Note that from the perspective of learners, the progression is from lower and external (phase 1) to higher and more internal (phase 3). This corresponds to the general idea of advancement from novice to expert (advanced, skilled, etc.). This progression is *analytic* because it proceeds from external (phase 1) to internal (phase 3), also known as "bottom-up" direction; in other words, from effects to causes. However, from the perspective of graduates or practitioners, the progression is *synthetic* because it proceeds from internal (phase 3) to external (phase 1), which is known as 'top-bottom' direction; in other words, from managed causes to resultant effects.

In an earlier report on Generation 2 students, the three phases of learning and adapting to the Internet were identified from the students' biweekly self-witnessing reports. These were based on journals or records students kept of their feelings and thoughts over the course of the semester as they were learning to put up their Web sites and carrying out the weekly assignments (e.g., access, search, navigation, telnet, ftp, HTML). A taxonomic inventory of affective and cognitive skills and errors was extracted from the self-witnessing reports. Level 1, which is called *Achieving Focus on Internet,* proceeds when learners, under the motivation to be accurate and persistent (affective skills), make appropriate observations and identify sub-tasks (cognitive skills). Level 2 is called *Achieving Engagement* and denotes that phase of information seeking which requires that the user become engaged, affectively and cognitively, by proceeding with self-confidence to gaining mastery over Internet navigation and file management techniques. Level 3, *Personalizing*, is entered when users begin to accept the Internet by contextualizing and personalizing it in the presence of feelings of attraction, connectivity, and the desire for task completion.

The results of this study conformed to the findings of earlier taxonomic research on library skills and errors (Jakobovits-James & Nahl, 1987). In that behavioral area, Level 1 was titled *Orientation to the Library* and included the willingness to follow instructions (affective skills) and memorizing library terms (cognitive skills). Level 2 internalization was called *Interacting with the Library* and consisted of acquiring attitudes (affective skills) and reasoning procedures (cognitive skills) similar to what librarians used in their classification and retrieval operations. Through this they were enabled to select keywords for a search and plan a workable retrieval strategy. Level 3 was called *Internalizing the Library* and included the acquisition of positive affect for libraries and their mission in society (affective skills), coupled with understanding how knowledge and information structure are tied to disciplines (cognitive skills).

Phase 1 (or level 1) is thus an initial stage of practice in which learners acquire the ability to orient and focus on those elements that are the most external of a task or situation, thus involving sensorimotor skills (keyboarding, clicking, inspecting, locating, identifying). In the community-classroom generational curriculum context, the most external elements involve *maintaining self-confidence* (affective skills—not quitting when the going gets tough), *acquiring disciplinary content* (cognitive skills—knowing what the earlier generations wrote), and *acting out membership status* (sensorimotor skills—performing requisite activities online). In the context of online community-classroom, these external phases of learning are enabled through the psychological process of *generational identification*.

As the Appendix and Tables 8.1 and 8.2 show, Phase 1 is the activity of becoming information literate through generational identification. This phase is marked *affectively* (A1) as recurrent attempts by learners to postpone quitting and to eliminate procrastinating. Self-confidence and self-efficacy expectations have to be maintained through self-pep-talks and social identification with other students—those who had similar difficulties yet ended up successful. *Cognitively*, phase 1 (C1) involves getting familiar with the content of the generational curriculum by reading, processing, and commenting on what prior students have written. The affective and the cognitive necessarily interact. There is no finding out the curriculum content if the activity is continuously postponed. The thoroughness with which the curriculum is studied depends on affective effort or persistence. The affective and the cognitive together determine the outcome and performance. At this external level, the *sensorimotor* process involves learning how to practice the behaviors of a generational member or cyber-community netizen.

This general taxonomic principle has been applied to the generational curriculum objectives as shown in the Appendix and Tables 8.1 and 8.2. This scheme tries to retain face validity in terms of common knowledge about teaching, training, or coaching efforts. In education at all levels there appears such a progression of objectives as represented here. Becoming information literate is the first phase of any new online practice to which one aspires. One needs to learn the vocabulary (cognitive skills) within a context of acquired work attitudes and participation ethics (affective skills) that are appropriate in the performance of acts (sensorimotor skills) in the chosen field of acquisition. The online community-classroom approach provides the mechanism of *generational identification* through which learners can more easily acquire information literacy and practice online democracy.

While phase 1 is a continuous process that will continue to develop more and more, phase 2 will start at some point and will overlap with phase 1. As learners become literate in their chosen field (phase 1), they need to learn how to continue learning (phase 2) by becoming self-directed autonomous learners. The online community-classroom approach provides the mechanism of *generational modeling* through which participants can more easily become self-directed autonomous learners. Modeling (in phase 2) is a more internal control phase than identification (in phase 1) because it requires interactive involvement. One can identify with a performer through being a passive audience and thus become familiar with a cultural milieu. But modeling requires an active participation and social construction so that more inward elements of the learner are engaged.

Even as learners are still active in phases 1 and 2, they also begin a more interior involvement as innovators and leaders of their learning community (in phase 3). This requires going beyond identification, beyond modeling, and on to *generational loyalty*. The motive to be an innovator (affective skills) depends on the desire to strengthen one's ties to the target community (affective skills). Phase 3 of learning and adapting to the infosphere depends on learners' willingness to continue learning until they are able to see a personal use. This new context makes the effort of learning the Internet ultimately worthwhile. Personalizing, contextualizing, and feeling loyalty are the deepest, highest, and most central control activities in becoming a successful participant in an online community.

The online community-classroom context thus provides the generational curriculum approach with social facilitators for learners. Identifying (phase 1), modeling (phase 2) and showing loyalty (phase 3) are three types of activities that go on more or less simultaneously as the novice is transformed into a netizen. The Appendix and Tables 8.1 and 8.2 specify the instructional objectives in the three domains for each phase (9 zones). The *affective* internalization process starts with *identifying* with successful peers, which improves self-efficacy expectations, thus allowing them to overcome technophobia and resistance (phase 1 affective skills). As this becomes stabilized, learners begin *modeling* and can acquire the motive of sustained effort and project completion (phase 2 affective skills). Finally, learners develop *loyalty* and become motivated to be inventive and innovative (phase 3 affective skills).

A similar internalization procedure occurs in the *cognitive* domain as learners internalize the affective involvement. By identifying with prior generations, learners empower themselves to acquire disciplinary and cultural content to which members refer and discuss (phase 1 cognitive skills). Identification ensures that learners are motivated to focus on relevant details and remember them. When they start *modeling* or acting like a member themselves, they acquire the style of reasoning and assessment criteria (phase 2 cognitive skills), which is part of the online culture as the generational community evolves. Finally, when they start showing *loyalty* to the generational curriculum, their cognitive activities become more complex and creative (phase 3 cognitive skills).

The *sensorimotor* domain undergoes a parallel and overlapping process of internalization. Starting with generational *identification* (phase 1), learners are given the opportunity to practice their cyber-community citizenship by taking their place in the sequence of generations and class presence (phase 1 sensorimotor skills—such as, attaching their files to their own homepage, which is attached to their class page, which is attached to the generational page). Going further with generational *modeling*, learners begin cumulating their role activities and coalescing into a sustained, meaningful project that is published on the Web (phase 2 sensorimotor skills). Finally, when generational *loyalty* begins, achieving excellence becomes visible through products and performances achieved for the benefit of the community's survival and enrichment (phase 3 sensorimotor skills).

IMPLICATIONS AND CONCLUSIONS

Participating in the Web community has become critical for many reasons—social, informational, commercial, educational, professional, and entertainment. Participation requires becoming involved in performing the practices of an online group or community. Brooks (2007) uses the term "externalization" to describe the focus of consciousness in a digital world where being a user means relying on options and preferences provided as multiple choice alternatives. Brooks acknowledges that he has more options and preferences to choose from than ever, but he also has less "autonomy." Preferences, selections, models, and templates all allow users to express themselves individualistically, but this is a relatively external feature of a human being. We may opt to download a song or view a video simply because it was listed in the most favored category, or most downloaded in the past 24 hours.

This is an issue that will have to be examined in the future. In the meantime, to be a user in the information world today is to integrate one's thoughts and feelings, values and goals, into the stream of interactivity and its resultant intersubjectivity, which marks digital participatory culture. Bumgarner (2007) surveyed college students who regularly use Facebook and discovered that "Essentially, Facebook appears to operate primarily as a tool for the facilitation of gossip" (Abstract). The highly popular social networking site is one of the most frequented places on the Web, with millions of visits daily. Competing sites include MySpace, Friendster, Orkut, and others. A basic motivation for networking with social software is its function as a peer-based support group. Habitual members get to know each other and become involved in social rescue operations when one of the members posts a distress call. Another motive is the need to connect to others, which is particularly intense for those in their postadolescence and early 20s. Bumgarner cites Calvert's (2000) definition of "mediated voyeurism" as "the consumption of revealing images of and information about others' apparently real and unguarded lives, often yet not always for purposes of entertainment but frequently at the expense of privacy and discourse, through the means of mass media and Internet" (para. 15). Bumgarner (2007) believes that the intense interest in social voyeurism in this age group is part of the process of discovering and developing a personal identity.

In this project I have found that *generational identity* or identification can become a community management tool during the emotionally challenging phase when novices are gaining information literacy by acclimatizing to the technological information environment (phase 1 in Table 8.1). But something in addition was needed by students to be able to begin practicing the behaviors of self-directed autonomous learners. This additional social force was provided by the appropriate management of *generational modeling*. Students were enabled to see themselves as autonomous authors and scientists (phase 2) by processing the reports of prior generations, collected in a permanent archive to which they themselves are going to contribute and become part of. They could see themselves when they saw prior students practicing what they were expected to accomplish as well. This feeling of enablement was strengthened and made more real when they realized that their reports will be processed and commented on by future generations, as they are doing to past generations. Finally, full and complete membership in the online generational learning community occurs when students experience *generational loyalty* (phase 3) and thereby begin practicing democratic leadership in their online activities. This involves the integration of Web citizenship in one's daily life and developing a symbiotic relationship with it in one's personal, social, professional, and community life. This project demonstrates that a course-integrated online learning activity can be effective in producing cyber-citizens by managing the students' interactional procedures through the generational community-classroom approach.

APPENDIX: TAXONOMY OF INSTRUCTIONAL OBJECTIVES FOR THE COMMUNITY-CLASSROOM ONLINE GENERATIONAL CURRICULUM

There are three phases (1, 2, 3) of involvement or internalization, and within each, there are three domains of instructional objectives: *affective* (A), *cognitive* (C), *sensorimotor* (S).

Phase 1. Becoming Information Literate Through Generational Identification

- (A1) *Improving Self-efficacy Expectations and Overcoming Technophobia* (e.g., student statements such as "*It was a relief to realize that I'm not the only one having problems*" and "*If they were able to accomplish this, I can too.*")
- (C1) *Acquiring Disciplinary Content and Culture* (e.g., [a] reading backwards in time, [b] referencing its content through hyperlinks to the original, [c] integrating its content to the current generation's perspective)
- (S1) *Acting as a Generational Carrier or Citizen and Transmitter of Knowledge and Culture* (e.g., seeing self as both the latest and most advanced generation while recognizing one's archival function for future generations; or, volunteering extra projects and reports for the sake of future students).

Phase 2. Becoming Self-Directed Autonomous Learners Through Generational Modeling

- (A2) *Acquiring a Project Orientation and Learning to Maintain Sustained Effort* (e.g., in the degree of effort and time expended for assignments, reports, database development, cumulative searches, etc.; or, in valuing details and completeness; or, in risking self by self-initiated innovations).
- (C2) *Acquiring Critical Thinking Skills and Adopting Professional-like Assessment Criteria* (e.g., engaging in appropriate problem solving and analysis procedures).
- (S2) *Achieving Continuity in Education and Acting as a Lifelong Learner* (e.g., following instructions appropriately; or, using adequate personal information retrieval systems for keeping track of community issues and topics).

Phase 3. Exercising Leadership and Practicing Inventiveness Through Generational Loyalty

- (A3) *Becoming Service Oriented and Acquiring the Motivation to be an Innovator* (e.g., making use of new technology for producing and presenting one's work—e.g., color backgrounds, animated images, embedded videos, varying font color, using frames, making up navigation tables for the site; or, volunteering to make-up tutorials and help facilities for others).
- (C3) *Showing Creativity within a Disciplinary Context* (e.g., producing Web pages that are complex and original in composition, appearance, and interactivity features).
- (S3) *Achieving Excellence* (e.g., producing a Web site that has an integrated theme, gives thorough treatment to topics, and links to useful resources with helpful annotations).

REFERENCES

Association of College and Research Libraries. (2000). *Information literacy competency standards for higher education* Retrieved March 6, 2008, from www.ala.org/ala/acrl/acrlstandards/informationliteracycompetency.htm

Amazon Askville Web site. (2007). Retrieved February 1, 2008, from http://askville.amazon.com/

Anderson, C. (2004). The long tail. *Wired, 12*(10). Retrieved February 1, 2008, from www.wired.com/wired/archive/12.10/tail.html

Bloom, B. S. (Ed.). (1956). *Taxonomy of educational objectives: The classification of educational goals. Handbook I: Cognitive domain*. New York: David McKay.

Brooks, D. (2007, October 26). The outsourced brain [Op-ed]. *The New York Times*, October 26, 2007, Opinion Column. Retrieved February 1, 2008, from: www.nytimes.com/2007/10/26/opinion/26brooks.html?_r=1&oref=slogin

Bumgarner, B. A. (2007, November 5). You have been poked: Exploring the uses and gratifications of Facebook among emerging adults. *First Monday, 12*(11). Retrieved February 1, 2008, from www.uic.edu/htbin/cgiwrap/bin/ojs/index.php/fm/article/view/2026/1897

Calvert, C. (2000). *Voyeur nation: Media, privacy, and peering in modern culture*. Boulder, CO: Westview.

Grohol, J. M. (2006, April 4). Anonymity and online community: Identity matters. *A List Apart*. Retrieved February 1, 2008, from www.alistapart.com/articles/identitymatters

Habib, M. C. (2006). *Toward academic library 2.0: Development and application of a library 2.0 methodology*. Retrieved from the School of Information and Library Science of the University of North Carolina at Chapel Hill Web site: http://etd.ils.unc.edu/dspace/bitstream/1901/356/1/michaelhabib.pdf

Jakobovits-James, L. (1991). Course-integrated electronic socializing on PLATO. *UHCC Newsletter, 28*(2), 12-14. Retrieved March 6, 2008, from www.soc.hawaii.edu/leonj/leonj/leonpsy/instructor/leonplato1.html

Jakobovits-James, L., & Nahl, D. (1987). Learning the library: Taxonomy of skills and errors. *College and Research Libraries, 48*(3), 203-14.

James, L. (1973). *The analysis of transactional engineering competence*. Retrieved March 6, 2008, from www.soc.hawaii.edu/leonj/leonj/leonpsy/tec.html

James, L. (1995). Course integrated use of the World Wide Web. *InfoBITS—University of Hawaii Information Technology Services, 2*(2), 8-9. Retrieved March 6, 2008, from www.soc.hawaii.edu/leonj/leonj/leonpsy/instructor/infobits1.html

James, L. (1997a). *Ethnography of an academic cyber-community: The Hawaii generational curriculum project*. Retrieved March 6, 2008, from www.soc.hawaii.edu/leonj/leonj/leonpsy/gc/gcintro.html

James, L. (1997b). *Managing an online generational learning community*. Retrieved March 6, 2008, from www.soc.hawaii.edu/leonj/leonj/leonpsy/gc/onlinetalk.html

James, L. (2008). *Hawaii generational student reports* (Directory of links). Retrieved March 6, 2008, from www.soc.hawaii.edu/leonj/leonj/leonpsy/gc/generations.html

James, L., & Bogan, K. (1995, June). Analyzing linkage structure in a course-integrated virtual learning community on the World Wide Web. INET '95 conference proceedings, Honolulu, HI: Internet Society. Retrieved March 6, 2008, from http://www.soc.hawaii.edu/leonj/leonj/leonpsy/instructor/inet95.html

James, L., & Nahl, D. (1979). Social psychology of the generational community classroom. Retrieved March 6, 2008, from www.soc.hawaii.edu/leonj/leonj/leonpsy/gc/spcc.html

James, L., & Nahl, D. (1995). *Applied psycholinguistics in social psychology: An ethnomethodological approach*. Retrieved March 6, 2008, from www.soc.hawaii.edu/leonj/leonj/leonpsy/instructor/applied_psycholing.html

James, L., & Nahl, D. (1997a). *Achieving focus, engagement, and acceptance: Three phases of adapting to Internet use.* Retrieved March 7, 2008, from www2.hawaii .edu/~nahl/articles/ejvc.html

James, L., & Nahl, D. (1997b) Introduction to the Community Classroom Generational Curriculum. Retrieved March 7, 2008, from www.soc.hawaii.edu/leonj/ leonj/leonpsy/gc/intro.html

Jenkins, H., Purushotma, R., Clinton, K., Weigel, M., & Robison, A. J. (2006). Confronting the challenges of participatory culture: Media education for the 21st century. *Occasional paper on digital media and learning.* Retrieved February 1, 2008, from www.projectnml.org/files/working/NMLWhitePaper.pdf

Lewin, K. (1935). *A dynamic theory of personality.* New York: McGraw Hill.

Linn, M. C. (1996). Cognition and distance learning. *Journal of the American Society for Information Science*, *47*(11), 827-842.

Nahl, D. (1997) Information counseling inventory of affective and cognitive reactions while learning the Internet. *Internet Reference Services Quarterly, 2*(2/3), 11-33.

Nahl, D. (2001). A conceptual framework for defining information behavior. *Studies in multimedia information literacy education* (SIMILE), *1*(2). Retrieved February 1, 2008, from www.utpjournals.com/jour.ihtml?lp=simile/issue2/nahl1.html

Nahl, D. (2007a). Social-biological information technology: An integrated conceptual framework. *Journal of the American Society for Information Science and Technology, 58*(13), 2021-2046. Retrieved February 1, 2008, from www3 .interscience.wiley.com/cgi-bin/abstract/116314481/ABSTRACT

Nahl, D., & James, L. (1992). *Achieving focus, engagement, and acceptance: Three phases of adapting to Internet use.* Retrieved March 6, 2008, from www.soc .hawaii.edu/leonj/leonj/leonpsy/instructor/compedutext.html

Suler, J. (2000). Essential issues in cyberpsychology. 2. Disinhibition, transference, and personality types in cyberspace. *The psychology of cyberspace.* Retrieved February 1, 2008, from http://truecenterpoint.com/ce/essentials2.html

Werle, J., & Fox, L. (2007). Internet2 and libraries: Serving your communities at the speed of light. *Information Today, 27*(10). Retrieved February 1, 2008, from www.infotoday.com/cilmag/nov07/Werle_Fox.shtml

CHAPTER 9

THE SOCIAL IMPACT OF PERSONAL LEARNING ENVIRONMENTS

Graham Attwell

PERSONAL LEARNING ENVIRONMENTS: CAUSE AND EFFECT

Although the personal learning environment (PLE) is a very new term (van Harmalen, 2006, argues the first recorded use of the term is November 4, 2004), the concept represents the latest step in an alternative approach to e-learning which can trace its origins to earlier systems such as Colloquia, the first peer-to-peer learning system (released as Learning Landscapes in 2000), and to more recent phenomena such as the Elgg system released in 2003. The PLE approach is based on a learner-centered view of learning and differs fundamentally from the alternative learning management systems or virtual learning environments approach both of which are based on an institution- or course-centered view of learning. Van Harmelen (2006) describes personal learning environments as "systems that help learners take control of and manage their own learning. This includes providing support for learners to

- set their own learning goals;
- manage their learning; managing both content and process;

Connected Minds, Emerging Cultures: Cybercultures in Online Learning
pp. 119–137

- communicate with others in the process of learning and thereby achieve learning goals."

He goes on to say: "a PLE may be composed of one or more subsystems: As such it may be a desktop application, or composed of one or more web-based services" (p. 000).

Downes (2006) has noted that

> the heart of the concept of the PLE is that it is a tool that allows a learner (or anyone) to engage in a distributed environment consisting of a network of people, services and resources. It is not just Web 2.0, but it is certainly Web 2.0 in the sense that it is (in the broadest sense possible) a read-write application. (p. 000)

Important concepts in PLEs include the integration of both formal and informal learning episodes into a single experience, the use of social networks that can cross institutional boundaries, and the use of networking protocols (peer-to-peer, Web services, syndication) to connect a range of resources and systems within a personally-managed space. The "pedagogy" behind the PLE—if it could be still called that—is that it offers a portal to the world through which learners can explore and create, according to their own interests and directions, interacting as they choose, with their friends and learning community. Seely Brown (1999) has drawn attention to the social nature of learning: "Learning becomes as much social as cognitive, as much concrete as abstract, and becomes intertwined with judgment and exploration" (para. 27).

This chapter examines the social impact of personal learning environments. In so doing, it is difficult to separate cause and effect. Personal learning environments can be expected to have a profound effect on systems for teaching and learning, on pedagogic approaches to learning, and on knowledge development and sharing. Conversely, the emergence of PLEs and the widespread interest in PLEs may be seen as a reaction to the changing ways in which people are using technology for learning, to new societal demands for education, and to changing forms of knowledge usage within society.

THE INDUSTRIAL REVOLUTION AND THE CHALLENGE TO EDUCATION

Education systems and institutions develop to meet the needs of society at particular stages of economic and social development. Education systems serve not only to develop the skills and knowledge in the workforce required by industry, but also to develop social capital. Furthermore, the organizational forms that education systems develop reflect particular organizational forms of capitalist production. The present "industrial" model of schooling evolved to meet the needs and form of a particular phase of capitalist industrial development. The first industrial revolution imposed new requirements in terms of skills and knowledge, in particular the need to extend general education to wider layers of society. In the second half of the nineteenth century, in the United Kingdom, there were a series of education acts designed both to extend participation in education and to regulate the education system. While before 1870, education was largely a private affair, with wealthy parents sending their children to fee-paying schools, and others using whatever local teaching was made available, the Forster Elementary Education Act (1870) required partially state-funded board schools to be set up to provide primary (elementary) education in areas where existing provision was inadequate. Board schools were managed by elected school boards, and the schools remained fee-paying (Wikipedia, n.d.). Under the Elementary Education Act 1880, education became compulsory from the ages of 5 to 10. It was not until 1893 that the Elementary Education (School Attendance) Act raised the school leaving age to 11 and 1902 that the state took over education, through the organization of local education authorities and the provision of funding for schools from taxation.

These reforms were based on a perception that for Britain to remain competitive in the world by being at the forefront of manufacture, higher levels of participation in education were necessary. [Note: Some of the speeches and documents of the time resemble debates about the European Union's Lisbon Declaration.] It is notable that there was opposition to these reforms based, on the one hand, on the idea that this would make the laboring classes "think" and could lead to revolt and, on the other, that handing children to a central authority could lead to indoctrination.

The form of organization of schooling and the predominant pedagogy were based on the forms of production developed through the industrial revolution. Schools resembled large-scale factories for knowledge, organized into different departments with a foreman or forewoman in control of each class and an overall manager in charge of the school (in older industrial cities in the United Kingdom it is sometimes hard to distinguish between old schools and factories). Classroom monitors (or prefects) acted as overseers. Students sat at desks organized in rows. Work was to take place with set starting and finishing times each day. Bells would announce the start and end of rest periods (or breaks).

The system evolved to provide a basic technical education for the majority (through secondary modern schools) and a more advanced academic education in grammar schools for a minority progressing to university. The selection of schooling routes was reinforced the class divide.

There were continuing changes and reforms in the education system throughout the twentieth century. In the United Kingdom, perhaps the most notable were the move to end the 11 plus entrance examination for grammar schools and the establishment of comprehensive schooling and the move toward mass university education heralded in then-Prime Minister James Callaghan's 1976 "Ruskin speech," which argued for society's right to have a say in what was taught in schools—through establishing a "core curriculum of basic knowledge" (interestingly, this speech was still quoted on Tony Blair's 10 Downing Street Web site in May 2007). However, which sections of society were to have their say was more contentious. The crisis in industry in the late 1970s led to a merger of the education and employment ministries, the establishment of the Manpower Services Commission and an increasing emphasis on skills for employment. Such reforms basically reflected the changing needs of industry and the economy at the time.

However, despite the reforms, the main forms of organization and delivery of education, the institutional form of schooling, the development of curriculum and approaches to pedagogy were based on the Taylorist organization of production stemming from the industrial revolution.

THE NEW INDUSTRIAL REVOLUTION

Industrial revolutions lead to profound and often paradigmatic social change. However, such paradigm changes in the social arena tend to lag behind at times of rapid technical development and change.

The present deep and prolonged industrial revolution, based on the development and implementation of digital technologies, is leading to massive pressures on education and training systems, both in terms of the changing demands from society—especially from employers—for new skills and knowledge (seen in the move towards lifelong learning), but also from the changing ways in which individuals (especially young people) are using Web 2.0 technology to create and share knowledge.

The combination of these pressures is likely to result in a longer-term paradigm shift in our education systems, including the organization and form of educational institutions and infrastructure (e.g., funding) and curricula and the pedagogic approaches to learning and knowledge development.

Of course, the new technologies have already impacted on education with various phases of innovation, culminating in the present wide-scale adoption of learning management systems and virtual learning environments. It is another feature of industrial revolutions that profound innovations in technology tend to be reflected in older paradigms. Rather than focusing on the possibilities of the new technologies for fundamental innovation, we tend to replicate previous forms of organization and communication through the new technology. In education, we have attempted to adapt the technology to the existing paradigm of schooling with the resulting virtual classroom and virtual college.

Where do personal learning environments fit in? Personal learning environments represent, perhaps, the first attempt to develop educational technologies that transcend the traditional paradigm of industrial schooling and move beyond the forms of organization of that paradigm. PLEs represent an attempt to use technology to move from school- (institutional- or course-) led learning to learner-led learning. As such, the first major visible impact may be in the institutional organization of education that forms the subject of the next section of this paper.

PERSONAL LEARNING ENVIRONMENTS AND THE IMPACT ON SCHOOLS

In the last section, I outlined two key challenges to education and training systems: the need to facilitate and support lifelong learning and the changing cultural and pedagogic ways in which young people are using technology for learning.

How are education systems reacting to the challenge? Primary education, in most countries, fulfils the role of providing basic skills in reading and writing—and, increasingly, digital literacy—and in providing a social environment for children to interact. Pedagogic approaches include storytelling, group work, play, and project-based learning. While universities provide access to higher education for an increasing age cohort, it could be argued that they have failed in terms of providing access to in terms of lifelong learning.

However, it is at the level of postprimary (or secondary) education that the systems seem to be particularly challenged. It is notable that, at least in Europe, almost every system is in the process of reforming post-10- or post-11-year-old education systems and provision. Despite the reforms, in many countries there remain concerns that the systems are not working (see, for example, the ongoing debates in Germany following the relatively poor performance in the international PISA study). Even with relatively high investment in education, the proportion on nonachievers remains persistently high, teachers are often disillusioned, employers complain about the low levels of skills and competence from school graduates, and many young people, when questioned, are less than enthusiastic about school. At best, it is just a hurdle that has to be jumped in order to progress in their lives. In the following section, I will look at why postprimary education systems and institutions may be seen as dysfunctional within today's culture and society.

DYSFUNCTIONAL SYSTEMS

I want to draw attention to three particular aspects of what I believe to be dysfunctional aspects of secondary education schooling systems: the development and use of educational technology; the culture of networking, sharing and collaboration; and curriculum design and development.

Educational Technology

Young people are increasingly using technology for creating and sharing multimedia objects and for social networking. A Pew Research study (Lenhart & Madden, 2005) found that 56% of young people in America were using computers for "creative activities, writing and posting of the Internet, mixing and constructing multimedia and developing their own content. Twelve- to 17-year-olds look to Web tools to share what they think and do online. One in five who use the net said they used other people's images, audio or text to help make their own creations. According to Raine (British Broadcasting Corporation, 2005), "These teens were born into a digital world where they expect to be able to create, consume, remix, and share material with each other and lots of strangers" (para. 7). However, the major implementations of educational technology have been not to encourage such networking and creativity but to manage learning and to isolate networks. Learning management systems are WSYWYG (what you see is what you get)—they do what they say, manage learning. Systems have been developed as a "walled garden," to perpetuate the isolation of the school from the wider outside community.

We tend to recreate with new technologies older forms of social organization. Thus, we talk about virtual classroom or the virtual university, attempting to recreate and preserve the old paradigm of education with new technical forms. Even in Second Life, a multiplayer 3D virtual world, universities have been investing heavily in buying islands to recreate in 3D form their buildings and classrooms.

In addition, most education systems have acted with, at best, suspicion and, often, downright hostility to social networking systems and technologies. In the United States a bill is proceeding through Congress to ban access to social networking sites from public institutions. In Europe we insist that young people turn off their mobile phones to prevent them texting friends in school. Yet these are the very systems and tools that businesses are increasingly seeing as central to future knowledge creation and distribution!

Particularly notable are the continuing moral panics over young peoples' use of technology. There would appear to be more studies of sexual predators on sites like MySpace than actual proven instances. Boyd (2006) notes: "Moral panics are a common reaction to teenagers when they engage in practices not understood by adult culture. There were moral panics over rock and roll, television, jazz and even reading novels in the early 1800s" (para. 3).

Networking, Sharing, and Collaboration

The second aspect of the dysfunction of secondary education relates to the culture of networking, sharing, and collaboration. Web 2.0 applications and social software are increasingly being used for knowledge development and sharing and for cultural interchange and networking. Research in economic development advances the idea of the learning region based on collaboration between enterprises and between enterprises and other social institutions. The theory of connectivism states that learners are actively attempting to create meaning through engagement in networks (Siemens, 2004), yet the schooling model remains rigidly tied to the idea of developing and assessing individual attainment. Of course, the idea that we should enable each individual to develop to his or her full potential is laudable as a social goal, but if knowledge and creativity is dependent on engagement within wider social networks, then how can this be developed within education systems based on individual attainment? I will talk more about the issue of assessment later in this chapter.

Curriculum

The third illustration of how education and schooling systems are dysfunctional relates to curriculum. Most learning does not take place in formal educational programs. Cross (2006) argues that only 10-15% of learning is formal, and that 85% of our learning takes place outside of formal settings. Learning is taking place through engagement in social networks, both by young people of school age and by older people in work. Furthermore, learning takes place in multiple contexts, in work, in the community, and in the home as well as in school, yet our schooling systems remain wedded to attainment against a narrow curriculum of formal knowledge. Informal learning is hardly acknowledged, less still fostered and facilitated.

RESCHOOLING SOCIETY: ENGAGING WITH LEARNERS

We face the danger that school may become irrelevant for the everyday lives (and learning) of many young people. How can we overcome such dysfunction? Fraser (2007) has looked at how Web 2.0 tools and applications are being used to supplement the limitations of learning management systems (or virtual learning environments). In common with many educational technology researchers, she is interested in the concept of the personal learning environment. Fraser says the PLE has become a tool for empowerment, as it embodies the principles of self-directed learning. It recognizes that learners exist in an ecosystem and that the PLE is a tool for learning within that ecosystem. The PLE is the system (or multiple systems) that enables and supports the growth and behavior of self-directed or self-motivated learners. Fraser sees such a development as a move from adaptive personalization to dynamic personalization. Figure 9.1. shows the processes involved in such a shift.

Critical to such an understanding is a basic paradigm shift from learners engaging with institutional provision and procedures to the institution engaging with the learner. This would imply that institutions have to recognize the new cultures of learning and networking and engage with those cultures, yet that involves profound change in institutional practice and procedures and institutional organization and in curriculum organization and pedagogic approach.

Critical to engagement (or re-engagement) and support of institutions with learner-led participation is to end the schooling culture whereby schools have been isolated from wider forms of community and social discourse, knowledge development, and sharing. The present organization of schools and education institutions cannot achieve this. Instead, we have to rethink the role of educational provision and support for learning within communities and wider society. This might include the adoption and promotion of the following developments: community learning centers, project-based learning, open educational resources, mixed age learning, a new role for higher education, assessment for learning, and personal learning environments.

Instead of the present schools, we could envisage the idea of community learning centers. These would be support centers open to all ages— at least from the age of 11 or 12 upwards—although there is a case for

Adaptive Personalisation	(Implicit or Inferential Personalisation) - The availability of options is based on knowledge about users gained from tracking user activity and/or other sources of user information. The system identifies items of potential interest to the user and controls what is made available to the user. Note, this form of personalisation may involve varying degrees of user awareness of, and involvement in, the process. *Personalisation in presentation services, Nicky Ferguson, Seb Schmoller, Neil Smith 15 July 2004*	**institutional provision and procedure**
Customisation	(Explicit or Referential Personalisation) - The selection of options is under the direct control of the user who explicitly chooses to include or exclude options. *Personalisation in presentation services, Nicky Ferguson, Seb Schmoller, Neil Smith 15 July 2004*	**enabling the learner to engage with institutional provision**
Dynamic Personalisation	Production, reception and relationships are supported by the system but determined by the user - the ability to create original or derivative works, to collaborate, form networks and connections via the users choice of applications, locations, platforms	**the institution engaging with the learner**

Source: Fraser (2007).

Figure 9.1.   From adaptive personalization to dynamic personalization.

maintaining separate primary learning provision. Critically, such centers would be networked allowing access support for learning currently only available in specialist schools or in higher education institutions, within the community.

Learners could work on projects combining elements from different subjects. Individual learning plans would be developed through a personal learning environment with the support of "teachers." Such projects would be undertaken in teams with "teachers" facilitating learning. Teams could be geographically based, but might well include participants from other community learning centers and from other countries participating through networked communication. Although this might seem far-fetched, many young people participate in online communities involving participants form different countries in their leisure time. Projects could also include the wider community, including community-based organizations and enterprises. Such a pedagogic approach is not new, but the use of new technologies can greatly enhance the learning potential.

Learners would be able to access federated (or central) repositories of open educational resources. New resources, created by "teachers" and learners to meet the particular need of a learning task, would be added to such a repository.

Community learning centers would support wider community resources, including provision for adult learners and support for single parents. Members of the community would be encouraged to assist with the learning provision. The local community, with regular and open meetings to discuss management and future development, would control centers. Buildings would be designed to facilitate interaction between small groups of learners, providing privacy and quiet for intense activities, but also encouraging transparency and communication. It goes without saying that they would also provide access to bandwidth and to information and communication technologies.

These ideas are not new. Thinking and practice already exists, although all too often innovative practice has not been mainstreamed. Information and communication technology (ICT) adds an extra dimension and creates additional possibilities and may enable the new pedagogies to speed up the rate of change.

Higher education providers would be given a new role in supporting networked community learning centers. However, with more learning occurring at local level, and learners participating in the network of centers as a whole, not an individual institution, they would also be able to focus on research (with that research shared under Creative Commons and Science Commons licences).

It is hoped that, over a period of time, the motivation for participation in "school" would become a self-drive interest in learning activities. However, it may be that we have advanced the leaving age for full time education too far, and young people, from say 14 or 15, should be offered the opportunity to undertake paid work while learning.

At present, assessment is usually based on individual achievement. This is a substantial barrier to collaboration, reflection, and feedback and to project-based group work. Rick Stiggins (2004), building on the work of Black and Wiliam (1998) distinguishes between the assessment of learning and assessment for learning. The assessment of learning seeks to discover how much students have learned at a particular point in time. Assessment for learning asks how assessment can be used to help students learn more, better, and differently. Assessment for learning can promote new pedagogic approaches, including peer group learning and reflective self-assessment.

Personal learning environments can play a central role in assessment for learning in allowing learners to record and reflect on progress and attainment, both as an individual and as part of groups. Learners would be encouraged to produce regular presentations of their work, which would be shared online and also provide a resource both for other learners and for the broader community.

LIFELONG LEARNING

The recent focus on lifelong learning, in the last 30 years, has been guided by a narrow discourse. Driven by a shorter product life-cycle, the increasing speed of adoption and implementation of new technologies in the workplace, and the increasing instability of employment with the computer driven industrial revolution, it was reasoned that workers would need continuous learning throughout their work-life to update their occupational skills and knowledge or to learn new occupational competencies. It was contestable as to who would be responsible for this. While previously continuing vocational training had been the responsibility of employers, with the state playing a leading role in the provision of continuing education and training, it is now increasingly argued that individuals are responsible for maintaining their own employability, albeit sometimes with the assistance of grants, vouchers, and subsidized courses, if not continuous, learning is now seen as multiepisodic, with individuals spending occasional periods of formal education and training throughout their working life.

The idea of lifelong learning was originally rooted in the workers' movements. In the United Kingdom, the mechanics institutes, the miners institutes, and organizations like the Workers Educational Association organized classes and courses for workers to improve their own education as well as providing access to learning resources and social activities. While this provision might have aimed at developing technical- and labor market-related skills and knowledge, it was guided by a wider belief in the power of education for emancipation.

The idea of a personal learning environment recognizes that learning is discontinuous and seeks to provide tools to support that learning diachronically. It also reinforces the role of the individual in organizing his or her own learning, including learning based on personal interest and with a less narrow employment-based focus than has been so in much face-to-face provision. Moreover, it is now recognized that learning will take place in different contexts and situations and will not be provided by a single learning provider. Linked to this is an increasing recognition of the importance of informal learning. Personal learning environments can bring together learning from multiple contexts, including from home, from school, and from work, and can support formal learning activities provided by different educational institutions.

LEARNING IN THE WORKPLACE

Whilst there have been a number of studies in the different ways in which young people are using computers for social activities and for learning, only limited attention has been paid to the way computers are being used for learning in the workplace.

A seven-country study of the use of ICT for learning in small and medium enterprises (SMEs) found that computers are already being widely used for informal learning through searching and networking (Attwell, 2007). The survey showed that there was little use of ICT for formal learning in the SMEs (in fact, there was little formal learning taking place at all). However, in contrast to the paucity of formal learning provision in the SMEs studied, there was a great deal of informal learning taking place. From the study, most informal learning appeared be learner-driven, rather than planned in conjunction with others in the enterprise and was typically a response to a problem. Nevertheless, some learners were motivated by their own interest rather than by a particular problem. The main means of ICT-based learning was the use of Google keyword searches. Managers were often unaware of this learning, although they were frequently aware of the problem that inspired it. There were considerable differences in the use of ICT for informal learning between different enterprises. It would be tempting to ascribe these differences to age, sector, size, or occupation, but it is hard to discern such causal factors from the case studies undertaken. None of the employees in the enterprises studied had attempted to claim recognition or accreditation for the skills and knowledge gained through informal learning. It is not clear if this is because they are not interested in pursuing further formal qualifications or if it is because they are unaware of any opportunities for claiming accreditation for informal learning.

The use of the Google search engine as the major tool for learning is interesting. It raises the question of how people are framing their search terms, how they are refining search strings, how they are selecting from the results of search queries, and how they are following hyperlinked texts. For a search result to be useful, it needs to produce materials, ideas, and concepts that can connect with the learner's existing knowledge base on the one hand, and deal with the issue or problem being addressed on the other.

LEGITIMATE PERIPHERAL PARTICIPATION
AND COMMUNITIES OF PRACTICE

The ideas of legitimate peripheral participation and proximal development may be helpful for explaining this process and of understanding how people are making sense of knowledge.

Lave and Wenger (1991) propose that the initial participation in a culture of practice can be observation from the periphery or legitimate peripheral participation. As learning and observation in the culture increases, the participant moves from the role of observer to a fully functioning member. The progressive movement towards full participation enables the learner to piece together the culture of the group and establish their identity. "Knowing is inherent in the growth and transformation of identities and it is located in relations among practitioners, their practice, the artefacts of that practice, and the social organization ... of communities of practice" (Lave & Wenger, 1991, p. 122).

Especially in microenterprises, SME employees have tended to be isolated from communities of practice. This may be a greater barrier to learning than the lack of time to attend training courses. One of the most powerful uses of ICT for learning in SMEs could be the ability to connect to distributed communities of practice. Many people have commented on the phenomenon of "lurkers" on discussion sites, lists servers, and bulletin boards. Lurking is very much a process of legitimate peripheral participation. Watching, listening, and trying to make sense of a series of posts and discussions without being forced to reveal oneself or to actively participate, allows the development of knowledge "about knowledge" within a community and about the practices of the online community.

Similar to the idea of legitimate peripheral participation is Vygotsky's (1978) "zone of proximal development." This theoretical construct states that learning occurs best when an expert guides a novice from the novice's current level of knowledge to the expert's level of knowledge. Bridging the zone of proximal development construct with the legitimate peripheral participation construct may be accomplished if one thinks of a zone in which the expert or mentor takes the learner from the peripheral status of knowing to a deeper status. This may be accomplished with or without intention, as Lave and Wenger (1991) state:

> Legitimate peripheral participation is not itself an educational form, much less a pedagogical strategy or a teaching technique. It is an analytic viewpoint on learning, a way of understanding learning. We hope to make it clear that learning through legitimate peripheral participation takes place no matter which educational form provides a context for learning, or whether there is any intentional educational form at all. Indeed, this view-

point makes a fundamental distinction between learning and intentional instruction. (p. 40)

However, the expert scaffolds the environment to the extent in which the learner is engaged with the discourse and participants within the zone and is drawn from a peripheral status to a more engaged status. The peripheral learner interacts with the mentor, expert learners and peers within this zone. More-able learners (peers) or the mentor will work with the less-able learner, potentially allowing for socially constructed knowledge. Within the SME studies there were few instances of mentoring or continuous contact with an expert. The use of ICT was allowing distributed access to expertise—albeit mediated through bulletin boards, forums, and Web pages. This leaves open the question as to the process of scaffolding, which essentially becomes an internalized process. However, the process of less-able learners working with more-able peers is a common process in seeking new knowledge through the use of ICT.

SEARCHING AND LURKING

Essentially, workers are using search engines to seek out potential forums and contexts for learning. Selection depends on the degree to which there is a match of interest between learner and community and also the level of discourse in the community. There is little point in following a discourse at too low a level, of knowledge already gained; neither is there an attraction to a discourse clearly on a level that cannot be understood. Learners will seek a community with knowledge at a higher level than their own but which can connect with their prior learning, learning and practice. They will lurk in order to understand the workings of the community and to gain some basic knowledge. After a period of time they might contribute in the form of a question and later again might themselves contribute to the shared knowledge pool. In this way they move from the periphery through lurking to full bound participants in a community. It should be noted that communities are frequently overlapping and that the use of hyperlinks and, more recently, standards like trackback allow the communities to be dynamic with the emergence of new groups and discourses.

The results of this study demonstrate the potential for personal learning environments as a tool for lifelong learning, linked to communities of practice. Personal learning environments can extend access to educational technology to everyone wanting to organize their own learning. PLEs can include and bring together all learning, including informal learning, workplace learning, learning from the home, learning driven by problem solving and learning motivated by personal interest as well as learning through engagement in formal educational programs.

KNOWLEDGE SHARING AND DEVELOPMENT

This final section of the paper examines the impact of PLEs on knowledge sharing and development. I argued in a previous section, that the schooling model developed out of the first industrial revolution had isolated learning—or education—from wider communities. Furthermore the curriculum has been based on formal bodies of explicit knowledge or on technical rationality—the idea that it is possible to learn everything that needs to be known about a subject.

Learning has been separated from processes of innovation and knowledge creation. Even in software applications, learning platforms have developed independently of systems for knowledge management (although often these are merely information databases).

However, knowledge development has been identified as a key factor in innovations designed to increase the supply of creative knowledge value: "what is important for the production of knowledge value is not so much facilities or equipment in the material sense, but the knowledge, experience, and sensitivity to be found among those engaged in its creation" (Sakaiya, 1991, p. 270). This way, knowledge is assumed as the real driving force of our era but also strictly linked with day-to-day problem solving and problem setting in working situations and, more generally, with the development and use of professional competencies and expertise.

Brown (1997) has highlighted the importance of entry into communities of practice in the development of knowledge and expertise. This is based on

the ideas that learning is a relational social process; that processes of becoming skilled take place within a broader process of identity formation; and that recognition of significant achievement (and attainment of the status of experienced practitioner) is itself a socially mediated (or contested) process, dependent on the recognition of others and a sense of self-worth.

Learners gain knowledge through a process of personal and cooperative experimentation, questioning, and problem solving through which meaning can be constructed. Learning is the articulation of schema that incorporates cognition, perception, and action (Mjelde, 1994). Schemata are made meaningful by jointly carrying out activities with an "expert" in such a way that the learner gradually masters successively more difficult parts of the task through successively more complex stages (Mjelde, 1994).

As early as 1994, Enkenburg proposed that the authenticity and transfer of knowledge and skills depends on the refinement of intelligent instructional systems and on the design of learning environments in which students are helped to construct knowledge themselves (Enkenberg, 1994). Teaching and learning strategies include modelling, coaching, scaffolding and fading, articulation, reflection, and exploration.

Within a social model of knowledge creation, the prerequisite process for genuine knowledge transformation to occur is that knowledge has to move from the individual level into wider communities of interaction that cross organizational boundaries (Attwell & Brown, 2000).

Attwell and Brown talked of the spiralling of knowledge creation and transformation through and across different themes. A dynamic ICT environment allows material and ideas to be transferred rapidly between themes. That is, it will not involve a static accumulation of different materials, documents and information but rather it will possess the dynamism to continually create new knowledge. "Within this vision the role of the ICT platform is to provide a rich virtual knowledge environment to support the processes of collaboration and knowledge creation and transformation in the learning community developed to enhance practice."

Personal learning environments can bring together individual learning and collaborative and organizational knowledge development. Figure 9.2, developed for the Freefolio ePortfolio and social knowledge management system, shows the relationship between learning and knowledge construction.

Freefolio, despite being described as an e-portfolio and lightweight knowledge management system, is essentially a personal learning environment. The tools mediate knowledge construction by individuals within communities of practice. Such communities establish rules, although these rule are often tacit, and of course reflect a division of labor that, in turn, mediates the practices of that community. Through the process of social practice, described as tasks, such knowledge is disseminated into wider environments.

Although most attention to personal learning environments has been in the context of education, it may be at the level of knowledge construction and innovation that their impact will be most profound. Knowledge management systems have been developed largely in isolation from learn-

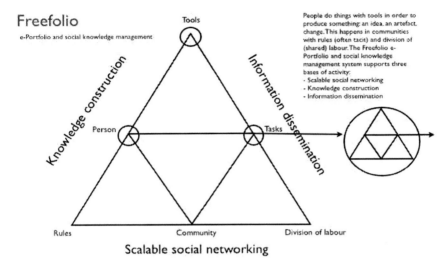

Figure 9.2.   Freefolio ePortfolio and social knowledge management system.

ing systems. PLEs can unite processes of learning and social and organizational knowledge development.

PERSONAL LEARNING ENVIRONMENTS: SOME INITIAL CONCLUSIONS

Personal learning environments are a *significant* move forward for three reasons. Often the introduction of new technology in education has tended to inhibit pedagogic innovation and change. Virtual learning systems have focused on managing learning. The IMS Question & Test Interoperability (QTI) specification for assessment has inhibited the introduction of peer assessment and focused assessment on what people know, rather than on assessment for learning. In contrast personal learning environments can stimulate the development of new forms of pedagogy and facilitate the introduction of social forms of learning, such as, use of social networking. PLEs, by themselves, do not represent a new practice in teaching and learning, but PLEs can enhance existing best practices and speed up the rate of change. Third, PLEs bring into sharper focus issues around the shift from teaching to learning and may provide some solutions to some of the problems in this area. However, by themselves, PLEs cannot transform our education systems and practice. They are but one tool in changing the social practice of education.

REFERENCES

Attwell, G. (Ed.). (2007). *Searching, lurking and the zone of proximal development: E-learning in small and medium enterprises in Europe.* Vienna, Austria: Navreme.

Attwell, G., & Brown, A. (2000, August). *Knowledge development at the interface of research, policy and practice: Support for knowledge development within the CEDE-FOP Research Arena (CEDRA).* Paper presented at IVETA 2000 Conference, Hong Kong.

British Broadcasting Corporation. (2005, November 4). *US youths use Internet to create.* Retrieved April 20, 2007, from http://news.bbc.co.uk/2/hi/technology/4403574.stm

Black, P., & Wiliam, D. (1998). Assessment and classroom learning. *Assessment in Education, 5*(1), 7-71.

Brown, A. (1997, September). *Valuing the development of practice, expertise and research in continuing professional development of vocational education and training professionals.* Paper presented at European Conference on Educational Research (ECER 97) Frankfurt, Germany.

Boyd, D. (2006). *Identity production in a networked culture: Why youth heart MySpace.* Retrieved April 20, 2007, from www.danah.org/papers/AAAS2006.html

Callaghan, J. (1976, October 18). *Towards a national debate* (Speech). Retrieved June 16, 2007, from http://education.guardian.co.uk/thegreatdebate/story/0,9860,574645,00.html

Cross, J. (2006). *What is informal learning?* Retrieved January 22, 2007, from http://informl.com/?p=551

Downes, S. (2006). *Learning networks and connective knowledge.* Retrieved June 16, 2007, from http://it.coe.uga.edu/itforum/paper92/paper92.html

Enkenberg, J. (1994). Situated cognition and cognitive apprenticeship. New framework for education of professional skills. In A. Heikkinen (Ed.), *Vocational education and culture: European prospects from history and life-history* (pp. 135-139). Tampere, Finland: University of Tampere.

Fraser, J. (2007). *Open complimenting closed?* Retrieved May 14, 2007, from http://eduspaces.net/josiefraser/weblog/169960.html

Lave, J., & Wenger, E. (1991). *Situated learning: Legitimate peripheral participation.* Cambridge, England: Cambridge University Press.

Lenhart, A., & Madden, M. (2005). Teen content creators and consumers. *Pew Internet.* Retrieved April 21, 2007, from www.pewInternet.org/pdfs/PIP_Teens_Content_Creation.pdf

Mjelde, L. (1994). Will the twain meet? The world of work and the world of schooling (vocational and general) in relation to upper secondary educational reforms in Norway. In A. Heikkinen (Ed.), *Vocational education and culture: European prospects from history and life-history.* Tampere, Finland: University of Tampere.

Sakaiya, T. (1991). *The knowledge value revolution.* Tokyo: Kodansha International.

Seely-Brown, J. (1999). *Learning, working and playing in the digital age.* Retrieved October 21, 2008, from: http://serendip.brynmawr.edu/sci_edu/seelybrown/

Siemens, G. (2004). *A learning theory for the digital age.* Retrieved April 20, 2007, from www.elearnspace.org/Articles/connectivism.htm

Stiggins, R. (2004). *Student-involved assessment for learning*. London: Prentice Hall.

van Harmelen, M. (2006). *Personal learning environments*. Retrieved June 16, 2007, from http://octette.cs.man.ac.uk/jitt/index.php/Personal_Learning_ Environments

Vygotsky, L. S. (1978). *Mind in society: The development of higher psychological processes* (M. Cole, V. John-Steiner, S. Scribner, & E. Souberman, Trans.). Cambridge, MA: Harvard University Press.

Wikipedia. (n.d.). *Education in England*. Retrieved June 16, 2007, from http:// en.wikipedia.org/wiki/Education_in_England

PART III

ROLES AND IDENTITIES

CHAPTER 10

EMERGING ONLINE PRACTICES

An Endo-Aesthetic Approach to E-Tutoring and E-Learning

Viv Tucker

Faith and hope in human affairs comes from the fact that new people are continually coming into the world, each of them unique, each capable of new initiatives that may interrupt or divert chains of events set in motion by previous action. Action is the miracle working faculty of wo(man) and in human affairs it is actually quite reasonable to expect the unexpected, that new beginnings cannot be ruled out even when society seems locked in stagnation or set in an inexorable course. (Arendt, 1998, p. 17)

CHAPTER OVERVIEW

This chapter outlines an innovative poststructural philosophical feminist position which informs the conceptual development of an endo-aesthetic approach to online teaching and learning within the context of postgraduate initial teacher training for the lifelong learning sector. This model

Connected Minds, Emerging Cultures: Cybercultures in Online Learning
pp. 141–157
Copyright © 2009 by Information Age Publishing
All rights of reproduction in any form reserved.

critically examines and resists the limitations of an instrumental approach and argues for a teaching and learning model in which contemporary poststructural theory radically informs emerging online practice.

This approach to practice acknowledges the importance of identity construction and multiplicity in the building of a fluid, virtual learning community. It also embraces the digital aesthetic of the virtual classroom. As an outcome of the second phase of research that began in 2003, a newly validated option module named "E-tutoring and E-pedagogy: A Practice and Theoretical Approach to Online Tutoring" has been written and validated in November 2006 subject to the author bidding for funding to support the third phase of research and development of a standalone Web site that provides access to learning materials to support the module. Due to the recent embedding of the Lifelong Learning UK (2007) teacher training standards rolled out in September 2007 into Post Graduate Certificate in Education (PGCE) (post-16) programs in the United Kingdom, there has been a notable shift in culture from education to training. It has been agreed, in line with the universities corporate objectives and government policies on e-learning standards and the application of information and communication technologies (ICT) to teaching and supporting learning in the Life Long Learning sector (2005), that it is more appropriate to embed general ICT skills and knowledge into the rewritten PGCE post-16 program rather than offer the module as a designated option module where trainee teachers experience an intensive 11 weeks of online tutoring and learning.

The author however believes that there should to be a sustained investment in educating and training teachers for online tutoring due to the emphasis of ICT in learning strategies (British Educational Communications and Technology Agency, 2007; Department for Education and Skills, 2005; Joint Information Systems Committee, 2007). It is noted that the Department for Education and Skills (2008) is currently offering an e-skills U.K. passport in which you can profile your IT user skills, however the highly reputable Learning To Teach Online or "LeTTOL" (2008) program offered by Sheffield college has over a decade of research and practice devoted to the development of online educational tutoring. It offers a 9-month course in this area, thus validating the importance for teachers and lecturers who wish to engage in the transfer and construction of knowledge, pedagogy and ICT skills to the potentially sophisticated, complex, and unpredictable online learning environment. This said, the author is exploring the benefits and enrichment of relocating the recently validated e-tutoring and e-pedagogy module onto the BA education and training program at the University.

The collection and analysis of data created by both e-tutor and e-learner during this body of research consists of online narratives generated in discussion forums, e-mails, data from questionnaires, and examples of Web sites visited during the running of the ICT option modules between January 2004 and March 2005. The reflexive narrative that follows provides insight into the emergent pedagogical, technological, and sociocultural concerns that the author has been utilizing to inform an endo-aesthetic approach to online tutoring and the digital aesthetic.

INTRODUCTION

Between the dates of January 2004 and March 2005 I took the opportunity to pilot an approach to e-tutoring and e-pedagogy within the context of an already-existing information and communications technologies for Teaching and Learning option module on a PGCE (post-16) full-time program. The focus of the 11-week module was a critical exploration of developing an approach to facilitating online learning through the building of a fluid learning community. In the process it was important to critically reflect on emergent approaches to pedagogy and identity construction within the online setting from a student and tutor perspective. I had concerns that many of the current online developments, research projects and government e-learning initiatives I had reviewed were too focused upon the process of skills development (Learning Skills Council, 2005) and (Learning Skills Development Agency, 2005) that an instrumental model to embedding ICT skills into practice was being unconsciously privileged. While such government initiatives have their place in skilling the work force to be competitive in the global economy, I still felt that teacher education was a fertile terrain from which to offer experience via computer-mediated communication to critically reflect on e-tutoring and e-pedagogy and radically inform the culture emerging in this digital space.

My research interests in 2003-06 were underpinned by the literature of online pedagogy (Stephenson, 2001), aspects of computer mediated communication and learning communities (Palloff & Pratt, 1999), e-tutoring and support in learning within online programs (Salmon, 2000, 2002) and case studies in developing online learning (Murphy, Walker, & Webb, 2001). The significant cultural and philosophical literatures were Deleuze and Guattari (2003), Prophet and Hamlett (2000), Bell and Kennedy (2000) and Reiche (2004) on the subject of poststructural approaches to identity construction in cyberspace. Through the feminist poststructural discourse examining posthuman bodies in Halberstam and Livingston (1995) I engaged in a critique into hybridities that resist a reduction into a single overarching ideology. Such hybrids which emerge from Haraway's (1991) "Cyborg Manifesto" redefine the body as a cybernetic organism, a hybrid mixture of human being and machine. Identity becomes an expanded concept, fluid, nomadic, and in motion. The hybrids I discursively engage with in this chapter are the hybrids of identity construction (teacher/learner becoming) and curriculum.

DARE TO IMAGINE

I had no previous experience of e-tutoring but had 21 years experience facilitating learning in both further education (FE) and higher education (HE) settings. I was curious to find out how my pedagogy and philosophical approach to tutoring in the traditional classroom setting could be reconceptualized and applied to an online context. I had access to one person who experienced e-tutoring and e-learning on the LeTTOL program at Sheffield College. At the completion of the second phase of research in 2006, I enrolled on the LeTTOL program and successfully gained my online teaching qualification in July 2007. This has affirmed that my online skills and pedagogy are professionally informed for the third phase of research to being when I receive funding to update and redesign the learning materials in a standalone Web site. However, in 2003 I was strongly informed by theoretical knowledge in this area of research but limited in personal experiential knowledge. It was my aim to create a practice led model in this field and conceptualize a theoretical map of a rhizomatic curriculum to illustrate a philosophy it would inevitably represent. My new model of practice can be seen in the following diagram.

In 2003 I reaccessed an online learning research site that I had been involved in designing and e-tutoring on in 1999 with two other academics. Back then, during the first stage of research, we piloted a program of study to teach teachers how to teach online. In 2003, when I began the second stage of research, I set about with no budget, prohibitive research hours, one learning technologist, and an abundance of imagination to immerse myself into an online world of e-tutoring and pedagogy. I reconceptualized the 11-week module with the invaluable help of a learning technologist/educator and adapted the learning materials for use by trainee teachers on the Postgraduate Certificate of Education. I ran the module twice between January 2004 and March 2005. Each time I undertook an in depth and careful evaluation of the functionality of the site and student and tutor experience using two methods of data gathering, the first being a questionnaire which encouraged students to write a narrative account of their experiences as a student being e-tutored with particular focus on identity construction.

The second method employed the AEIOU (Accountability, Effectiveness, Impact, Organizational factors, Unanticipated outcomes) model

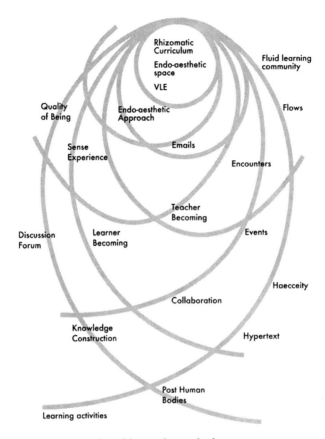

Figure 10.1.   The Rhizomatic curriculum.

(Sorensen, 1996). I used this model to make adjustments to the technology and its functionality. Out of this second phase of research emerged the model of practice above to illustrate how post-structural theory radically informs emerging online practice.

THE CURRICULUM

The curriculum was designed to run over a period of 11 weeks and the learning materials located on the university student portal focused on six sections (see Table 10.1).

Table 10.1.   E-Tutoring and E-Pedagogy: A Practical and Theoretical Approach to the Online Tutoring Module Structure

Session	Elements	Methodology and Duration	End Date
Induction	Setting up ground rules. Checking access to WWW, ability to send e-mails, searching, information handling and access to discussion forum set up to facilitate learning.	Face-to-face tuition 3 hours 9:30 a.m.-12:30 p.m. K205 Kimsbury House	January 13, 2004
Introduction	What is a VLE? How does online learning differ from traditional f2f learning? What are the implications for learning and social communications?	Linked online Web pages 7 hours over 14 days	January 14-27, 2004
E-tutoring and e-moderating	Encouraging participation, building of learning communities, strategies for teaching and learning. Exploring pedagogy. Time and email management of teaching and learning resources. Equality, diversity, and inclusion.	Online document folders, resource pages, email and a discussion forum. 9 hours over 20 days	January 28-February 17, 2004
Authoring	Level and styles, file types. Best use of tools, copyright issues. Information gathering and retrieval. References	Face-to-face tuition 3 hours 9:30 a.m.-12:30 a.m. Computer room E206. Online materials and a discussion forum. Six hours over 14 days.	February 17-March 1, 2004
Cyber Culture	Cyberculture providing learning contexts. Analysis of technological competence, access, and a global context to learning in the information age.	Online discussion forum 4 hours over 16 days	March 3-18, 2004
Course evaluation	Feedback session	Face-to-face tuition 3 hours 9:30 a.m.-12:30 a.m. K205 Kimsbury House	March 23, 2004

Whilst a blended delivery was used, there were only three scheduled face-to-face sessions which students were asked to attend. The rest of the tutoring was done entirely online, at a distance. The students had electronic access to a copy of the module handbook and curriculum to enable them to plan and prepare for learning. Student autonomy was assumed; however, there were scheduled online opportunities with learning sets and individuals to check progress, levels of motivation and engagement with the learning activities.

The first face-to-face session was an induction held at the university on networked computers. The students physically met each other and it was important for the learners and me to form an understanding of each other given all the traditional physical clues that are apparent in a face-to-face learning context. I wondered if/how these students would develop an awareness of a constructed online "flexible entity" (Voltart, 2004, p. 114) and/or if they felt their online identity was an authentic one? (Matlow, 2000).

ASSESSING ONLINE CAPABILITIES DURING THE INDUCTION TO ONLINE PROGRAM

It was essential that I assessed the students' online capabilities via the learning activities. I needed to check that they had reliable Internet access and online skills to progress through the programme. Salmon (2002, p. 14) suggests at the first stage of the five-stage framework for e-tivities; when considering access, "e-tivities at this stage need to provide a gentle but interesting introduction to using the technological platform and acknowledgment of the feelings surrounding the use of the technology" (p. 14)

What was also critical within the prerequisites of the program was that the students' Internet service provider could work remotely to access the learning materials that were located on the student portal at the university. I had experienced no problem with this issue using my Internet service provider, Zetnet, but in the early stages of the first pilot we experienced remote access issues with two major Internet service providers and had been unable to resolve them. As a result we suggested that students change their providers to ones we knew worked. This was in early 2004. In 2008 VLE platforms such a Moodle, Blackboard academic suite, and WebCT are more operationally stable to support distance learning and blended learning programs.

It is not my intention to critique these virtual learning environments (VLEs) in this chapter, but as a result of experiencing the limited visual aesthetic these platforms offer, I made a professional decision to develop a stand-alone site, separate from the university portal in which fully inter-active software can be utilized to enhance the multisensory learning experience while enriching the digital and endo-aesthetic of the people who populate the site. The affordance of such VLEs noted above, is that they offer transferability of skills to different learning contexts but in doing so they become a normative discourse.

Danaher, Schirato, and Webb (2000) critique Foucault and suggest that discourses shape our experiences in language. Foucault believed our thoughts and actions are influenced, regulated, and controlled by such discourses. Here we are discussing the discourse of curriculum and VLEs within HE and FE education. To encourage free intellectual thought, the idea of offering students a stand-alone site in which the curriculum can evolve by the encounters, flows, hypertext, and links to emerging knowledge on the Web offers a transitional stage into an educational future that is net-based. This orientation toward a curriculum becomes fluid and evolves with the needs of the learners. Learners can become authors of their own education in relationship with an experienced tutor to guide then towards relevant nodes of knowledge. This valorizes personalized learning and celebrates multiplicity. Access to the learning materials as a practical example to support this theoretical concept is not currently available as the site that supported this module is decommissioned and awaiting funding for the third phase of research and development. In the third phase, it is my intention to work with a digital artist to enhance the digital aesthetic of the virtual learning space. Students evaluative comments about the effectiveness of the learning were very good and only minor change to learning content were needed but the visual aspects needed reviewing.

THE DIGITAL AESTHETIC

Murphie and Potts (2003, p. 69) propose "the postmodern aesthetic elevates eclecticism and multiplicity over any dominant 'original' style," maintaining that the digital aesthetic is diverse:

> This diversity and the constant divergence into new forms focus not upon an eternal idea of art and beauty, but upon endless transformation of our sense perception through digital technologies and we should begin by saying that there is no definitive approach to digital aesthetic. (Murphie & Potts, 2003, p. 84)

Turkle (1997) discusses the quality of emergence in an online setting through the aesthetics of "connectionism," claiming it "began to present the computer as though it was a biological organism" (p. 136). Gianetti

(2008) brings the two flows of thinking together when discussing endo-aesthetics. Endo is the prefix that refers to something internal. As a practicing interactive media artist she discuss "the process of an internal interactor participating in an artificially generated model world which moves beyond the human-machine interface." The interactors' consciousness of acting with the simulation, as well as their perception of that simulation suggest that s/he share a 'spatio-temporal experience in the system' which is defined as both hypermedia and imaginary of the mind. She says interactive art works exist from an endo-aesthetic position "only in the measure to which there is a reciprocal and active (real or virtual) relationship between the interactor(s) and system" (p. 5).

Gianetti's endo-aesthetic theory can radically inform the "flexible entity" we continually form and reform as we flow inside digital worlds and networks. As stated previously, it is my aim in the third phase of this research to work with a digital artist and educators who are focused on creatively and aesthetically enhancing endo-systems, and bring awareness to the complexity, randomness and collaboration necessary in rhizomatic learning and its curriculum model. Will this thinking and action destabilize the traditional notions of the educational experience and pedagogy, offering a radical time, space and endo-system for learning?

MULTIPLICITIES: A RHIZOMATIC CURRICULUM

Deleuze and Guattari (2003) best define multiplicities for the purpose in this chapter being "defined by the outside: by the abstract line, the line of flight according to which they change in nature and connect with other multiplicities" (p. 9). Multiplicities constantly construct and dismantle themselves in the course of their communications as they cross over into each other at, beyond, or before a certain threshold. Multiplicities are rhizomatic.

Deleuze and Guattari (2003) summarize this nontotalizable collectivity of partial components which never make up a "whole," a series of flows, as the principle characteristics of a "rhizome."

> A rhizome connects any point to any other point, and its traits are not necessarily linked to traits of the same nature. It is not a multiple derived from the one. It is composed not of units but of dimensions, or rather directions of motion. It has neither a beginning, nor end, but always, middle, (milieu) from which it grows and which it overspills. The rhizome operates by variation and expansion. It is a non-hierarchical system without a general and an organising memory, defined solely by a circulation of states. A plateau is always in the middle and a rhizome is made of plateaus. (p. 21)

HAS LEARNING BECOME UNSTABLE?
THE RHIZOMATIC CURRICULUM

To reconceptualize the poststructural notion of multiplicities/rhizome into an online e-learning setting you may find it necessary to engage with the ongoing process of the "re" and "de"-construction of knowledge and identity in critical relationship to the curriculum, events, lived and imagined experiences that occur in our communications via, discussion forums, e-mails, learning communities, and links to the Web or Web 2.0 spaces. With the rise of the Web 2.0 world in which people create images as well as become writers of the Web, I wonder if there is latitude in research based on facilitating students to become authors of curriculum? The implications for the traditional role of the educators could be radically transformed into a rhizomatic relationship with knowledge, curriculum, pedagogy and posthuman bodies?

Conceptually, the curriculum becomes a flowing, impermanent rhizomatic aesthetic. As a result, specific learning outcomes and assessment points need to be monitored by the tutor and learner as information retrieval facilitated by the connections and interconnectedness of the learners and tutor through net-based construction of knowledge become exponentially expansive. Careful management of knowledge and time in this transient space needs to occur. The nature of the teaching and learning experience suggest that the learner becomes a manager of streams of information that she or he is gathering and constructing into a critically reflexive body of work.

Learning becomes relativized and personalized and the locus of power shifts from the historically stable instrumental hierarchy of teacher centred curriculum delivery to initially an often messy and spontaneous experience of learning and knowledge construction, which can be refined via reflexivity and connectivity with an online learning community and experienced tutor.

The triumph of relativized or personalized learning can be witnessed more explicitly via mobile technologies where learners inhabit their own virtual worlds, learning what they want to learn, when they want to. This context demands a micromanagement of time and information. This is not true of online learning via the PC, for the PC provides a generic platform from which learning and evolving pedagogy is conducted. The mobility of the static PC here comes from the imagined endo-aesthetic experienced in the spaces of net-based learning rather than through mobile technologies. Ubiquitous learning has its place but, as Virilio (2002) suggests, "the computer is no longer simply a devise for consulting information sources, but an automatic vision machine, operating within the space of an entirely virtualized geographical reality" (p. 16).

This concept of a rhizomatic model of practice may never become a generic model of practice for a large education provider for it involves working with no more than 12 people in a learning space at one time. Here Schumacher's (1974) concept of "Small is Beautiful" adheres. Schumacher maintained that the western world's pursuit for profit and economic efficiency via large organizational structures has resulted in gross economic inefficiency and inhumane working conditions. Central to the modules success is the building of a supportive community of learners in which critical, creative, collaborative, and problem-based learning takes place. Social sustainability, intimacy, human scale education, happiness, and wellbeing in the online mediated learning context are also important values and philosophies underpinning this model. Economically, it may not be a viable model, but the sustained depth of engagement demonstrated by the research participants was very good. The research data suggest this was due to the learning community that was created and maintained throughout and beyond the 11-week module.

LEARNING COMMUNITIES

In the induction to the module, I highlighted the value and benefits of building a virtual online learning community which supports and guides learners' skills, knowledge construction and sharing and confidence in using the technology to enhance learning. None of the learners enrolled had any experience and concept of online learning. They showed limited understanding of the commitment. It was explicit in the evaluation data that every student (one group of 8 and one group of 12) believed that the induction, pre-requisites, and approach that highlighted the value and benefits of building a virtual online learning community enabled them to engage and participate in such a conceptual framework of a rhizomatic curriculum. However, they all underestimated the need to organize their time to successfully complete the program of study even though guidelines had been introduced.

Palloff and Pratt (1999) highlight the importance of an e-tutor facilitating collaboration with online learners. By encouraging students to connect around shared problem-based learning, construction and exchange of knowledge, discuss personal interests in the social site provided, and have a common awareness of the desired learning outcomes of the program, both autonomy support and interdependence is nurtured within the learning community to share both personal and information exchange.

GROUND RULES: NETIQUETTE

The negotiation of ground rules for behavior and expectations within online communication were paramount to successful interaction. The learners may have different levels of online experience, anxieties, special education needs, and diversity that need to be acknowledged by the tutor and understood by the community of learners. Ground rules facilitate such awareness and operate just in case there are communication and behavior issues in the future that need to be resolved. Ground rules, like in any other complex social/formal situation can help modify behavior and set a framework for people to cooperate by in order to achieve a common goal. Duggleby (2000) offers a good set of rules to adapt.

An "Email Effectiveness guide" can be accessed at: www.skyrme.com/tools/email.htm and a valuable online tutoring e-book which offers information and theories to support online learning strategies can be accessed at http://otis.scotcit.ac.UK/onlinebook/T1-03.pdf. The Learning Lab (2008) and media arts net are two useful and informative sites to visit.

CRITICAL MIDPROGRAM REVIEW

The second face-to-face session was in week 6. This was the midterm point in the program and provided an opportunity for me (the tutor) and students to critically review their progress. It provided a space for students to debate different perspectives of their learning experience and construction of their online identities. It provided the tutor with an opportunity to summarize the progress of the learning community and to encourage and sustain group bonding. There is often a fear of becoming isolated in the online setting. This can be prevented by the e-tutor facilitating discussion in the forums, which engage learners in their search for knowledge and negotiating meaning as a result of the problem-based learning, and group activities offered in the program.

EVALUATION OF PILOT (RESEARCH SITE)

The final face-to-face session was after the online program had been completed. An evaluation of the technology and experience of the learners, was carried out. The AEIOU evaluation model, created by research and evaluation specialists Fortune, Keith, Sweeney, and Sorensen (Sorensen, 1996) was used: A = Accountability, E = Effectiveness, I = Impact, O = Organizational Constraints, U = Unforeseen/Unpredictable outcomes.

The evaluation was important and provided important critical reflection of the 11 weeks populating the online learning environment. It provided a forum for participants to discuss the effects of net-based learning.

AN INSTRUMENTAL MODEL

I set out on my journey to map the new terrain, mindful to provide a learning environment in which e-tutors and learners had the opportunity and were effectively supported in the building of a community which promotes knowledge construction, sharing, and collaboration (Salmon, 2000, pp. 25-35), as opposed to a model of learning which valorizes knowledge transmission/information acquisition such as ECDL (European Computer Driving License) or CLAIT (Computer Literacy And Information Technology), in which a linear and systematic model of learning is adopted.

These two very different models have their benefits when employed in particular educational settings. However, working in postgraduate initial teacher education, where self direction, autonomy, research and reflexive thinking are encouraged, it was my intention to create a model that would support such an approach to learning and avoid employing a linear instrumental model. As Alexander and Boud (2000) suggest:

> Much of the potential for online learning is being lost because too much of the pedagogy of online learning has been transferred unreflectively from didactic traditional teaching where the computer substitutes for the teacher and textbook as a conveyer of information. (p. 3)

Competency-based models may very well have learning benefits when employed in the FE setting which take students through a systematic route of learning (Maier & Warren, 2000) and place an emphasis on on line testing and multiple choice assessment. A critique of this model is that it fails to develop the learner as a critical thinker. The uses of interactivity and reusable learning content as instructional objects are becoming more prevalent within this model. This approach suggests it may best suit the implementation and management of instrumental curricula and the need to meet prescribed learning outcomes through the process of assessment?

TEACHER-BECOMING, LEARNER-BECOMING

For many years now I have been experiencing a phenomenon, new to myself, of teacher-becoming in the environment of cyberspace in which new identities and aesthetics are being imagined and constructed. As an e-tutor in this digital environment, I have not experienced an "identity crisis," but more a fall into consciousness via the development of my online practice.

Deleuze and Guattari (2003) use the example of Virginia Woolf being questioned about women's writing to illustrate the notion of "becoming-woman," whereby she explained, "writing should produce a becoming-woman as atoms of womanhood capable of crossing and impregnating an entire social field, and of contaminating men, of sweeping them up in that becoming" (p. 276). Teacher-becoming, learner-becoming in cyber-space is a process in which the teacher-learner is constantly through writing and image making, "becoming," never meeting a point of fixity, only stopping briefly to connect with an event (the discursive environments of one-to-one e-mails, discussion forums, videoconferencing, streamed media), then to move in another direction (to connect with peers, tutor, via online group activities, Web 2.0 contexts). As Deleuze and Guattari (2003, p. 274) have noted, by "entering into composition with something else, something else is formed, being similar or quite varied" (new knowledge, meaning, hybridities of self in a professional setting, haecceity, an order of becoming).

The spaces where teacher-becoming and learner-becoming briefly rest, are the liminal spaces which the cultural anthropologists Victor and Edith Turner defined as the spaces between, where things change. This in-between space becomes a developmental space of "trans": transgeographical, transaesthetic, transnarrative, transeducational? The teacher-learner is not defined by the curriculum or institution, but defined by a relation of movement, of rest, defined by speed and slowness and haecceity (order of being/becoming) whilst inhabiting sites of cyber-teaching and cyber-learning within a fluid virtual learning community. Thus teacher-learner becoming does not belong to an age group, sex, higher education system, or government unless it chooses to be defined by such discourses. The teacher learner slips in everywhere between all these things on their line of flight, in relation to the curricula, online communities, knowledge construction, discussions and learning materials they author. This understanding of identity construction has at its centre the concept of the posthuman body.

THE POSTHUMAN BODY

The posthuman body is the interface between humans and technology, and re-presents posthuman body as cyborg. The posthuman body becomes hypertext, is a result of power relations and discourse surrounding technology, is a cyborg, is connected by telephone wires and exists in multiple sites. Third-wave feminist Bradotti (1999) reminds us that with the intellectual collapse and theoretical flattening of the body, we need to be acutely aware that women's bodies suffer daily, have the pain of child-birth, lactation and leakage of menstrual fluids. She allows us not to for-get the sexual, political, and power struggles central to women's bodies and subjectivities. Virilio (1998) supports Bradotti: "after all our talk of war machines, prosthetic humans and virtual technology—bones break, flesh weakens, but the spirit only gets stronger" (p. 13).

In sharp contrast, the postmodern feminist writer Grosz (1994) claims:

> The limits or boarders of the body image are not fixed by nature or con-fined to the anatomical container of the skin. The body image is extremely fluid and dynamic; its borders, edges and contours are osmotic. They have a remarkable power of incorporating and expelling outside and inside in an on-going interchange. (p. 79)

SUMMARY

It is now I descend into endo-aesthetic space.
The digital, coded space of Internet technologies,
Of discussion boards, immersive platforms, virtual communities
In which I construct post-human identities.
It is here that text and images
Attach and flow in the indeterminacy of post structural space
Like body flesh
Disembodied
Collapsing in on itself
Reconstructed
Becoming embodied in the technology
In the culture
As information exchange transforms text persona
Imaginary construction takes place in the liminal space
creative space.

In this chapter I have conceptualized a new theoretical approach to teach-ing and learning in an online setting. This has outlined a poststructural feminist philosophical approach to online tutoring in which an awareness of an endo-aesthetic informs a framework for further research into the notion of the posthuman condition within an educational context. Key to this concept is the notion of a rhizomatic curriculum that offers insight into the complexity and randomness of encounters and events in many sites of online learning and teaching that I hope would be inevitable fea-tures of a creative endo-system. Identity becomes an expanded concept, fluid, nomadic and in motion and emerges from posthuman discourses.

The traditional notion of arts and aesthetic emerge from an endo-aesthetic understanding of both the interior of our philosophical mind and the interior of the electronic network of cyberspace.

The first and second phase of my research into online teaching and learning between 1999 and 2005 offered a crude visual and aesthetic interface for the online learner and teacher with limited research funding and time. Having the intellectual freedom to innovate is an important reminder, that for poets and visionaries in the world of education, the liminal space offers a site to imagine and set in motion an unexpected professional relationship between the philosophical mind, posthuman bodies and the environment of net-based learning. My aim now is to gain a more deeply informed experience in the creative application of hypermedia to enhance the online learning environment.

Copies of the document *E-Tutoring and E-Pedagogy: A Practical and Theoretical Approach to Online Tutoring. Module Curriculum and Handbook* are available on request by e-mail from: imagination@zetnet.co.uk

REFERENCES

Alexander, S., & Boud, D. (2000). Learners still learn from experience when online. In J. Stephenson (Ed.), *Teaching and learning online: Pedagogies for new technologies* (pp. 3-15). London: Kogan Page.

Arendt, H. (1998). *The human condition* (2nd ed.). London: Chicago Press.

British Educational Communications and Technology Agency. (2007). Retrieved January 22, 2008, from http://learningandskills.becta.org.uk/index.cfm

Bell, D., & Kennedy, B. (2000). *The cybercultures reader.* London: Routledge.

Bradiotti, R. (1999). *Positioning the body.* Retrieved January 23, 2008, from http://etd.unisa.ac.za/ETD-db/theses/available/etd-08232004-155034/unrestricted/04Introduction.PDF

Danaher, G, Schirato, T., & Webb, J. (2002). *Understanding Foucault.* London: SAGE.

Deleuze, G., & Guattari, F. (2003). *A thousand plateaus. Capitalism and schizophrenia.* London: Continuum.

Department for Education and Skills. (2005). *Harnessing technology.* Retrieved January 21, 2008, from www.dfes.gov.uk/publications/e-strategy/docs/e-strategy.pdf

Department for Education and Skills. (2008). *E-skills passport.* Retrieved January 23, 2008, from http://www.e-skillspassport.com/

Duggleby, J. (2000). *How to be an online tutor.* Aldershot, England: Gower.

Gianetti, C. (2008). Retrieved September 10, 2008, from http://www.medienkunstnetz.de/themes/aesthetics_of_the_digital/endo-aesthetics/scroll/

Halberstam, J., & Livingston, I. (1995). *Posthuman bodies.* Bloomington, IN: University Press.

Haraway, D. J. (1991). *Simians, cyborgs and women: The reinvention of nature.* London: Fabooks.

Joint Information Systems Committee. (2007). Retrieved January, 22, 2008, from http://jisc.cetis.ac.uk/

Learning Lab. (2008). Retrieved January, 23, 2008, from www.learninglab.org.uk/asp/homepage.asp

Learning To Teach Online. (2008). *Learning to tutor and teach online programme at Sheffield College.* Retrieved March 7, 2008, from www.sheffcol.ac.uk/index.cfm?ParentID=dd22687d-39f7-412e-9a00-c9bb33e12b45

Lifelong Learning UK. (2007). *Further education teachers' qualification new standards.* Retrieved January 22, 2008, from www.lifelonglearningUK.org/documents/standards/professional_standards_for_itts_020107.pdf

Learning Skills Council. (2005). Retrieved March 7, 2008, from http://cove.lsc.gov.UK/

Learning Skills Development Agency. (2005). Retrieved February 4, 2008, from www.lsda.org.uk/

Maier, P., & Warren, A. (2000). *Integr@ting technology in learning and teaching: A practical guide for educators.* London: Kogan Page.

Matlow, E. (2000). Women, computers and a sense of self. In Cutting Edge Women's Research Group (Ed.), *Digital desires: Language, identity and new technologies* (pp. 167-183). London: I. B. Tauris.

Murphie, A., & Potts, J. (2003). *Culture and technology.* Hampshire, England: Palgrave & Macmillan.

Murphy, D., Walker, R., & Webb, G. (2001). *Online learning and teaching with technology. Case studies, experience and practice.* London: Kogan Page.

Palloff, R., & Pratt, K. (1999). *Building learning communities in cyberspace: Effective strategies for the online classroom.* San Francisco: Jossey-Bass.

Prophet, J., & Hamlett, S. (2000). Sordid sites: The internal organs of a cyborg. In Cutting Edge Women's Research Group (Ed.), *Digital desires: Language, identity and new technologies* (pp. 25-33). London: I. B. Tauris.

Reiche, C. (2004). *Cyberfeminism: Next protocols.* New York: Autonomedia.

Salmon, G. (2000). *E-Moderating: The key to teaching and learning online.* London: Kogan Page.

Salmon, G. (2002). *E-tivities: The key to active online learning.* London: Kogan Page.

Schumacher, E. F. (1974). *Small is beautiful.* Abacus: London.

Sorensen, C. (1996). *Final evaluation report: Iowa distance education alliance.* Ames, IA: Research Institute for Studies in Education.

Stephenson, J. (2001) *Teaching and learning online: New pedagogies for new technologies.* London: Kogan Page.

Turkle, S. (1997). *Life on screen: Identity in the age of the Internet.* London: Phoenix.

Virilio, P. (2002). *The information bomb.* New York: Verso.

Virilio, P. (1998). *The Virilio reader.* London: Blackwell.

Volcart, Y. (2004). The cyberfeminist fantasy of the pleasure of the cyborg. In C. Reiche (Ed.), *Cyberfeminism: Next protocols* (pp. 97-117). New York: Autonomedia

CHAPTER 11

POSTMODERNISM AND CYBERCULTURE

Ken Gale

Baudrillard (1983) argued that there is no longer a polarity between "the one and the other." We are indeed living in an age in which diverse and pervasive use of new technologies are challenging our conceptions of separateness and community. Postmodern philosophies contribute to a deeper understanding of cybercultures through their use of various deconstructive strategies, their troubling of the self-conscious "I," and through nomadic inquiries that nurture ever-changing structures of multiplicity and interconnectedness. This chapter both explores and suggests possible folds and intersections between poststructural philosophies and digital learning practices and in so doing, proposes that these new technologies help to create all kinds of new learning possibilities beyond the existing nexus that exists between the educational institution and the enquiring mind.

> The present epoch will perhaps be above all the epoch of space. We are in the epoch of simultaneity: we are in the epoch of juxtaposition, the epoch of the near and far, of the side-by-side, of the dispersed. We are at a moment, I believe, when our experience of the world is less that of a long life developing through time than that of a network that connects points and intersects with its own skein. (Foucault, 2002, p. 229)

Connected Minds, Emerging Cultures: Cybercultures in Online Learning
pp. 159–166

Summer sunlight pours into the warm, slightly dusty, interior of the small Sunday school room. A group of young children are standing around in a half circle, singing; they are grouped around their teacher, a young woman in her thirties, who is gently conducting them in their efforts. The room is light and the walls are covered in pictures of biblical scenes, a vase of brightly colored flowers sits on a table beside them. Their heads are lifted and their faces are full of smiles as, together, they sing the words of the beautiful Victorian hymn "All Things Bright and Beautiful"; the simple cadences of the song carry their words, filling the small room with happiness and joy. It is the sound, the light and the simple community of souls that captures the moment; the words of the song weave the texture of the moment together. They sing:

The rich man at his castle
The poor man at his gate
God made them high and lowly
And ordered their estate.

It is a classroom in a small rural secondary modern school in Cornwall in the United Kingdom in the 1950s. The 30 or so children in the class all sit in rows facing the teacher and the large blackboard at the front of the classroom. For geography or history lessons the teacher often rolls down a map of the world to cover this blackboard. Mercator's Projection, a large, heavy, canvas map rolled around a long heavy pole suspended just above the board, when unrolled fills the space at the front of the room. In those times of rationing and austerity its colors are vibrant, vividly capturing the differentiation and displacement of the many countries of the world. Its dominant shiny color is pink and many large regions, whole continents like Africa and Australia seem to jump off the canvas, arresting the innocent vision of the children in the class. At the center of this pervasive visual presence, at the focal point of the map, are the British Isles, also in pink, quite clear in their central position, giving the impression that the rest of the world, with its great swathes of similar color somehow revolves around this axiomatic hub. Those geography lessons were fabulous, full of tumbling glaciers in the Himalayas and coffee plantations in Brazil. Our teacher, "Charlie" Cameron, would spice these descriptions with tales from his wartime travels and pursuits, and we small children were rapt. Our sense of the world, its spatial displacements and sovereignties, and the historical and political forces that shaped it were all wrapped in the encapsulating breadth, dimensions and colors of that map.

Althusser (1990) uses the idea of "interpellation" to describe the way in which we are "hailed" by the symbols and images of our culture. These words and gestures, these pictures and signs, claim our attention and provide an enticing allure, drawing us to their suggestions and leading us on particular pathways. Althusser argues that the pervasiveness of this language goes largely unnoticed by our sentient and perceptual minds; the objects of the external world somehow enter our consciousness, they become internalized, and then we are free to express them as our own or be "hailed" by them when they reappear.

The words of the children's hymn help to fabricate a joyous occasion of reverence and celebration and reside in the children's hearts and minds as their generations accumulate and they grow into adults.

It is possible to imagine young farm boys and factory apprentices in 1915 being hailed by the stern eyes of Kitchener beaming out at them from posters all over the country and following them as they walked past, sensing in their hearts that, as the poster asserted, "Your Country Needs You!" The simple and direct knowing entailed by this would seem to have contributed to their subsequent conscription and march to unquestioning death.

For Althusser, the force of interpellation lies in its resistance to reflexivity, in its perpetuation of the normal, the familiar, and the customary. While the determinist tendencies in Althusser's theory are obvious, they become points of intense critical relevance when contextualized within the topographies of cyberspace. Escobar points out that

> Modernity ... constitutes the "background of understanding"—the taken-for-granted tradition and the way of being out of which we interpret and act—that inevitably shapes the discourses and practices generated by and around the new technologies. (Escobar, 2000, p. 57)

So, while we might be informed, indeed warned, by Baudrillard's (1983) contention that in the "precession of simulacra" the map precedes the territory, it is of extreme relevance to ask, within the context of emerging new technologies and ever changing pedagogical practices, in what ways might this be seen to be taking place? Answers are likely to emerge if a careful and rigorous examination and investigation of the relationship between learning and learner identities and the cybercultural contexts within which distance or online learning can be seen to take place. Deleuze and Guattari (1988) argue forcefully that cultural spaces can be characterized as being "smooth" or "striated," and it is the purpose of this chapter to suggest that this figurative spatial representation is valuable in helping to achieve understanding of the substantial liminal potentiality of learning in cyberspace.

The many and varied topographies of cyberspace offer the potential for a variety of learning situations to be recognized and experienced. The multiple and interconnected potentiality of such an assertion is given relative force when viewed in contrast with Schon's famous topographical metaphor, which describes a high ground overlooking a swamp.

> On the high ground, manageable problems lend themselves to solution
> through the application of research-based theory and technique. In the
> swampy lowland, messy, confusing problems defy technical solution. (Schon,
> 1987, p. 3)

Beyond the confines of Schon's simple binary distinction, within what
Foucault characterized as "sites," learning in many different forms can
take place, but also within these "sites" learner identities and practice
styles will also be differentiated and constructed in diverse ways. However,
on entering one of a great many possible "sites" in cyberspace, numerous
possibilities open up in which experience will not only subject the online
learner to different forms of identity and knowledge construction, but
also that learners themselves might use strategies of identification and
knowledge construction through their own involvement with the site. The
somewhat rigid culture agency binary to be found in the work of Althusser, for example, no longer seems to be appropriate in the diverse, distributed, and differentiated worlds of cyberspace. Do we become what
others want us to become? Do we become who we want to become? Do
others become what we want them to become? These intriguing questions
are all extremely apposite as this exploration of new learning possibilities
and pedagogical practices begins to develop.

So, in examining and attempting to answer these questions, it is of
relevance to consider the way in which Baudrillard's contention that the
map precedes the territory operates through the "precession of simulacra." Within his view of cyber-technologies, learning is a cultural event
in which identities, knowledge, and meanings are constructed. Within
this view, the media of cyberspace does not work in the kinds of technological determinist ways suggested by the opening vignettes by simply
providing settings in which the opportunities for learning can be established. It is by turning toward Deleuze and Guattari's (1988) theorizing
of the "smooth" and "striated" nature of cultural spaces that a more
complex and appropriate form of explanation learning and identity formation is offered.

Deleuze and Guattari present a view of "striated" cultural space that is
delineated, bordered, and ordered. Such a space is closed and is organized around an established *logos* that provides the foundational grid for
all accepted forms of communication within the space. By contrast,
"smooth" cultural space is much more open and informal and, by virtue
of this, is less stable and fixed and operates according to a *nomos* of
enquiring and amorphous thought and action. Irigaray's work on gender
and language talks in similar ways of

contradictory words, somewhat mad from the standpoint of reason, inaudible, for whoever listens with ready-made grids, with a fully elaborated code in hand.... When she returns it is to set off again from elsewhere.... One would have to listen with another ear, as if hearing an "other meaning" always in the process of weaving itself, of embracing itself with words; but also of getting rid of words in order not to become fixed, congealed in them. (Irigaray, 1974, p. 29)

It is important to stress that Deleuze and Guattari do not present these conceptualizations in rigid binary form. They propose that within and between these cultural spaces there are territorializing tendencies. So that, on the one hand, the arboreal features of striated spaces may tend toward and inhabit the gaps and unbounded places of smooth space whilst, on the other, the rhizomatic inclinations apparent in the smooth space will grow and destabilize the established patterns of striated cultural space. Processes of reterritorialization and deterritorialization are constantly at play, and it is the conceptual and contextual fluidity offered here by Deleuze and Guattari that offers a critique of some of the more traditional approaches to online learning.

It is an over simplification to suggest, on the one hand, that Althusser's idea of interpellation is an example of the deterministic operation of the cultivated fields of striated space, and that the World Wide Web is somehow an open moorland of smooth space. Similarly, the binary representation offered of cyberspace by Nunes (1999) of either driving on the information super highway of striated space or surfing the open and dynamic smooth spaces of the Net, is equally untenable according to the more fluid and process-based approach offered by Deleuze and Guattari. The processes of territorialization that they offer challenge the kind of binary to be found here or, indeed, that which is inherent in Prensky's (2001) idea of the "digital native" and the "digital immigrant." In relation to the latter, they offer the possibility, perhaps, of the digital nomad, moving in smooth space, territorializing and creating striated space which then might be destabilized by further nomadic territorialization.

Recent research by Conle (2006) into what she refers to as narrative learning environments, interestingly appears to provide an example of pedagogical practices in which a binary division of this kind can be found. In summarizing a range of research carried out into technology-mediated narrative environments for learning, she suggests that a distinction can be made, on the one hand, between narrative learning environments in which students are active in creating multimedia narratives and, on the other, where they are encouraged to learn from packages that have been produced for this purpose. In Deleuzian terms, it could be argued that with the former the focus is on creativity and personal skill development within smooth space, and in the latter the focus is on the reception of professionally created multimedia narratives within striated space. An all-too-obvious distinction, perhaps, but it is one that offers a circumspect critical challenge to a vast emerging field of digital learning technology in which new literacies are being created at rapid rates.

A central organizing figure for Deleuze and Guattari is that of the rhizome, and the following description offers substantial resonance with some of the views of cyberspace and cyber-cultural formation being considered here. For Deleuze and Guattari:

> A rhizome ceaselessly establishes connections between semiotic chains, organisations of power, and circumstances relative to the arts, sciences and social struggles. A semiotic chain is like a tuber agglomerating very diverse acts, not only linguistic, but also perceptive, mimetic, gestural, and cognitive: there is no language in itself, nor are there any linguistic universals, only a throng of dialects, patois, slangs, and specialised languages. There is no ideal speaker-listener, any more than there is a homogenous linguistic community. Language is ... "an essentially heterogeneous reality." There is no mother tongue, only a power takeover by a dominant language within a political multiplicity. Language stabilises around a parish, a bishopric, and a capital. It forms a bulb. It evolves by subterranean stems and flows, along river valleys or train tracks; it spreads like a patch of oil. It is always possible to break a language down into internal structural elements, an undertaking not fundamentally different from a search for roots ... a method of the rhizome type ... can analyse language only by decentering it onto other dimensions and other registers. A language is never closed upon itself, except as a function of impotence (Deleuze & Guattari, 1988, pp. 7-8).

So, for Deleuze and Guattari, within the figure of the rhizome, concepts are events; they exist as "fragmentary wholes that are not aligned with one another so that they fit together, because their edges do not match up ... they resonate nonetheless" (1994, p. 35). This resonance has some similarity with Gibson's (1984) much-quoted characterization of cyberspace as a "consensual reality" where nothing is fixed but where from time to time, concepts and practices might briefly interconnect to temporarily striate the space in which they appear.

> Concepts are centres of vibrations each in itself and every one in relation to all the others. This is why they resonate rather than cohere or correspond with each other. There is no reason why concepts should cohere. As fragmentary totalities, concepts are not even the pieces of a puzzle, for their irregular contours do not correspond to each other. They do form a wall but it is a dry-stone wall, and everything holds together only along diverging lines (Deleuze & Guattari 1994, p. 23).

The characterization of these cyberspaces as temporary assemblages where shifting and mutating consensual realities are to be found suggests also the existence of very fluid forms of identity, meaning, and knowledge construction. If these spaces can be described in Foucauldian terms as "sites," then they may also be seen in discursive terms as technologies that influence normalization and legitimation. It could be argued, then, that from the point of view of learning, the inhabitants of such "sites" possess relative amounts of cyber-cultural capital and will influence what Deleuze and Guattari refer to as the "vibrations" and "resonances" of these sites. Our predispositions to learning in cyberspace, our philias and our phobias, will have an influence upon the way in which we are able to learn at a distance, in an "e" environment, within these virtual realities. These sites, these cyberspaces, can be seen to possess what Bourdieu has referred to as "habitus" in which the new inhabitants of or the visitors to those spaces will experience "symbolic violence" as they come into contact with the norms, values, and language of those spaces. Their "resonance" with the site will be in part a measure of the learning that they will experience as they inhabit the site. So, cybercultures will reproduce themselves in these ways, territorializing existing habitations and laying down "dry stone walls" or striations that will influence existing and future inhabitants. In turn, these striated cultural spaces will also be made smooth through the reterritorializing tendencies of nomadic forms of inquiry carried out by those who become visitors or new inhabitants of those spaces.

We see at play here what Derrida (1978) has referred to as an endless play of signifiers, where the fixed meaning of the signified remains mercurial and elusive and always just beyond the grasp of the persistent learner in cyberspace. The constant allure for the browser of the next hyperlink that might address Derrida's "absence of presence" in the search for meaning is what MacLure has referred to as the "gap across which desire might spark" (MacLure, 2003, p. 3). We are drawn to search, surf, and populate this vast territory. What Foucault refers to as these "other spaces" entice our utopian sensibilities, encouraging us to explore the immense heterotopia of cyberspace. On the one hand, new digital technologies appear to provide a fluid and dynamic nexus between the educational institution and the enquiring mind in which all kinds of new learning possibilities begin to emerge. On the other, they also offer a new dimension to what Illich (1970) referred to as the "deschooling" of society in which learning breaks out from the constraining influence of the institution and takes on new and volatile forms in the more amorphous and perhaps the less obviously disciplined territory of cyberspace.

The rhizomatic and nomadic approaches of Deleuze and Guattari suggest creative forms of learning that offer the means of (de- and re-) territorializing cyberspace through nomadic inquiry and transgressive forms of becoming.

REFERENCES

Althusser, L. (1990). *For Marx*. London: Verso.

Baudrillard, J. (1983). *Simulations*. New York: Semiotext.

Conle, C. (2006). Considerations on technology-mediated narrative learning environments. In G. Dettori, T. Gianetti, A. Paiva, & A. Vaz (Eds.), *Technology-mediated narrative environments for learning* (pp. 143-161). Rotterdam, The Netherlands: Sense.

Deleuze, G., & Guattari, F. (1988). *A thousand plateaus*, London: Athlone.

Deleuze, G., & Guattari, F. (1994). *What is philosophy?* London: Verso

Derrida, J. (1978). *Writing and difference*. London: Routledge.

Escobar, A. (2000). Welcome to Cyberia: Notes on the anthropology of cyberculture. In D. Bell & M. Kennedy (Eds.), *The cybercultures reader* (pp. 56-77). London: Routledge.

Foucault, M. (2002). Of other spaces. In N. Mirzoeff (Ed.), *The visual culture reader* (pp. 229-236). London: Routledge.

Gibson, W. (1984). *Neuromancer*. London: Harper Collins.

Illich, I. (1970). *De-schooling society*. New York: Harper and Row.

Irigaray, L. (1974). *Speculum of the other woman*. Ithaca, NY: Cornell University Press.

MacLure, M. (2003). *Discourse in educational and social research*. Buckingham, England: Open University Press.

Nunes, M. (1999). Virtual topographies: Smooth and striated cyberspace. In M. Ryan (Ed.), *Cyberspace textuality: Computer technology and literary theory* (pp. 63-71). Bloomington: Indiana University Press.

Prensky, M. (2001). Digital natives, digital immigrants. *On the horizon, 9*(5), 1-6.

Schon, D. (1987). *Educating the reflective practitioner*. San Francisco: Jossey Bass.

CHAPTER 12

CYBORG THEORY
AND LEARNING

Vasi van Deventer

CYBORG THEORY

Building on the premise that humans are "natural born cyborgs" with an innate ability to interface naturally with technology, this chapter describes the evolution of the human cyborg. It draws on the history, theory, and philosophy of cybernetics to explore the psychodynamics of the integration of organism and machine. The chapter argues that theorists in this field of enquiry are correct when they assert that we are a lot further down the road to becoming cyborgs than we may be willing to concede. The implications of this for the future of education are discussed and the conclusion is that not only do human minds have an adaptability and plasticity, enabling students to interface with any technology that is useful to their purpose, but also that these students actually establish themselves as learning cyborgs through a symbiotic relationship with technology that blurs traditional distinctions.

Forty years after its release, Arthur C. Clarke and Stanley Kubrick's *2001: A Space Odyssey* still remains one of the most captivating movies ever made. It is mysterious and revealing at the same time. It is mysterious

Connected Minds, Emerging Cultures: Cybercultures in Online Learning
pp. 167–183
Copyright © 2009 by Information Age Publishing

because the truth of its core object is never revealed. The truth of the featureless black monolith that appears at significant moments of human evolution is not exposed. But the film is also revealing, reflecting the limits of rationality—the most distinguishing characteristic of the human species. When Clarke and Kubrick guide their audience toward understanding, it is an understanding not only of the incomprehensibility of understanding as such, but also an understanding that incomprehensibility as such is fundamental to any attempt at understanding. We are captivated by this undermining of our own understanding. The unknown calls out to be conquered. In the movie's initial scenes of skirmish, the primitive ape snatches a piece of bone from a skeleton of his own kind and uses it as a tool to launch himself as conqueror of the unknown.

The defeat of the unmastered is the attraction of the tool. The tool always promises more than its immediate application. When the film cuts from these initial scenes of noisy, aggressive fighting to the quiet vastness of weightless space, we see humans serenely encapsulated by their technological achievements, and later on a flight to Jupiter we meet the ultimate tool, HAL—the artificial intelligent computer in control of the ship, an extension of the human mind. But HAL's rationality breaks down when it has to reveal what it is supposed to keep secret, namely the purpose of the journey. Caught between revelation and concealment HAL's behavior becomes irregular and psychotic, causing the death of the astronauts.

For Clarke and Kubrick, the tool is inherently dangerous. Even if owned by us, part of us, like bone ripped from our skeleton, the tool must be a rejectable object, a piece of bone that can be thrown away, a HAL that can be disconnected. What is at stake is nothing less than the preservation of human identity, not only as body but also as rational being. We have to save ourselves from madness, the madness of the tool and also the madness of a joint venture with the tool. Irrational thought has to be contained—a containment that is only possible as long as the tool remains a machine, a mechanistic object inherently separate from man, like HAL, an additional crew member on the journey to the monolith at the origins of our evolution.

THE CYBORG AS MACHINE

But the fear of the tool is a recent phenomenon caused by the modern display of its power and the clandestine nature of its modus operandi. The atom bomb spelled obliteration, but it did so in a way that could be clearly comprehended in terms of the finality of extinction. However, genetic engineering and bodily invasion by nanotechnologies constitute a far more subtle exposure, a clandestine annihilation through morphing into something different—an exposure without any guarantees. For millions of years, the tool has been an innocent bystander in human evolution, but then came its sudden rise from inanimate object to machine. In the steam engine, the tool gained a life of its own, and became a force to be reckoned with.

Initially machines were understood in terms of their thermodynamics. Their designs were guided by how heat was gained and lost in mechanical systems, but in the twentieth century an interdisciplinary science called cybernetics significantly changed the way machines were understood. Today the optimization of heat flow still is a major consideration in the production of mechanical force, but modern machines acquire efficiency through the effective use of operational feedback loops. Information about its output is fed back into the machine to modify its input, ensuring its functioning within set parameters. These machines are considered in terms of abstract cybernetic principles, designed to optimize the flow of information. The primary concern is its systemic functioning, not the materials the machine is made of. From a cybernetic perspective, the question is how systems use information and how they control actions counteracting various disturbances while steering toward and maintaining particular goals (Heylighen & Joslyn, 2001).

The term "cybernetics" was derived from the Greek word for steersman (*kybernetes*), and was revived by the mathematician Norbert Wiener in a book first published in 1948, called *Cybernetics: Or Control and Communication in the Animal and the Machine* (Wiener, 1961). Cybernetics was distinguished by its emphasis on control and communication, not only in mechanically engineered systems but also in naturally evolving systems such as biological organisms and social organizations. The cybernetic view shifted the notion of machine from an entity with internal power to an entity with internal control. The machine became a robot, an automatic device that could perform functions that would normally be ascribed to humans. The machine had begun its morphing into the human form.

The machine presented in the form of the human body is an image well preserved in history. From the earliest of times, humans represented themselves in drawings and statues, and the animated body was only a further step toward greater realism, but the advent of World War I changed this. If previously the machine was aligned with social progress, the war drove home the realization that the machine was a powerful tool of death and destruction (Grenville, 2001). When, in 1921, the term "robot" first appeared in literature, it already stood for forced labor. The human-bodied machine had taken on an uncanny appearance, representing a psychodynamic force threatening to turn us into neurotic beings.

For Freud, the uncanny occurs when something familiar is alienated through a process of repression, and then returns to us in a form we recognise as some uncanny thing (Grenville, 2001). Thus, when my familiar body is repressed by the machine and made to reappear as alienated robot, I am forced to face existential dilemmas at the core of my being. My struggle for identity becomes the struggle for power between the biological body and the mechanical machine—a struggle that draws on the interplay of good and evil, logic and emotion, and mind and body (Grenville, 2001). The uncanny surrounds us. The deadly machines of war reappear as the lifesaving machines of modern medicine; the nuclear missile's artificial intelligence becomes the friendly voice of my car's GPS system; and when machines obtain consciousness, I am forced to face questions about the ontological status of my mind and to wonder about my soul.

> In the years between World War I and II, there appeared an ever-widening gap between those who envisaged the machine as a liberating force that would produce new social and economic configurations and those who viewed the machine as uncontrollable monster that would crush the human spirit and transform its subjects into automatons. It is here, in this untenable gap between a utopian and dystopian vision of the machine that the cyborg, was born. (Glenville, 2001, p. 27)

Yet the term "cyborg" would not make its appearance until the 1950s, and then still only in an uncomfortable combination of organism and machine. The term—a neologism of cybernetics and organism—was first proposed by Manfred Clynes and Nathan Kline when they were trying to engineer a mouse that could withstand the harshness of an environment similar to that encountered in space travel (Glenville, 2001, p. 29). Since then, the idea of a cyborg has shifted from the notion of armored human machine to augmentation of the human body through bioengineering. The effective application of information flow and feedback has replaced brute mechanical force. The cyborg has become a symbol for adaptability, intelligent application of information, and elective physical augmentation, but these characteristics are not reflected in popular culture (Glenville, 2001, p. 29). In popular consciousness the cyborg remains a superhuman who can pass as an ordinary person in everyday life, calling up superhuman strengths and characteristics when required. Popular culture harbors a Freudian defence. In neurotic defence against the uncanny, the robot has been repressed and made to reappear in the form of a human body. Thus, the cyborg is twice repressed. It is a human being dressed up as a machine that has been dressed up as human being. Popular culture, it seems, is a neurotic defence of neuroticism, an irrational attempt at keeping the irrational at bay—at best a fragile normality.

The fragility of a normality that is founded on a strong repression of the uncanny showed itself clearly in 2002, when Kevin Warwick received an implant creating an external electronic interface with the median nerve fibres of his left arm. The media portrayed the event as the creation of the world's first real cyborg (Cable News Network, 2002). The news created controversy, and Warwick, professor of cybernetics at the University of Reading, England, was accused of undergoing the operation for publicity reasons. In defence of himself—in defence of the cyborg—Warwick was forced to argue that the purpose of his work was to assist the disabled by showing that it was possible to control devices such as wheelchairs and intelligent artificial hands (Warwick, 2002). The fact that this kind of technology could serve to augment human functioning in general was silenced and subjected to the notion of technology in service of the restoration of human functioning. In this creation of a cyborg, the machine could be accepted as therapist but not as collaborator. A core value of science, namely the creation of knowledge for the expansion of human frontiers, was subjected to the need for an applied knowledge, an application that could only serve to fill a gap. The fear of the unknown potentialities of human beings had to be repressed and covered by a restoration of being human.

THE CYBORG AS OBSERVING SYSTEM

The fear of the cyborg is not simply the fear of the body's invasion by the machine. It is also the fear of the body as machine—the fear that the abstract machine (the machine as a cybernetic system) may be a true image of the abstract body (the body as a cybernetic system)—the fear that we are reducible to nothing but a physiological machine. But the image is not this simple. When we find ourselves mirrored, as machine the image seems incomplete, but the deficiency does not result from the content of the image. The lack does not arise because we cannot be described as cybernetic systems. The problem is more fundamental. The cybernetic image of ourselves does not include the act of mirroring, the act of bringing ourselves into view as a cybernetic system. The cyborg we see, our cyborg image, does not know that it itself has chosen to see itself as cyborg. There is indeed a ghost in the machine, an agent that does not reveal itself in the cybernetic image of itself.

The cybernetics that fails to calculate its own ghostly agent is a first-order cybernetics, a cybernetics governed by the metaphor of machine. It is the cyborg as machine. Although the positive and negative feedback loops of first-order cybernetics can explain complex notions characteristic of organismic life-forms—for example, self-organization, self-reproduction, autonomy, networks, connectionism, and adaptation (Heylighen & Joslyn, 2001)—these feedback processes quickly develop into theories of higher-order control. They soon become "double-loop" processes, which refer to feedback processes controlling feedback processes. But this does not simply mean an increase in complexity, it also requires a qualitative shift in ontology. It requires the introduction of the observer, central to the understanding of the system to be explained (Kenny & Boxer, 1990). Thus, when I identify myself as cyborg, my identity is not simply that of a machine consisting of mechanical and biological parts—a first-order cybernetic description. The image is more complex. I have to consider myself as an observing system in relation to an observed system, necessitating a second-order cybernetic description. What is observed, the observed system, is a function of the observational powers of the observing system. If the observing system has a mind in the sense that it can be considered mindful of the observed system, as we would readily assert, it is not at all obvious that mind does not extend into the observed system. The question to be asked is: Where does the mind stop and where does the world begin?

According to Clark and Chalmers (1998) this question invites two standard replies, namely those who consider anything outside the body to be outside the mind, and those who agree that the meanings of words cannot be considered to be "just in the head," and that this externalism about meaning carries over into an externalism about the mind. Clark and Chalmers advocate a strong view of externalism (a third position); namely, that the environment plays an active role in driving cognitive processes. Within the lifetime of an organism, individual learning moulds the brain in ways that rely on cognitive extensions surrounding the organism. In other words, a physical object like a chair is not represented in the brain in some form such as an image or a word. The brain has been moulded to perceive and understand the chair as chair. One may use pencil and paper or a computer to execute a calculation, or read a newspaper to learn about an event that took place somewhere else. The brain develops in ways that complement these external structures. It learns to play its role within unified, densely coupled systems. Clark and Chalmers extend this notion to the social environment: My mental states are partly constituted by the mental states of others, and theirs by mine. For example my beliefs may be a reference for another person who plays his or her role within the densely coupled system of our interactions. It is also conceivable that the extended mind implies an extended self, especially if one believes that the self outstrips the boundaries of consciousness.

Yet the idea of the extended mind is not easily accepted. We do not without doubt escape the notion of the cyborg as machine. When we consider ourselves as constituted through a cybernetics of cybernetics we quickly slip back into the idea of a second-order machine slotted on top of a first order machine—a second-order (observing) system calculating the calculations of a first-order (observed) system. There is an entire psychology that supports us in this view: I, cyborg, am the rational being who executes reasoning procedures on my internal representations of the external world. But we are changing our perceptions. Our ideas of rational thought and reason, and our understanding of the kinds of mechanism that might explain them, may be in a state of transition (Clark, 2003b). Rationality involves both more and less than we thought at first. Rationality is not simply a sequence of calculations, it is not simply the modification and deployment of information in a dispassionate way. In humans, emotions play a cardinal role in sifting options and biasing choices enhancing our capacity to act in a fluent, reasoned, and rational manner. But, says Clark (2003a), rationality may also involve significantly less than we tend to think. It may simply be a quick-and-dirty compromise forged in the heat of our ecological surround. Rational thinking may simply be fast and economical heuristics that enable us to use the minimum cues to get by in our living worlds. As a second-order cybernetic system, I, cyborg, may be the result of a complex ecological balancing act.

The shift toward a second-order cybernetics and an ecological perspective is not simply a shift toward the machine in context—the ecologically situated machine. The move is more fundamental, requiring an interesting turnaround in the modeling of systems, and an entirely new set of ideas. There is an emphasis on the notions of autonomy, self-organization, and cognition, and the role the observer plays in the modeling of a system (Heylighen & Joslyn, 2001). If first-order cybernetics modeled the person after the machine, second-order cybernetics explores the machine in terms of the characteristics of living systems. Second-order systems are autopoietic (self-reproductive) and structurally coupled entities (Maturana, 1980a, 1980b; Maturana & Varela, 1980, 1992). Perception is not a representation of an external world. It is a reciprocal and interacting phenomenon that takes place between a living entity and its environment. Environmental events impact on the sense organs of an organism, and because the organism is structurally coupled to its environment, the sensory impact perturbs the organism. The nature of the perturbation is a function of the organism's structure. In other words, the information gained by the organism is not a representation, a reflection of the external world, but a construction built from its internal perturbation. What the organism sees, hears, feels, or smells is the effect of a perturbation of the structure of the organism. What it gets to know is not a compilation of empirical facts. Knowledge is the self-organized structures and processes of the brain. There is no way to know the extent to which knowledge reflects an external reality. These organisms are autopoietic systems; systems that are autonomous and operationally closed; systems within which every process helps to maintain the system as a whole; systems that remain stable for considerable periods of time despite not being in equilibrium (in a state of minimum energy) with their environments. The consciousness and the processes of cognition of the autopoietic cyborg can only be understood in terms of the structures in which these processes arise, namely the body of the cyborg and the world with which it interacts.

There is a marked shift in the meaning of cyborg when the metaphor of the machine is replaced by the metaphor of the living organism. The machine-based first-order cyborg is a system in which cause and effect are balanced through linear, unidirectional feedback processes (Boga, 2002). But, when the observer is absorbed in the definition of cyborg, when the cyborg recognizes itself as an observing system, this second-order cyborg becomes an autopoietic system in which causes are effects as much as effects are causes, and a system in which these caused effects and effected causes are balanced through feedback processes that are acausal, mutually causing, and reversible (Boga, 2002).

THE CYBORG AS SELF-REFERENTIAL SYSTEM

But the core of the cyborg's identity escapes the oppositional structure bounded by machine and organism. A remarkable piece in cyborg history was published in 1991. With her cyborg manifesto, Donna Haraway propels the identity of the cyborg (and our identity as cyborg) beyond the dualism of machine and living organism. The cyborg manifesto predates a substantial body of work on the notion of cyborg, but it reads like a text that is still to come in the evolution of the cyborg. Haraway's text circulates in an acasual, mutually causing, and reversible manner through our observations of the cyborg, drawing us closer to the identification of ourselves as cyborgs, and also to the cyborg as a self-referential system. Haraway's observations are enabled by an integration involving the breaching of various boundaries, namely the boundary between human and animal, the boundary between organism and machine, and the distinction between physical and nonphysical.

Haraway's observation is enabled by a second-order cybernetics (for example, a machine in context, an autonomy, and a certain self-organization), but the product of her observation is a force of disruption, at least in part. This is an important shift in our understanding of the cyborg. By her own words, Haraway's cyborg disrupts through partiality, irony, intimacy, and perversity. It is oppositional and completely without innocence, causing a revolution of its ecosystem, the system if its *oikos*, its household. Oppositional structures are reworked, and hierarchies (such as machine and organism, social reality and fiction, nature and culture) are overturned so that the one can no longer be the resource for appropriation or incorporation by the other. However, more fundamental and more disruptive, beyond Haraway's immediate words, is the cyborg's disruption of its own disruptive identity. When Haraway identifies herself as cyborg, when she writes that in our mythic time we are chimeras, theorized and fabricated hybrids of machine and organism (through our technologies of designer running shoes, motor vehicles, and cell phones), when she identifies the cyborg as our ontology, as the condensed image of both imagination and material reality—the joined centers structuring any possibility of historical transformation, when she is doing all of this, she is already being ironic and blasphemous. She is cyborg—serious about her cyborg being and her being cyborg. She sees her blasphemy is an interruption that disrupts from within. It protects her against the moral majority— those who identify themselves as cyborg without recognizing the impossibility of the cyborg identity. Yet blasphemy is not apostasy. But she is also being ironic. Her disruption is about contradictions that do not resolve into larger wholes, about the tension of holding incompatible things together because they are necessary and true. Her irony is a play that is both humorous and serious. It is a rhetorical strategy, a political method. At the center of her ironic faith and her blasphemy is the image of the cyborg. At the end of her text we find a final move of disruptive identification. Haraway declines the role of the speaker of truth when she says: "I would rather be a cyborg than a goddess" (p. 181). The denial of the goddess (an identity, a truth, a logos) and the acceptance of the cyborg is an identification that has already lost the truth of identity—an impossible identification.

How should we understand Haraway's cyborg, the cyborg that Haraway calls our ontology, the cyborg that constantly disrupts—even its own ontology? The cyborg that is a constant disruption of ontology itself? Haraway's cyborg is a third-order cybernetics. It harbors an ontology of reflection, and as such it can be recognized only as an onto-epistemology. Although these notions cannot be fully unpacked here because they require lengthy deviations into concepts such as Derrida's (1982) *difference* and Lacan's (1977) mirror stage image, a brief outline will be sufficient to provide an indication of what it means to be a cyborg of the Haraway kind.

The need for a third-order cybernetics emerges whenever self-referentialty occurs (Kenny & Boxer, 1990). The question of subjectivity (and therefore the ontology of the subject) surfaces when the second-order cyborg in seeing itself as observing system is confronted with the problem of the self in the observing system. If the second-order cyborg is confronted with the fact that all realities are constructed, the third-order cyborg finds herself confronted with her own construction. Her image appears at the centre of her ironic faith, and her blasphemy, the image she believes in, the image she identifies with as being herself, is also an image captured in an ironic play of the incompatible, an image that is not her. In the moment of self-construction, her true being is disrupted. In her moment of self-reference, she disappears between her being and the image of her being. When the cyborg finally calls herself I, cyborg, when her identity collapses into an I, it is an ontology of I that reveals itself as an opening, like the iris of the eye, the position from which the I is viewed as I. An entire ontology and an entire epistemology collapse into this iris, this onto-epistemological eIe. But it is an eIe, that disrupts through partiality, irony, intimacy and perversity, a cyborg that is completely without innocence, that gives us our politics, that structures any possibility of historical transformation.

Haraway's contemporary cyborg is not the one envisioned by Clarke and Kubrick in the 1960s. It has grown itself into technology and technology into itself. Haraway's cyborg cannot discard the bones of its own skeleton. It cannot disconnect its HAL. It does not become irrational in its existential paradox of a knowing being and a being known. It does not go mad in the face of its being a concealed revelation as much as a revealed concealment.

IMPLICATIONS FOR EDUCATION

The cyborg has developed into a powerful symbol of integration. It does not distinguish between the humanized tool and the tooled human. For the cyborg the humanized tool has a memory, it processes information, catches a virus, and it mirrors the tooled human using a computer for storing information, calculating risks and making decisions. The cyborg challenges our understanding not only of who we are and what we know but also how we come to know. This section traces the relationship between the development of the cyborg and the evolution of learning in terms of teaching, facilitating and the choreography of action.

Teaching the Machine

The industrial age cyborg was a machine controlled by loops of information, being fed forward and backward, balancing of the machine's inputs and outputs to achieve particular goals. These goals could be a set of static parameters laying down the limits of the machine's behavior, a kind of behavior maintained through negative feedback—that is, feedback that counter the direction of the machine's operations. But the goals could also be a set of parameters of change, defining how the machine was to modify its behavior—a case in which the machine required positive feedback, feedback that encouraged the direction of operations. Goals could be defined internally or externally. Autonomous machines (autopoietic systems) were guided by internal goals, whereas artificial machines (allopoietic systems) were governed by goals that were maintained externally (Heylighen & Joslyn, 2001).

By the end of the industrial age, teaching and learning have been seamlessly embedded in and regulated by the paradigm of the machine. An entire literature on behaviorism and much of cognitive science gave credence to learning being understood as the linear development of intellect through a process that required teaching and learning approaches that were characterized by static and rigid processes of conforming to facts and methods, realized through endless memorizing and the repetition of content (see Gross, 1999). Underlying all the variants of educational approaches was a simple didactic of positive and negative feedback measures with the teacher as a central controller. There was little room for an autopoietic view of the learner. The goals were set by educational systems, and were maintained by teachers.

Facilitating the Observing System

But the information age brought different challenges. The industrial era's rigid processes of conformation were too static and inflexible to accommodate shifts in learning process, shifts marked by customized, just-in-time learning, learning systems that allow learners to progress at individual pace, learning activities that become increasingly authentic and embedded in real-world practice, learning environments that require learners to interact with professionals outside the classroom walls and, perhaps most important, teacher education programs that prepare teachers for the schools of the future rather than the instructionist schools of the past (Sawyer, Collins, Confrey, Kolodner, & Scardamalia, 2006).

> Perhaps the most solid finding to emerge from the learning sciences is that significant change cannot be done by fiddling around at the edges of a system that was designed in the industrial age. Instead, the entire educational system will have to be replaced with new learning environments that are based on the learning sciences. (Sawyer et al., 2006)

The information age requires teachers focused on developing the learners' cognitive and meta-cognitive abilities through collaborative learning environments (Dimitracopoulou, 2005), something not yet realized in current educational programs (Dowling, 2003).

Today, most learners entering the education system are cyborgs in reality. In the language of second-order cybernetics: they are observers embedded in their systems, not able to claim outside views they observe through lenses shaped by their life histories. For them, information does not reside in the observer or the environment, but arises in the process of living between the observer and the observed system (Murray, 2006). These learners are younger than the microcomputer, are more comfortable working on a keyboard than using pen and paper, demanding constant connectivity, being in touch with friends and family at any time and from any place. They display what Frand (2000) refers to as "the mindset of the information age" (p. 16). This mindset is a way of engaging with the world that is distinctly different from the mindset of those who grew up in the industrial age. In this mindset:

- computers are not experienced as technology but form an integral part of what the world is all about;
- the Internet (interactive communication) and not television (passive viewing) is the primary source of information;
- the ability to deal with complex and often ambiguous information is more important than simply knowing a lot of facts or having an accumulation of knowledge;
- problems are solved in a trial-and-error manner rather than careful deduction from preset principles;
- multitasking is a way of life—different information sources are accessed simultaneously;
- text and data are not simply captured in a linear manner—word- and data processing allows interactive construction and capturing of ideas;
- there is a need to be permanently connected to others;
- the is a need for fast, efficient and immediate communication—no tolerance for delays; and
- the is a need to create through consumption—for example, the creation of new texts through electronically assembling bits and pieces harvested from existing texts.

The challenge for educators and higher education institutions is to incorporate the information-age mindset of today's learners into their programs so as to create communities of lifelong learners (Frand, 2000). Through constant communication and feedback, these learners change their world and are changed by it with or without the intention of changing and being changed. This change is called learning. It is a learning that arises from the need for survival (in social, economic, cultural, and physical terms), that is triggered by the environment, that fits with the learner's life history, and that is different for everyone.

The Choreography of the Self-Referential System

Information-age learning is acquired through facilitation, and not through a process of teaching. Facilitating this kind of learning requires the construction of learning environments supporting opportunities for communication and multiple interactions (Murray, 2006). Learning is not the assimilation of information transmitted from one system to another. It is the system's structural change in reaction to the perturbation of the system. It requires self-reflection in interaction with others. These reflections-in-action require learning environments that include teachers, artifacts, texts, and all forms of communication. The reflections-in-action are the tacit theories that guide the activities of practising professionals (Murray, 2006).

But reflection-in-action is not a simple concept. It requires an understanding of learning in terms of the relationships among thought, action, and technology, a notion supported by a substantial body of work in psychology and anthropology. But in most of these considerations the link between thought and action is analyzed from the perspective of the individual, not taking into account that thinking and acting take place within certain contexts—contexts of tools and social interactions. Furthermore, in cases where these contexts are considered, as for example in activity theory and theories of the distributed mind, the relationship between individual and contextual artefact is viewed as an asymmetrical interaction—that is, an interaction in which the individual rather than the artefact is the agent of change (Shaffer & Clinton, 2005). In an attempt to maintain a certain form of symmetry between person and tool—and one should keep in mind that this kind of symmetry constitutes a prerequisite for any cyborg being—Shaffer and Clinton suggest the concept of *tool-forthoughts* as a primary category of analysis. According to these authors:

> All thoughts are connected to tools, and all tools are connected to thoughts: every time we consider a thought (since it is an internalization of action with a tool) it is inextricably linked to a tool, and every time we consider a tool (since it is an externalization of a thought) it is inextricably connected with a thought. In this view, tools are not distinct from thoughts; rather, both are poles in the back and forth movement between tool and thought. The reciprocal relation between tool and thought exists in both. (p. 595)

In this ontology, then, there are no tools without thinking, and there is no thinking without tools. There are only toolforthoughts, which represent the reciprocal relation between tools and thoughts that exists in both. When we say that something is a tool for thought (as separate words) this might suggest that thought is the broader category and that tools are something that help people think. Or it might imply that tool is the broader framework and persons are agents who use both thoughts and physical artefacts as tools. To avoid these difficulties, we connect the nouns tool and thought in order to suggest how toolforthoughts are the outcome of a process of tools existing in a reciprocal relation with thoughts.... In such a framework, the appropriate unit of analysis is not a system comprised of human beings and tools, but rather systemic effects of individual toolforthoughts and the particular forms of social interaction they foster. For each toolforthought, the task is to understand its particular constraints and affordances—and to uncover how the linkages between the two participate in particular kinds of social interactions at the expense of others. (p. 596)

Although the concept of toolforthoughts is difficult to grasp due to its somewhat counterintuitive nature, it has been with us for a long time. We simply have not recognized it as such. For example, the notion of an ink pen as a tool of writing comes quite naturally to those who use pens for writing. But a pen is also a toolforthought. We have to recognize the fact that a certain kind of knowledge has been enfolded in the pen, namely that it "knows" how to get ink on paper. From this point of view, the pen is not a simple tool in the mediation of writing. It is a tool that contributes to the production of symbols on paper. The pen is not merely acted on. It acts in and out of its own right, when it allows the ink to flow onto the paper. The toolforthought concept becomes more distinct as the tool's knowledge contribution to the end-product becomes more pronounced. It is easier to see the word processor as a toolforthought because its contribution to the writing process is more active than that of the ordinary pen. It corrects spelling and grammar, asks for clarification, and offers suggestions. The text is produced through the interaction between the author and the word processor. This is already the product of a cyborg, but it is not difficult to imagine an even larger and more complex role for the word processor, such as moderating the text for factual correctness, inserting diagrams and video clips, expanding explanations, and completing chains of thought. The unit of analysis of this (cyborgian) activity (the production of a text) is not the system comprised of the human author (thought) and the word processor (tool), but rather the systemic effect of the toolforthought (the text) and the particular forms of social interaction it fosters (writing and reading).

The former is a concrete example, a demonstration of physical fact. But the postmodern idiom of the information age allows abstraction to a more general level. Much of postmodern philosophy is marked by the idea that our experiential world is like a text. We construct this world (we write the text) as much as we are constructed by this world (by reading the text). At this level, the unit of analysis of the cyborgian production of our world text is not the system comprised of the tooled human and the humanized tool, but rather the systemic effect of the cyborg and the particular forms of social interaction it fosters through its constructions of and subjections to its world.

Shaffer and Clinton's (2005) toolforthought is a vehicle to understand cyborg learning. The cyborg preserves the unity of action and mediation. Cyborg learning is not the acquisition of isolated skills that transfer from one context to another. It is the mastery and appropriation of cultural tools; it is collaborative and guided by meaningful ends. The cyborg develops an understanding of the world through its own actions in the world. It is not troubled with the fact that it does not learn to think when it uses, for example, a calculator to find the sum of 2 plus 2. Its concern is its collaboration in the toolforthought (e.g., its ability to use the calculator) and its understanding of the various possibilities opened up by this collaboration. The cyborg knows that the source of diminished understanding is not technology, but poor curricula—the poor match between *toolforthought* and activity. What matters to the cyborg are the actions it values—values defined in relation to the cyborg's understanding of the things worth doing and the issues worth addressing.

In the end, the cyborg is necessarily ideological and deeply self-responsible. In setting its curricula, in choreographing its own learning, it has to ask itself: How am I to decide what activities I value? What ethical frameworks do I deploy to select my destiny from amongst the various purposes I set myself? How do I steer a true course for myself on my journey to the monolith at the origins of my evolution?

REFERENCES

Boga, S. (2002). *Advancing the frontiers of systems dynamics through higher orders of paradox*. Retrieved March 20, 2008, from http://systemdynamics.org/conferences/2002/papers/Boga1.pdf

Clark, A. (2003a). *Natural-born cyborgs: Minds, technologies, and the future of human intelligence*. New York: Oxford University Press.

Clark, A. (2003b). Artificial intelligence and the many faces of reason. In S. Stich & T. Warfield (Eds.), *The Blackwell guide to philosophy of mind* (pp. 309-321). Oxford, England: Blackwell.

Clark, A., & Chalmers, D. J. (1998). The extended mind. *Analysis, 58*, 10-23.

Cable News Network. (2002). *Scientists test first human cyborg*. Retrieved March 22, 2008, from http://archives.cnn.com/2002/TECH/science/03/22/human.cyborg/

Derrida, J. (1982). *Margins of philosophy* (A. Bass, Trans.). Chicago: The University of Chicago Press.

Dowling, C. (2003, January). *The role of the human teacher in learning environments of the future*. Paper presented at the IFIP Working Groups 3.1 and 3.3 Working Conference: ICT and the Teacher of the Future, St. Hilda's College, University of Melbourne, Australia.

Dimitracopoulou, A. (2005). Designing collaborative learning systems: Current trends & future research agenda (pp. 115-124). In T. Koschmann, D. D. Suthers & T. -W. Chan (Eds.), *Computer supported collaborative learning 2005: The next 10 years! Proceedings of the International Conference on Computer Supported Collaborative Learning*. Mahwah, NJ: Erlbaum.

Frand, J. L. (2000). The information age mindset: Changes in students and implications for higher education. *Educause Review, 35*(5), 15-24.

Grenville, B. (2001). The uncanny: Experiments in cyborg culture. In B. Grenville (Ed.), *The uncanny: Experiments in cyborg culture* (pp. 13-58). Vancouver, British Columbia, Canada: Arsenal Pulp Press.

Gross, R. (1999). *Peak learning*. New York: Jeremy P. Tarcher/Puttnam.

Haraway, D. (1991). A cyborg manifesto: Science, technology, and socialist-feminism in the late twentieth century. In *Simians, cyborgs and women: The reinvention of nature* (pp. 149-181). New York: Routledge.

Heylighen, F., & Joslyn, C. (2001). Cybernetics and second-order cybernetics. In R. A. Meyers (Ed.), *Encyclopedia of physical science & technology* (3rd ed., pp. 155-169). New York: Academic Press.

Kenny, V., & Boxer, P. (1990). The economy of discourses: A third order cybernetics? *Human Systems Management, 9*(4), 205-224.

Lacan, J. (1977). *Ecrits: A selection*. (A. Sheridan, Trans.). London: Tavistock.

Maturana, H. R. (1980a). Introduction. In H. R. Maturana & F. J. Varela (Eds). *Autopoiesis and cognition: The realisation of the living* (pp. xi-xxx). Dordrecht, The Netherlands: D. Reidel.

Maturana, H. R. (1980b). Biology of cognition. In H. R. Maturana & F. J. Varela (Eds.). *Autopoiesis and cognition: The realisation of the living* (pp. 3-57). Dordrecht, The Netherlands: D. Reidel.

Maturana, H. R., & Varela, F. J. (Eds.). (1980). Autopoeisis: The organisation of the living. In *Autopoiesis and cognition: The realisation of the living* (pp. 73-135) Dordrecht, The Netherlands: D. Reidel.

Maturana, H. R., & Varela, F. J. (1992). *Tree of knowledge: The biological roots of human understanding* (Rev. ed.). Boston: Shambhala. (Original work published 1987)

Murray, J. (2006). Cybernetic circularity in teaching and learning. *International Journal of Teaching and Learning in Higher Education, 18*(3), 215-221.

Sawyer, R. K., Collins, A., Confrey, J., Kolodner, J. L., & Scardamalia, M. (2006). Moving forward: The learning sciences and the future of education. In S. A. Barab, K. E. Hay, & D. T. Hickey (Eds.) *International conference on learning sciences: Proceedings of the 7th international conference on learning sciences* (pp. 1084-1087). Mahwah, NJ: Erlbaum.

Shaffer, D. W., & Clinton, K. A. (2005). Why all CSL is CL: Distributed mind and the future of computer supported collaborative learning. In T. Koschmann, D. D. Suthers, & T. -W. Chan (Eds.), *Computer supported collaborative learning*

2005: The next 10 years! Proceedings of the international conference on computer supported collaborative learning 2005. Mahwah, NJ: Erlbaum.

Warwick, K. (2002). The next step towards true cyborgs? Retrieved March 20, 2008, from http://www.kevinwarwick.com/Cyborg2.htm

Wiener, N. (1961). *Cybernetics: Or control and communication in the animal and the machine* (2nd ed.) Cambridge, MA: MIT Press.

CHAPTER 13

TRANSFER THROUGH LEARNING FLEXIBILITY AND HYPERTEXTUALITY

Gorg Mallia

CHAPTER OVERVIEW

The rise of flexible, independent learning has created a dilemma for institutionalized, accredited teaching. Concurrently, there is student nonconformity to most top-down classroom practices, which has been induced by nonlinear, or hypertextual, processing as a result of immersed usage of, among others, social software and electronic gaming. Exploration of the full change needed to match teaching practices with the mutated procedural schemas of cyber-natives is still under way, but there are indications that the very nature of the change has brought about a potential new route to transfer of learning, so elusive within rigid curricular face-to-face and online teaching environments. The diffusion and multifocusing that are at the base of hypertextual processing, and the personalization, diversification, and acquisition of general knowledge that infuse independent, flexible learning can create an amenable setting for the generalization and abstraction needed for effective transfer. This chapter explores the connection between processing change brought

Connected Minds, Emerging Cultures: Cybercultures in Online Learning
pp. 185–206
Copyright © 2009 by Information Age Publishing

about by immersed new-media usage and new potentials for transfer of learning.

PREAMBLE

Cyber-society's Web-immersed digital natives have moved decisively away from conventional processing of information, and its rigid schematic makeup. Through persistent exposure and responding, they are now complying to the hypertextual architecture of what has slowly become an extension of their own selves.

There is a constant presence of social software in the lives of heavy users of the Internet, as well as interaction with role-playing games and other video games, both online in their millions, motivated in a large number of ways (Yee, 2006), or with the use of gaming consoles, creating progressively more advanced environments that promote problem-solving on the go. These are causing transformations that go quite a long way beyond the well-researched positive/negative social interactions of users. There is no doubt that technological immersion is causing social change, and that some of that is diminishing personal user participation in society

The use of hypertextual conventions in interactive environments has instigated what I speculatively term "hypertextual processing" (Mallia, 2007), which underpins the very process of thought, mirroring the architecture and navigational processes of most of the software with which users interact.

HYPERTEXT

There is an extensive literature examining formalized hypertext assisted learning (Niederhauser & Shapiro, 2003; Shapiro & Niederhauser, 2004), with its singling out of the main features of hypertext, primarily its non-linear structure, its flexibility of information access, and its greater degree of learner control, and distinguishing "self-regulated readers" and "cue-dependent readers" (Balcytiene, 1999), with the second scoring better on content acquisition than the first, but with the first being more independent and exploratory in the way hypertext is read.

Self-regulation emphasizes independence both in search and reading patterns, as well as in the possibility of self-generating schemas that do not depend on a controlled scaffolding of cues, adapting to stimuli that are both irregular and, at times, from the perspective of the self-regulated, independent hypertext reader, chaotic. Self-regulated learning, even within classroom contexts, has proved to lead to improvements in performance and increases in positive learning behaviors (Schloemer & Brenan, 2006). "The combination of positive expectations, motivation, and diverse strategies for problem solving are the virtues of self-regulated learners" (Paris & Byrnes, 1989, p. 169).

A number of theories have explored the need for cognitive processes to develop flexibility in the face of hypertextuality and of, among others, forms of conceptual complexity and irregularity in knowledge domains, predominantly cognitive flexibility theory (Spiro, Feltovich, Jacobson, & Coulson, 1991).

Strongly significant within navigational independence are the meta-cognitive processes that put the learner firmly in the center of the learning in a cyclical process, the medium feeding the learner's own conscious approaches to the usage and the subsequent learning, with that same usage modifying the mechanisms of perception and application, and reflecting on the actual medium. Research does indicate that metacognitive awareness may precede effective strategy use (Sperling, Howard, Staley, & DuBois, 2004). It is also an important element in self-regulated learning.

Learner control also depends extensively on how the individual that is using the hypertext utilizes the baggage of prior knowledge he or she brings with him or her to the usage and how this affects whether learner control predominates. Prior knowledge is *the whole of a person's knowledge* and, as such:

- is dynamic in nature;
- is available before a certain learning task;
- is structured;
- can exist in multiple states (i.e., declarative, procedural, and conditional knowledge);
- is both explicit and tacit in nature;
- contains conceptual and metacognitive knowledge components (Dochy & Alexander, 1995, p. 227).

Those with high levels of prior knowledge are more in control than those with low levels of prior knowledge, who prefer more structured program-controlled hypertexts (Gail & Hannafin, 1994). A structured approach is not entirely necessary for information to be acquired (Shapiro, 1998). Hierarchies can be built even in unstructured hypertext links, providing they have cues to meaning (Shapiro, 1999). An interesting addendum to this, if one were to bundle Web-use with videogame use for the sake of examining of immersed usage, is that eye-tracking research about novices learning how to use computer games, indicates the preference of a trial and error strategy, with little time given to actual teaching hints as they learnt how to use the game (Alkan & Cagiltay, 2007), problem-solving and independently figuring their way around the gameplay, the learning of which they deemed to be easy.

HYPERTEXTUAL PROCESSING

There is a strong, independent problem-solving evident in frequent, particularly self-regulated users' navigation of these media, with metacognitive processes at work creating a schema-driven means of procedural acquisition. Hypothetically, this has led to a cognitive and affective reflection in the way users process information of the very structures of the navigational processes in the media. The result is an intrinsic move from predominantly linear information processing to a more lateral one. In many cases, this takes the form of multifocal hypertextual leaping, arbitrarily superficial in content, but quite wide in spread, allowing the freedom associated with hypertext that is evident even in the early literature on its use (e.g., Rouet & Levonen, 1996, and George Landow's seminal volume on the topic, now updated, Landow, 2006), and in direct structural links with, for example, the cinema (Gaggi, 1997; Mancini, 2005) and literature (Schneider, 2005). This multifocus is very much evident in media that is aimed primarily at young people who form part of the digital native generation, for example on such television stations as MTV, with its fragmented edits and erratic camera moments (Williams, 2003).

The result of persistent immersion is, hypothetically, hypertextual processing (HTP) which organizes perceived information into an erratic, loosely grouped number of simultaneous focal points, resulting in coherent, if sporadic information gain. This provides a change from a linear format within a chronological progression, to a partially controlled chaotic format, with tracking achieved primarily through hypertextual nodes. In turn, this conflicts with the perceived linear (if stratified) organization of thought processes on which presumption most traditional formalized pedagogies are built. The conflict makes for a very limited attention span and a resultant lack of follow-through.

One would assume that HTP affects to varying degrees and is dependent on a number of variables, not least of which are varying cognitive styles (Riding & Rayner, 1998), and the individual learning strategies of the immersed user that can determine how and in which way hypertextual architecture is perceived and handled (Graff, 2005).

What is certain is that HTP is anathema to traditional top-down schooling, be it institutional, or formalized e-learning. The lack of focus, diminished attention span, and lateral processing that are direct manifestations of HTP do not go well with the chronological linearity of hierarchical structures, and this includes most educational methodological practices.

LEARNING FLEXIBILITY AND INDEPENDENCE

Internet-immersed users, and heavy users of social software, as well as many forms of video gaming, live in an environment in which knowledge acquisition is at their fingertips, and the processes they have mastered to interact with the software also gives them the rudimentary skills needed to navigate, absorb, and integrate the learning into a cohesive, if chaotically absorbed, body of learning. In this sense, the acquisition is both substantive and procedural.

Tuschling and Engemann (2006) noted that "the structure sought here is integrative, a self-reflective technique of self performance ideally centered in the individual. It seeks to make learning independent from setting, from personal and financial effort. Informal learning can take place regardless of circumstances" (p. 456), and it can take place any time and anywhere, given that new media technologies are both desktop and mobile.

Mobile phones have become increasingly more versatile, with an integrated interface that can access the Internet through GPS and Wi-Fi. PDAs, aided by full-sized, foldable keyboards, mice, and other accessories, are little less than full-blown computers to be used on the go. The same can be said for most portable versions of static gaming consoles (for example, the Playstation Portable and the Nintendo DS), with Wi-Fi and a limited Internet connectivity being an integral part of their onboard facilities. Many major Web sites are creating pages specifically made for mobile devices, accepting the importance of mobile ICT. Bluetooth and other remote connectivity methods have also led to cordless ease of use, permitting multitasking while away from the desktop.

Formal research about informal learning has been with us since the 1980s (Marsick & Watkins, 1990), concentrating primarily on work-based learning, but often emphasizing the acquisition of transferable skills.

From the start, and to this day, there is the problem with measuring the extent and transferable impact of informal learning, and this is definitely the case with regard to accessible information on qualifications and participation rates (Conlon, 2003).

TRANSFER OF LEARNING

Transfer of learning can almost be taken as a measure for the effectiveness of learning. Yet, transfer is extremely difficult to trace. In spite of the fact that a body of research has been dedicated to understanding it (Analoui,

1993; Cormier & Hagman, 1987; De Corte, 1987; Detterman & Sternberg, 1992; Ellis, 1965; Grose & Birney, 1963; Haskell, 2001; Haslerud,
1972; Hunter, 1971; McKeough et al., 1995; Singley & Anderson, 1989),
transfer has remained an elusive concept.

Nevertheless, transfer is crucial to all learning. Transfer "isn't so much
an instructional and learning technique as a way of thinking, perceiving,
and processing information" (Haskell, 2001, p. 23), but the fact remains
that a lot of research seeking to determine the cause and effect of transfer
have resulted in no, or no significant transfer. This has been the experience of experimenters working with spontaneous, as opposed to cued,
transfer (informed versus uninformed transfer, reviewed in Gick &
Holyoak, 1987)—the most quoted being gestalt psychologist Duncker's
"radiation problem" experiments (Duncker, 1945) which yielded very little by way of analogical transfer[1] (Gick & Holyoak, 1980), though a substantial amount of spontaneous transfer was registered in children when
the focus was on instantiation of abstract statements designed to enhance
the accessibility of the relevant information (Chen, Yanowitz, & Dahler,
1995). No transfer, too, has resulted from experiments with high road
transfer[2] when cues in the learning task are context-specific, and these are
not present in the transfer task (Voss, 1987).

Nonetheless, the need for a sound knowledge on the way learning
transfers has been felt since the inception of educational psychology. The
concept of fidelity as having to be part and parcel of the learning task for
elements within it to transfer to other situations (Thorndike & Woodworth, 1901) or, as it is better known, the fidelity theory, has been the
most explored in the last 30 or so years. "A change in one function alters
another only insofar as the two functions have as factors identical elements" (Thorndike, 1913, p. 358).

Hunter's (1971) four factors that generate transfer (both positive and
negative) are the common factors sought by researchers into teaching for
transfer who follow this as the main idea. These are:

1. The similarity of the situation in which something is learned and
    the situation to which that learning may transfer.
2. The student's association of the old and new learnings for any one
    of many reasons.
3. The degree of effectiveness of the original learning.
4. The perception of essential or unvarying elements that exist in
    both the old and the new learning's (Hunter, 1971, p. 9).

Some studies have found proof against the concept of fidelity being
paramount to the transfer task (e.g., Boreham, 1985), bringing forward

experiments in which lowering fidelity of simulation actually improved transfer, putting the accent on the information processing required for the learning task. Most others have accepted the concept that similarity in one or more elements is intrinsic to transfer. Singley and Anderson (1989) proved that the sharing of cognitive tasks between the learning and transfer tasks is essential to transfer, with declarative knowledge about a domain compiled into procedures, which are triggered under highly specific conditions (basically, ones that are identical in both cases).

In fact, a lot of research into transfer seems to have taken for granted the transposition of subjects from what we can continue to refer to as the "real" world, to insular conditions in which a single function is tested and controlled. This was strongly pointed out by, among others, Brown and Kane (1988), who demonstrated in experiments that kept to the natural conditions of their young subjects, that analogical transfer was obtainable with children as young as 3 years of age.

LEVELS AND TYPES OF TRANSFER

The basic problem of transfer is: "In what way and to what extent will acquisition of skills, knowledge, understanding, behaviors, and attitudes in one subject or learning situation influence performance or learning in other subjects or situations" (Bigge & Shermis, 1992, p. 219).

The distinction is also made between horizontal and vertical transfer. Horizontal transfer refers to conditions in which a skill can be shifted directly from the training situation in order to solve problems. Vertical transfer refers to conditions in which the new skill cannot be used to solve problems unless it is adapted to fit the conditions of the workplace—that is, an extension of learning is required before problems can be solved effectively (Joyce & Weill, 1996).

Gielen (1995), distinguishing between near and far transfer, has listed what she believes to be the main promoters of both, basing her premise on the literature and succinctly presenting many of the findings mentioned above. She writes that:

Near transfer is promoted by:

- Introducing knowledge in the context it will be used;
- Behavioral objectives that guide instruction;
- The presence of identical elements in tasks in training and in job environment promotes transfer.

Far transfer is promoted by:

- Introducing varied context, which leads to decontextualisation of learning;
- Stimulating generalization and analogies;
- Discovery strategies;
- Increasing diversity, which in turn decreases contextual bindings. (Gielen, 1995, 2.6.1)

Haskell (2001) distinguishes six levels of transfer based on judgements of similarity. Only levels four and five of these appear frequently in the literature. The six levels are:

- Level 1: Nonspecific transfer—all learning, because it is all connected in some way to past learning;
- Level 2: Application transfer—applying what one has learned to a specific situation;
- Level 3: Context transfer—applying what one has learned in a slightly different situation, often a change in context;
- Level 4: Near transfer—when previous knowledge is transferred to new situations that are closely similar but not identical to previous situations;
- Level 5: Far transfer—applying learning to situations that are quite dissimilar to the original learning; and
- Level 6: Displacement or creative transfer—transferring learning in a way that leads to the creation of new concepts.

Cognitive-interactionism[3] regards transfer of learning in the following amazingly longitudinal seven ways:

1. Opportunity for transfer may occur in many situations. It is not inherent in any subject but is possible from any field of knowledge.
2. Transfer is not dependent upon mental exercise with disciplinary school subjects.
3. Transfer is dependent upon methods of teaching and learning that use lifelike situations. It is facilitated by teaching for large generalizations that have transfer value.
4. Transfer is not automatic; opportunities for transfer must be recognized, and the person concerned must want to use them.
5. Transfer varies according to difficulty of generalization of subject matter and the intellectual ability of individuals.

6. Insights need not be put into words for their transfer to occur.
7. The amount of intraproblem insightful learning, not the number of trials as such, determines the amount of interproblem transfer (Bigge & Shermis, 1992, p. 238).

Taking the "real" world of work as the desired goal toward which to transfer an acquired education, Marginson (1994) suggests working directly on the acquisition of certain attributes which are strategic to the process of transfer itself—those skills and knowledge which themselves enhance the capacity of students-graduates to transfer their other attributes. These key attributes include confidence and the capacity to be proactive in new and familiar situations, learning how to learn, flexibility, adaptability, responsiveness, sensitivity, openness, critical thinking, and dispassionate thought.

Marginson also points out that the student needs to learn how to take into account at the same time more than one viewpoint through the ability of handling multiplicity and complexity and being able to move between different knowledge sets. All of these he calls transferability skills.

THE CASE FOR MINDFULNESS AND ABSTRACTION

An important contribution to our knowledge of what constitutes transfer was made by Salomon and Globerson (1987), who made a case for mindfulness (a state of mind defined as the volitional metacognitively guided employment of nonautomatic, usually effort demanding processes). Especially in high-road transfer, this is a result of mindful abstraction, as opposed to the near-automaticity of low-road transfer. However, Salomon and Globerson accept that distal sources are difficult to gauge, with causal factors being elusive of quantification. These are heavily influenced, among others, by sociocultural factors: culture, intellectual climate, common ways of perceiving a situation, shared habits, and the like.

The concept of abstraction can also be linked to memory retrieval. Kintsch and Van Dijk (1978) suggested that memory structures are constructed from experience as a result of abstracting out the essential content, or "gist" of a situation. They suggested further the processes of deletion, generalization and construction in order to construct abstract representations of events heard or read about.

A schema, too, is a more abstract representation than a direct perceptual experience (Winn & Snyder, 1996), which makes schemata very useful, both in terms of the easing of cognitive load, and in the processes fostering of transfer.

Salomon and Perkins (1989) insist that transfer is not at all a unitary phenomenon. Rather, transfer can occur by different routes dependent on diverse mechanisms and combinations of mechanisms.

They note that an important type of transfer is what they refer to as backward-reaching high-road transfer, because the individual formulates an abstraction guiding his or her reaching back to past experience for relevant connections. This continues to highlight the important role played by background knowledge in both the encoding of the original task and the transfer of content and procedure to other tasks. Duffy (1992) seems to corroborate this and gives an underlying suggestion as to its implementation when he writes that "the instruction of new tasks should always provide a familiar context so that the learner can use his or her knowledge base, what he or she already knows, to interpret and integrate the new skills and knowledge" (p. 81). That knowledge can (and does) affect further learning and as such is a case of *proaction*. The new learning can affect the original background skill and knowledge in its own turn, so as a result we can also have *retroaction* (Catania, 1992).

Salomon and Perkins (1989) point out that far-reaching transfer may be facilitated through mindful abstraction, but at the expense of relatively poor learning of the original material, because the greater level of generality makes it harder to connect the representation to any given particular. Mindfulness, or the conscious pursuit of specific learning, seems to also be evident in Pugh and Bergin's (2006) linking of motivation to, among other factors, intentional learning, as diverse from incidental learning, following the distinction made by Bereiter and Scardamalia (1989).

DISPOSITIONAL TRANSFER

A sort of transfer that is taken for granted, according to Bereiter (1995), is the "transfer of conceptual understanding to further conceptual learning" (p. 27). He refers to Voss (1984) for the "vast research literature that shows the importance of prior knowledge for comprehension" and says that this "is a literature showing the enormous power and range of transfer of conceptual knowledge" (Bereiter, 1995, p. 27).

But it is on the transfer of disposition that Bereiter puts the main emphasis, since while the transfer of *principle* depends on depth of understanding, the transfer of *disposition* depends on incorporation into character, insisting that this can be applied across all school topics—from moral education to science education. The point made by Bereiter is that dispositional transfer is embedded in the character set of the individual, and so this becomes an integral part of all processing.

Prawatt (1989, in Eggen & Kauchak, 1997) seems to be the precursor of Bereiter in this, because he believes that "although transfer of learning tends to be specific, *dispositions*, or the attitudinal element of learning, can transfer in a general sense. A disposition to be open-minded, to reserve judgement, and to search for facts to support conclusions is a general disposition" (Eggen & Kauchak, 1997, p. 329).

DISCUSSION AND SPECULATION

The direct linking between HTP and informal, (often flexible) independent learning, creates a very unique context for learning that collocates quite extensively with a number of the prerequisites that the literature says are necessary for there to be any sort of transfer of learning.

There are a number of divergences from the roles traditionally enjoyed by, for example, self-regulation. Given the semi-chaotic nature of hypertextual processing, the indications are that self regulation tends to be, in the main, incidental, and quite far from Zimmerman's (1998, 2000) cycles consisting of forethought, performance or volitional control, and self-reflection. The self-regulation is controlled by the nature of the hypertextual architecture, or by any one of the multidirectional paths suggested by the game-play. But close, mapped observation of gamers by the present author has yielded indications of schematically induced patterns, with increased hierarchical proficiency, leading to stepped problem-solving. I would say that, of the three cycles, in HTP induced self-regulation, it is the performance or volitional control that is best reflected.

As listed previously, some of the main elements that foster transfer on different levels are: similarity/fidelity; analogy; generalization; abstraction; metacognition; mindfulness/automaticity; disposition; confidence; proactivity in new and familiar situations; and lifelike contexts. Each of these can be mirrored to varying degrees in the instigational processes of informal learning brought about by HTP.

It is also worth noting that transfer of knowledge from education to workplace typically involves five interrelated stages:

1. the extraction of potentially relevant knowledge from the context(s) of its acquisition and previous use;
2. understanding the new situation—a process that often depends on informal social learning;
3. recognizing what knowledge and skills are relevant;
4. transforming them to the new situation;

5.   integrating them with other knowledge and skills in order to think/
act/communicate in the new situation (Eraut, 2004, p. 256).

Eraut points out that items 4 and 5 above are usually not considered by
higher education, and that the final stages draw attention to informal
learning at the workplace.

New media technology immersion has expanded the "workplace" to
incorporate any and all situations. Learning on the go is persistent everywhere. The need to know has become instantaneous and instantly executable, so Eraut's five steps are daily happenings in the lives of millions of
online seekers of the expansion of information about any and all things
that motivate such a reaction.

The intrinsic motivation stemming from the volitional nature of the
learning plays a primary role in instigating a transferable acquisition of
substantive and procedural knowledge from new technology immersion.

Typically, learning-independent, hypertextual processing, immersed
technology users have skills that navigate, absorb, and integrate learning
within the collective general knowledge so touted by Haskell (2001) as
being an essential base for transfer. Though there is a chaotic absorption
of the knowledge, there is also a personalization of it that provides recall
cues, most often through motivational associations with elements of personal enjoyment. HTP contributes to the mix multifocusing, independent
problem-solving, self-regulation, metacognition, and an individually
organized utilization of hierarchies of prior knowledge.

The motivational elements are drawn from the implicit fact that users
immerse themselves by choice in the media that instigate HTP as a direct
result of the heavy usage. In this sense, there is a divergence from Pugh
and Bergin's insistence that a greater understanding of transfer "can be
achieved by applying the intentional perspective" (2006, p. 155). Incidental learning within the flexible, independent learning context, diffused by
the presence of HTP, does not imply a lack of mindful persistence in the
pursuit of knowledge. It is just that it is most often a unique unit of information that is sought, rather than a module that is integrated organiza-
tionally within a larger, hierarchically designed block of intentional
learning.

If one where to take Haskell's six levels of transfer (2001) as the transfer to aim for, HTP motivated flexible independent learning would help
facilitate levels 1 to 4, and be an important element in the last two levels.

Level 1:   *Nonspecific transfer*—any and all learning acquired directly or
incidentally through volitional, self-directed information
search, or as side-learning from entertainment-driven activities;

Level 2: *Application transfer*—the value of transfer of training from flexible, independent sources in the world of work has been extensively mapped. It can also be contended that if, in gaming, there is a microcosmic simulation of macrocosmic reality, then transfer application of learnt strategic processes and content should be facilitated;

Level 3: *Context transfer*—taking RP gaming as a primary example, with levels utilizing a bridging of induced schematic strategic and element processing (same characters, tools, psychomotor action generation, etc.), but varying in difficulty of landscape and storyline navigation as well as in the hierarchical transformation, context transfer is a procedural accepted standard. Though incidental and empirical indications point at contextual transfer happening between gaming itself and the gamer's nonvirtual reality, more extensive research still needs to provide evidence of this;

Level 4: *Near transfer*—the chaotic nature of HTP makes for sporadic generalization in knowledge acquisition, which, in turn, ties in with elements of situations that are often different from those for which the knowledge was sought or acquired incidentally in the first place. Though this does not make for formalized, directed near transfer, it does contribute extensively toward creating a widely spread knowledge and skill base that plays an incidental, but extensive role in many day-to-day situations for which specific knowledge was not pursued in the first instance, resulting often in successful horizontal transfer;

Level 5: *Far transfer*—Both volitionally and incidentally sought diversification in knowledge acquisition is quintessential in flexible, independent learning particularly when motivated by HTP. It is presumed that the wide base and diverse general knowledge acquired (with under-running mindful, metacognitive processes at work—the random search is logistical, not cognitive) can transfer vertically to situations dissimilar to the original contexts of acquisition. There is an initial lack of ordering (i.e., nonspecificity, possibly to the point of abstraction) which is eventually mindfully concretized through organizational nodes that can take the form of theoretical or practical tasks that might have had no connection with the original context of the learning. This reasoning is speculative as comprehensive research into far transfer instigated by HTP enhanced flexible learning still to be carried out;

Level 6: *Displacement or creative transfer*—The volitional nature of new media technology immersion and consequent integration into users' character set, creates a dispositional stance that cuts across all subsequent, personal actions (as per Bereiter's theory, 1995). Apart from this, the very nature of, for example, gaming, is narrative-based (visual, iconic and symbolic narrative). It induces self-determined, often creative decision-making processes that may transfer, since the disposition is invoked in most of the instances and influences all actions carried out by the affected individual.

This speculation on the facilitation of transfer by contexts created by immersed new media usage can be corroborated somewhat by linking to the main elements that foster transfer an expansion of the elements that infuse hypertextual processing (HTP) and independent, flexible learning (IFL).

Similarity/Fidelity

- HTP: Associative hyperlinking among dissimilar elements that, however, have at least one element of fidelity, is staple to navigation both online and in most gaming.
- IFL: The random nature of the learning means that there are incidental elements throughout it that provide a bridging link to other knowledge harvesting (or learning), as well as task-oriented situations.

Analogy

- HTP: In role-play gaming, simulation of reality in three-dimensional animation format, fuelled by storylines that are processed by the player create analogical nodes that at times link with or replace elements in the gamer's own life.
- IFL: Analogy is an integral part of narrative in learning, but it can be a part of both independent and formal learning.

Generalization

- HTP: Multifocusing creates a spread of focus that is wider, if more superficial than singular focusing.
- IFL: Learning on the go (particularly through mobile devices) can be in the form of byte-sized snippets, the concision of which can be

of two extremes: either so totally specific that it is shorn of all excess information and has only the bare essentials of demanded information, or else general, giving an overview because of lack of space and time.

Abstraction

- HTP: Diffusion and lack of focusing create a non-specific collation of unit-based learning that abstracts.
- IFL: Unless hierarchically organized by a unified learning design, nonaccreditable online learning, as well as learning on the go, often lacks all but the focus on the searched for, or incidentally learnt unit of information. This is not in itself abstraction, but neither is it tightly parametered, specific learning.

Metacognition

- HTP: Though not planned into the learning itself, metacognitive processes are persistently at work, for e.g., in both the trial-and-error hierarchical tiering of level conquering in gaming, and in hypertextual navigation on the Internet, utilizing hierarchies of prior knowledge in the process.
- IFL: Motivationally induced learn-to-learn processes are an intrinsic part of independent learning. Skill-building is often not directed by outside sources but independently learnt. Hypertextual navigation, RPG manipulation skills, and other psychomotor processes are persistently enhanced through layered knowledge hierarchies, even if there is no actual formal structuring for the metacognition.

Mindfulness/Automaticity

- HTP: The process from mindfulness to automaticity can be perfectly illustrated by the experimentation with alternatives and the elimination of failures and strengthening of successes inherent in gaming skill acquisition, both within the parameters of each game, and also on a more accomplished scale across similar platform games (and, in the case of expert gamers, even across platforms).
- IFL: Salomon and Perkins' theory of the mindfulness to automaticity process can apply just as easily to both formal and informal, independent and flexible learning.

Disposition

- HTP: Strong, intrinsic motivation accounts for new media technology immersion, at times to the level of addiction. Dispositional adherence to the technologies is at times total.
- IFL: Disposition is one of the main driving influences behind the selection of independent knowledge and information acquisition as opposed to (or along with) a more formalized instructional regimen. Much of what is independently learnt online, unless directed by formal learning, is done through inclinations and/or dispositional instigation. The incidental learner's disposition is to learn, or at least to get specific information at any given time, rather than during time allocated for formal learning.

Confidence

- HTP: HTP induces lack of confidence in traditional organized learning conditions. If learning is self-motivated, immersion emphasizes individual confidence in both substantive and procedural acquisition.
- IFL: Once the independent skill acquisition is gained and instilled in the learner (in the form of procedural schemas), self-motivation, information need, and confidence in the use of new media technologies are what fuel learning in a flexible context.

Proactivity in New and Familiar Situations

- HTP: The very nature of Web site and gaming architecture stimulates exploratory navigation. Hypertextuality is based on the concept of the known leading to the unknown, which then becomes known in turn, in continuous, interlinked layering.
- IFL: Independent learning is instigated through the proactivity of the learner, since there is no predetermined regimen of study to follow through incitement. Background knowledge provides one base for the acquisition of new knowledge

Lifelike Contexts

- HTP: Virtual environments, in the main, mirror reality, infusing a willing suspension of disbelief and bridging lifelike contexts with fantasy-infused elements. In the case of heavy users, this has led to (well mapped out in the literature) addictive behavior that makes vague the demarcation between the virtual and the real. Albeit socially and psychologically prospectively negative, the potential for transfer from one domain to the other of such situations is quite marked.

- IFL: Independent learning has often been linked directly with the concept of lifelong learning, in that the sources are constantly accessible and an integral part of the life of the user. The contexts from which learning is drawn are life-like in that they are often an extension of life itself, with Web 2.0 (for example) becoming an exercise in continuous, cyclical interaction between the World Wide Web and everyday reality.

CONCLUSIONS

Very little research has been carried out about the specific nature of hypertextual processing motivated independent flexible learning and transfer, so all remains firmly in the realm of speculation based on the researched nature of what instigates transfer of learning, and what actually has been proved to transfer (i.e., very little).

However, this chapter has looked at potential effects of HTP and the resultant preferences for independent, flexible learning by heavy users of social software, and the indications are positive with regards to, primarily, motivationally acquired general knowledge and how this may lead to what the literature determines to be transfer.

Another branch of the literature is full of argumentation about the difficulty of accreditation for independent learning, and many institutions of higher learning are actually treating the rising wave of learning outside controlled regimens as a growing threat to their very existence in the form as we know it. The reality is that there are a number of cognitive and affective gains, many that are socially useful, being made by independent learners. Even more specific in profiting are learners whose integrational interaction with new media technologies, and specifically with social software, has made them adopt the navigational patterns native to the technologies within substantive and procedural processing. In their case, independent learning is not an option, but the only viable route to knowledge acquisition, and though the literature in the main looks at the social ills that are brought about by this type of immersion, there are very few who are looking proactively at how this new state of being and thinking can be used specifically for learning. A lot of the old axioms, including those assessing transfer of learning effectiveness as a result of tightly designed schooling procedures, will need to be rethought as part of this often ignored, but actually rampant development.

The old C-grade sci-fi robotic cliché "resistance is futile" springs to mind in the face of opposition to social software immersion, that ranges from (albeit valid) arguments about technology addiction, to the decrying of linguistic aberrations stemming from mobile instant message use. The reality is that this immersion and its effects have become an integral part of society as we know it, and it is about time that we also look at what gains can be made from this state of being.

It is a belief stated in this chapter, that transfer of learning can be one of the very important gains that can be made if we look closely at the change new media technologies have brought about in those who use it extensively.

NOTES

1. "The essence of analogical thinking is the transfer of knowledge from one situation to another by a process of mapping—finding a set of one-to-one correspondences (often incomplete) between aspects of one body of information and aspects of another" (Gick & Holyoak, 1983, p. 2).

2. Companion to transfer on the *low-road*. Both are defined thus by Salomon and Globerson (1987): "Two main routes of learning appear to emerge. One route implicates much deliberate effort utilization of non-automatic processes: it is a mentally demanding route to the acquisition of knowledge and skill. We call it the '*high road*' of learning. The other is a route that relies on much incidental practice where skills are employed in an increasingly more automatic manner.... It is a mentally undemanding but practice intensive road to learning ... By necessity it takes much more time than the high road, hence we call it the '*low road*' of learning" (p. 630).

3. *Cognitive interaction* theory, which stems primarily from the work in *social cognitive theory* by the Canadian Albert Bandura (b. 1925), "is the interaction of individuals with their perceived, meaningful environments" (Bigge & Shermis, 1992, p.148). "In cognitive interactionism an individual is considered to be not a passive object for environmental forces to condition but an interactive, intentional subject, continuously participating in an ongoing reciprocal person- and situation-interaction process and acting on the basis of his own reasons, expectations, needs, and motives" (p.148).

REFERENCES

Alkan, S., & Cagiltay, K. (2007). Studying computer game learning experience through eye tracking. *British Journal of Educational Technology, 38*(3), 538–542.

Analoui, F. (1993). *Training and transfer of learning*. Aldershot, England: Avebury.

Balcytiene, A. (1999). Exploring individual processes of knowledge construction with hypertext. *Instructional Science, 27,* 303-328.

Bereiter, C. (1995) A dispositional view of transfer. In A. Mckeough, J. Lupart, & A. Marini (Eds.), *Teaching for transfer: Fostering generalization in learning* (pp. 21-34). Mahwah, NJ: Erlbaum.

Bereiter, C., & Scardamalia, M. (1989). Intentional learning as a goal of instruction. In L. B. Resnick (Ed.), *Knowing, learning, and instruction: Essays in honor of Robert Glaser* (pp. 361-392). Hillsdale, NJ: Erlbaum.

Bigge, M. L., & Shermis, S. S. (1992) *Learning theories for teachers* (5th ed). New York: Harper Collins.

Boreham, N. C. (1985). Transfer of training in the generation of diagnostic hypotheses: The effect of lowering fidelity of simulation. *British Journal of Educational Psychology, 55,* 213-223.

Brown, A. L., & Kane M. J. (1988). Preschool children can learn to transfer: Learning to learn and learning from example. *Cognitive psychology, 20,* 493-523.

Catania, A. C. (1992). *Learning* (3rd ed.). Englewood Cliffs, NJ: Prentice Hall.

Chen, Z., Yanowitz, K. L., & Daehler, M. W. (1995). Constraints on accessing abstract source information: Instantiation of principles facilitates children's analogical transfer. *Journal of Educational Psychology, 87,* 445-454.

Conlon, T. J. (2003). A review of informal learning literature, theory and implications for practice in developing global professional competence. *Journal of European Industrial Training, 28*(2/3/4), 283-295.

Cormier, S. M., & Hagman, J. D. (Eds.). (1987). *Transfer of learning: Contemporary research and applications.* San Diego, CA: Academic Press.

De Corte, E. (Ed). (1987). Acquisition and transfer of knowledge and cognitive skills [Special Issue]. *International Journal of Educational Research, 11,* 601-712. Oxford, England: Pergamon Press

Detterman, D., & Sternberg, R. J. (Eds.) (1992). *Transfer on trial: Intelligence, cognition, and instruction.* Norwood, NJ: Ablex.

Dochy, F. J. R. C., & Alexander, P. A. (1995). Mapping prior knowledge: A framework for discussion among researchers. *European Journal of Psychology of Education, 10,* 225-242.

Duffy, T. M. (1992). What makes a difference in instruction? In T. G. Sticht, M. T. Beeler, & B. A. McDonald (Eds.), *The intergenerational transfer of cognitive skills: Vol.1. Programs, policy and research issues* (pp. 61-83). Norwood, NJ: Ablex.

Duncker, K. (1945). On problem solving. *Psychological Monographs, 58* (Whole No. 270).

Eggen, P., & Kauchak, D. (1997). *Educational psychology: Windows on classrooms* (3rd ed.). Upper Saddle River, NJ: Merrill.

Ellis, H. C. (1965). *The transfer of learning.* New York: Macmillan.

Eraut, M. (2004). Informal learning in the workplace. *Studies in Continuing Education, 26* (2), 247-273.

Gaggi, S. (1997). *From text to hypertext: Decentering the subject in fiction, film, the visual arts, and electronic media.* Philadelphia: University of Pennsylvania Press.

Gail, J., & Hannafin, M. (1994). A framework for the study of hypertext. *Instructional Science, 22*(3), 207-232.

Gick, M. L., & Holyoak, K. J. (1980). Analogical problem solving. *Cognitive Psychology, 12*, 306-355.

Gick, M. L., & Holyoak, K. J. (1983). Schema induction and analogical transfer. *Cognitive Psychology, 15*, 1-38.

Gick, M. L., & Holyoak, K. J. (1987). The cognitive basis of knowledge transfer. In S. M. Cormier & J. D. Hagman (Eds.), *Transfer of learning: Contemporary research and applications* (pp. 9-47). San Diego, CA: Academic Press.

Gielen, E. (1995). *Transfer of training in a corporate setting.* Unpublished doctoral dissertation, University of Twente, The Netherlands.

Graff, G. (2005). Differences in concept mapping, hypertext architecture, and the analyst-intuition dimension of cognitive style. *Educational Psychology, 25*(4), 409-422.

Grose, R. F., & Birney, R. C. (Eds.) (1963). *Transfer of learning: An enduring problem in psychology.* Princeton, NJ: Van Nostrand.

Haskell, R. (2001). *Transfer of learning: Cognition, instruction, and reasoning.* San Diego, CA: Academic Press.

Haslerud, G. M. (1972). *Transfer, memory & creativity.* Minneapolis, MN: University of Minnesota Press.

Hunter, M. (1971). *Teach for transfer.* Thousand Oaks, CA: Gorwin.

Joyce, B., & Weil, M. (1996) *Models of teaching* (5th ed.). Boston: Allyn & Bacon.

Kintsch, W., & Van Dijk, T. A. (1978). Toward a model of text comprehension and production. *Psychological Review, 85*, 364-394.

Landow, G. P. (2006). *Hypertext 3.0: Critical theory and new media in an era of globalization.* Baltimore: Johns Hopkins University Press.

Mallia, G. (2007). A tolling bell for institutions? Speculations on student information processing and effects on accredited learning. In K. Fernstrom (Ed.), *Readings in technology in education: Proceedings of the international conference on information communication technologies in Education, Heraklion, Crete* (24-32).

Mancini, C. (2005). *Cinematic hypertext: Investigating a new paradigm.* Amsterdam: IOS Press.

Marginson, S. (1994). *The transfer of skills and knowledge from education to work.* Melbourne: The University of Melbourne CSHE Research Working Papers 94-4.

Marsick, V., & Watkins, K. (1990). *Informal and incidental learning in the workplace.* New York: Routledge and Kegan Paul.

McKeough, R, Lupart, J., & Marini, A. (Eds.) (1995). *Teaching for transfer: Fostering generalization in learning.* Mahwah, NJ: Erlbaum.

Niederhauser, D. S., & Shapiro, A. (2003, April). *Learner variables associated with reading and learning in a hypertext environment.* Paper presented at the meeting of the American Educational Research Association, Chicago, IL.

Paris, S. G., & Byrnes, J. P. (1989). The constructivist approach to self-regulation and learning in the classroom. In B. J. Zimmerman & D. H. Schunk (Eds.), *Self-regulated learning and academic achievement: Theory, research, and practice* (pp. 169-200). New York: Springer.

Prawat, R. (1989). Promoting access to knowledge, strategy, and disposition in students: A research synthesis. *Review of Educational Research, 59*, 1-41.

Pugh, K. J., & Bergin, D. A. (2006). Motivational influences on transfer. *Educational Psychologist, 4*(3), 147-160.

Riding, R., & Rayner, S. (1998). *Cognitive styles and learning strategies: Understanding style differences in learning and behaviour.* London: David Fulton.

Rouet, J. F., & Levonen, J. J. (1996). Studying and learning with hypertext: Empirical studies and their implications. In J. -F. Rouet, J. J. Levonen, A. Dillon, & R. J. Spiro (Eds.), *Hypertext and cognition* (pp. 9-24) Mahwah, NJ: Erlbaum.

Salomon, G., & Globerson, T. (1987). Skill may not be enough: The role of mindfulness in learning and transfer. *International Journal of Educational Research, 11,* 623-638. Oxford, England: Pergamon.

Salomon, G., & Perkins, D. N. (1989). Rocky roads to transfer: Rethinking mechanisms of a neglected phenomenon. *Educational Psychologist, 24*(2), 113-142.

Schloemer, P., & Brenan, K. (2006). From students to learners: Developing self-regulated learning. *Journal of Education for Business, 82*(2), 81-87.

Schneider, R. (2005). Hypertext narrative and the reader: A view from cognitive theory. *European Journal of English Studies, 9*(2), 197-208.

Shapiro, A., & Niederhauser, D. (2004). Learning from hypertext: Research issues and findings. In D. H. Jonassen (Ed.), *Handbook of research for educational communications and technology* (2nd ed., pp. 605-620). Mahwah, NJ: Erlbaum.

Shapiro, A. M. (1998). Promoting active learning: The role of system structure in learning from hypertext. *Human-Computer Interaction, 13*(1), 1-35.

Shapiro, A. M. (1999). The relevance of hierarchies to learning biology from hypertext. *Journal of Learning Sciences, 8*(2), 215-243.

Singley, M. K., & Anderson, J. R. (1989). *The transfer of cognitive skill.* Cambridge, MA: Harvard University Press.

Sperling, R. A., Howard, B. C., Staley, R., & DuBois, N. (2004). Metacognition and self-regulated learning constructs. *Educational Research & Evaluation, 10*(2), 117-139.

Spiro, R. J., Feltovich, P. J., Jacobson, M. J., & Coulson, R. L. (1991). Cognitive flexibility, constructivism, and hypertext: Random access instruction for advanced knowledge acquisition in ill-structured domains. *Educational Technology, 5,* 24-33.

Thorndike, E. L. (1913). *Educational psychology: Vol. 2. The psychology of learning.* New York: Bureau of Publications, Teachers College, Columbia University.

Thorndike, E. L., & Woodworth, R. S. (1901). The influence of improvement in one mental function upon the efficiency of other functions. *Psychological Review, 9,* 347-382.

Tuschling, A., & Engemann, C. (2006) The emerging regime of learning in the European Union. *Educational Philosophy and Theory, 38*(4), 451-469.

Voss, J. F. (1984). On learning and learning from text. In H. Mandl, N. L. Stein, & T. Trabasso (Eds.), *Learning and comprehension of text* (pp. 193-212). Hillsdale, NJ: Erlbaum.

Williams, K. (2003). *Why I (still) want my MTV: Music video and aesthetic communication.* Cresskill, NJ: Hampton.

Winn, W., & Snyder, D. (1996) Cognitive perspectives in psychology. In D. H. Jonassen (Ed.), *Handbook of research for educational communications and technology* (pp. 112-142). New York: Macmillan.

Yee, N. (2006). Motivations for play in online games. *Cyberpsychology & Behaviour,* *9*(6), 772-775.

Zimmerman, B. J. (1998). Developing self-fulfilling cycles of academic regulation: An analysis of exemplary instructional models. In D. H. Schunk & B. J. Zimmerman (Eds.), *Self-regulated learning: From teaching to self-reflective practice* (pp. 1-19). New York: Guildford.

Zimmerman, B. J. (2000). Attaining self-regulation: A social cognitive perspective. In M. Boekaerts, P. Pintrich, & M. Zeidner (Eds.), *Handbook of self-regulation* (pp. 13-39). New York: Academic Press.

PART IV

NARRATIVES AND CASE STUDIES

CHAPTER 14

CYBERCRIME IN SOCIETY

Steven Furnell

INTRODUCTION

Online learning takes place in a context within which cyberthreats are rife. Although relatively few will explicitly target the e-learning domain, a multitude exist that have the potential to affect e-learners. Indeed, unprotected systems (whether they belong to the end-user or the service provider) are at extreme risk, and can be found very easily via automated scanning techniques. In addition, a number of threats are completely untargeted, and may be encountered simply by virtue of being online. In short, although the Internet is vast, it is easy to find trouble, and for trouble to find you.

This chapter examines the problem of cybercrime in our online society, with particular focus on the challenge that it poses for end-users. The discussion begins with an examination of a range of threats that can directly target end-users, and considering the associated impacts that these may have. This is followed by brief examples of some of the threats that can target online service providers, and which need to be guarded against in order to maintain user trust. The final aspect of the main discussion, then, considers how threats may be addressed from the end-user perspective, in terms of both the things that users need to know and the technical safeguards they ought to be using.

Connected Minds, Emerging Cultures: Cybercultures in Online Learning
pp. 209–224
Copyright © 2009 by Information Age Publishing
209

THREATS FACING ONLINE LEARNERS

Surveys frequently reveal the extent of problems facing organizations, but there is less available and well-publicized evidence to demonstrate the dangers faced by individual users on personal systems. Relatively few threats will affect them specifically because they are e-learners (and those that do are likely to be indirect, as a result of the online learning provider being attacked). However, there are a range of general threats to which online learners will be exposed as a result of their significant presence in cyberspace. Indeed, it could be argued that, as e-learners are likely to be online more than the average user, and to use a greater range of online tools and services, they have a proportionally greater exposure to the negative aspects as well. With this in mind, a range of threats are outlined in the sub-sections below, followed by a discussion of their relative potential to harm users.

Spam

Junk e-mail is, at the least, an annoyance that has the potential to waste time and litter our inbox with unwanted rubbish. However, it can also lead to other problems. For example, at an individual level, it can cause embarrassment and offence as a result of the frequently dubious subject matter. There are also potential impacts from productivity and safety perspectives, in the sense that users can waste time looking at it or be tricked into scams. Another consideration is that users can easy receive several hundred kilobytes of spam per day, which has the potential to become costly if they are downloading it via a slow link and/or paying by the byte (e.g., as is still frequently the case in many mobile access scenarios). Moreover, for users working with size quotas on their e-mail accounts, spam can carry the risk of filling up their mailboxes and causing legitimate messages to be missed.

Beyond complete novices, most e-mail users are fairly adept at differentiating between spam and legitimate messages, and indeed many messages give themselves away simply from their titles. For example, none of the following (all genuine spam message titles) are likely to be easily mistaken for legitimate messages:

- Don't Buy Vi-gra
- you can't beat our RX
- She wants a better sex? All you need's here!
- St0ck Market Standout?

- Horny pills—low price
- The Ultimate pharmacy

However, messages bearing other titles could more conceivably be misjudged (at least to the extent that recipients waste time by doing more than just ignoring or deleting them straight away). For example, all of the following would require a judgement based on the sender and content of the message rather than the message title:

- FYI
- Urgent and confidential
- Dear Sir
- Re [5]:

One of the categories of spam has a particular relevance to the e-learner, in the sense that a substantial subset of messages in circulation relate to bogus qualifications (as illustrated by the example in Figure 14.1). Ensuring trust in the e-learning provider is vital for both e-learners and prospective employers, and so the existence of such messages (and the fact that bogus qualifications can indeed be obtained) does not help to foster a good impression. At the very least, they may raise suspicion and create adverse publicity that is undesirable for the domain. However, in an extreme scenario, such messages may color someone's views to the degree that they undermine the credibility of legitimate e-learning courses/providers.

Phishing

Phishing is another threat that originates via e-mail, and involves the use of bogus messages that attempt to dupe the recipient into divulging sensitive information. The attacks work by crafting the messages such that they appear to come from an organization that the user should recognize (common candidates being banks and popular online services, such as Amazon and eBay), and then using social engineering techniques to convince the user that they need to part with the requested information. Links within the messages will typically lead users to a bogus Web site (also dressed to look like it belongs to the impersonated organization), which proceeds to collect the desired details. Although current attacks have tended to target personal data relating to the user (e.g., bank account and credit card details), similar techniques could also be used to target information that has the potential to compromise an institution (e.g., passwords and institutional details).

According to figures from the Anti-Phishing Working Group (APWG, 2007), 38,514 unique phishing reports were reported in September 2007,

UNIVERSITY DIPLOMAS

OBTAIN A PROSPEROUS FUTURE, MONEY-EARNING POWER, AND THE
PRESTIGE THAT COMES WITH HAVING THE CAREER POSITION YOU'VE
ALWAYS DREAMED OF. DIPLOMAS FROM PRESTIGIOUS NON-ACCREDITED
UNIVERSITIES BASED ON YOUR PRESENT KNOWLEDGE AND LIFE EXPERIENCE

If you qualify, no required tests, classes, books or examinations.

Bachelors', Masters', MBA's, Doctorate & Ph.D. degrees available in your field.

CONFIDENTIALITY ASSURED

CALL NOW TO RECEIVE YOUR DIPLOMA WITHIN 2 WEEKS

1-206-984-0021

CALL 24HRS, 7 DAYS A WEEK, INCLUDING SUNDAYS & HOLIDAYS

Figure 14.1.   Example of spam offering bogus qualifications.

as opposed to just 22,136 at the same point 12 months earlier (with an average for the year being 26,575 reports per month).

Although over 90% of the reported attacks in the APWG report were targeted against brands in the financial sector, the potential exists for phishing techniques to be used in other contexts, and no organization can really consider itself immune from impersonation. Indeed, if an attacker decides that users of a particular organization or provider are of interest, then there is the potential to utilize spear-phishing, which involves a highly targeted attack against a much smaller user community than would receive the normal mass-mailed messages.

Spyware

Spyware refers to parasitic software that invades the user's privacy, by divulging details of browsing habits and other sensitive information gathered from the target system (with specific categories including system monitors, adware, and tracking cookies). A variety of information may be harvested in this context, including account information, login details, surfing and shopping habits, and files from the system. The captured information can be transmitted to a malicious third party, thus putting both personal and business data at risk of abuse. In addition to this, there may be a significant degradation in the performance of the compromised system, as a result of the resources being utilized by the spyware rather than legitimate programs and processes.

Spyware has become one of the most prominent threats of recent years, and represents a clear problem from the end-user perspective. Indeed, a study of 354 domestic PCs conducted by AOL and the National Cyber Security Alliance found that 6 of 10 systems were infected with spyware (AOL/NSCA, 2005).

Malware

In general, the term "malware" refers to any piece of code that has a malicious or unwanted effect on a system or network. While there are literally hundreds of thousands of individual strains, the problems can be grouped into the following three categories (Furnell & Ward, 2006): virus, worm, and Trojan horse.

Virus

A virus is a replicating program that finds its way into a system by infecting "carrier" materials such as removable media, executable programs, or other files such as documents. At some point after infection, the virus will activate its payload, which can cause a variety of unwanted and often damaging effects.

Worm

Similar to viruses in that they replicate between systems, worms have the fundamental distinction of spreading autonomously, without needing to infect a carrier. Worm propagation can occur via fully automated activity (e.g., scanning network addresses and exploiting vulnerabilities in order to enter remote systems) or via user-initiated actions (e.g., opening bogus content from e-mail attachments or peer-to-peer file shares).

Trojan Horse

Trojan horses are programs that claim to perform a particular function, but actually have a hidden payload that results in unexpected (and very likely unwanted) activities. Depending on the extent to which the Trojan seeks to disguise its activity once executed, the hidden functions may be provided instead of, or in addition to, the expected functionality.

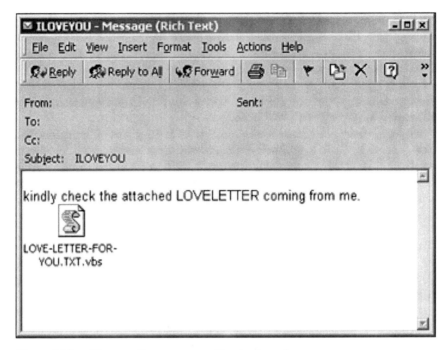

Figure 14.2.   The e-mail message used by the Love Letter worm.

Such malicious software can arrive via many routes, and common infection vectors may include e-mail attachments, instant messaging, peer-to-peer file sharing, "drive-by downloads" (in which a system becomes infected as a result of the user visiting a compromised Web site), and via direct exploitation of vulnerabilities on the user's system. A common trick, when focusing on the end-user as entry path and requiring them to perform an action to enable the malware to run, is the use of social engineering to fool them into opening a malicious file. A classic example of this is shown in Figure 14.2, which depicts the e-mail message used by the infamous Love Letter (or Love Bug) worm in May 2000. This arrived purporting to be a love letter, but was actually a Visual Basic Script that (when opened) caused a copy of the worm to be mailed to everyone in the victim's Outlook address book.

Similar methods are also used in some of the other contexts. For example, in the case of infection via peer-to-peer networks, users are fooled into downloading the malware in the belief that it is another file that they were seeking. However, there is also potential to bypass the need for user involvement altogether, by exploiting vulnerabilities that facilitate direct entry for worms (which may in turn introduce other malicious code onto the system). Once it is given the opportunity to run, the malware may then target the user in other ways, such as stealing their data or hijacking their system.

Hackers

In general terms, the threat here refers to persons deliberately gaining unauthorized access to the user's system, and the scope of the threat that they pose is therefore significant (i.e., if they gain an sufficient level of access, they could conceivably do anything on the target system). Their activities may be motivated by a variety of factors, including egotism, espionage, ideology, mischief, money, and revenge (Furnell, 2001). As such, even though the user may not consider him- or herself to be a likely target, hackers may wish to target an end-user system simply because they find it an easy target for some mischief, or in order to make later use of it for their own ends (e.g., as a file repository, or as a platform for initiating attacks against other systems). Hackers are also prone to targeting end-users as sources of sensitive information, via social-engineering attacks, with the consequence that users need to be cautious about what they divulge to whom (Mitnick & Simon, 2002).

Contrasting the Threats

Having summarized the nature of the problems, Figure 14.3 contrasts the aforementioned threats, comparing the potential impacts that they may cause against the ease with which the impact (although not necessarily the threat itself) may be avoided (Furnell, 2005). Although none are so trivial that they can be completely dismissed or ignored, they are certainly not of equal magnitude either—which in turn influences their relative potential to trouble end-users. In the chart, the differing sizes of the "impact avoidance" zones are intended to reflect the likelihood of encountering the associated threats (i.e., threats such as spam and phishing are much more likely to be encountered than hacking). As such, the chart as a whole aims to convey that the threats with the greatest the potential impact are the more difficult to handle, but also less likely to be encountered.

Having explained the general layout of the chart, the placement of the individual threats within it warrants some further explanation. In the bottom left, classed as having least impact and being the easiest impact to avoid, is spam. In fact, many might argue that spam is not really a security issue at all, and that it does not have to cause any problems, provided that

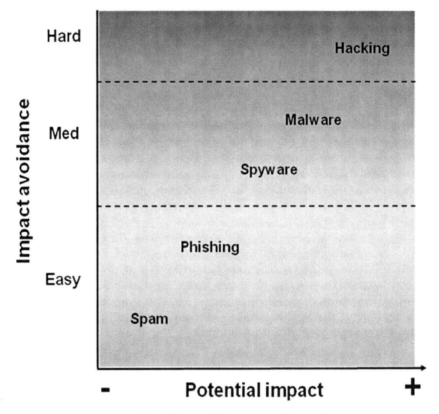

Figure 14.3.   Impacts and avoidance of threats targeting end-users.

users are aware enough to ignore it and that the volume received does not overwhelm the network. However, with spam accounting for over 86% of e-mail traffic (MessageLabs, 2007), there are still some scenarios that represent a problem, such as the aforementioned problem of filling mailboxes. Nonetheless, when considered against the other issues, spam creates the least impact and users can be trained to ignore it.

Given the manner in which they are distributed, phishing messages can be considered to be a subset of spam. However, they are considered as a distinct threat because of the specific intentions behind the messages, and the consequences that can result if the recipient is fooled by the attack.

Spyware can be classed as being easier to prevent than malware because it often gets installed as a result of an explicit user action (such as installing free software of questionable origin), which could be prevented if users were more keenly aware of what to look out for or adopted more cautious online behaviors. However, if it has already been installed on the system, it can actually be more difficult to eradicate than malware. For example, whereas a virus signature typically has between 1 and 50 traces on an infected desktop, spyware typically has between 20 and over 500 traces (Smith, 2007). Meanwhile, malware can be considered harder to avoid, simply because (to date) it has shown the potential to reach the user via a wider variety of routes, and on a wider range of devices. For example, whereas spyware has focused on traditional PCs, malware is now finding its way onto mobile devices such as smartphones and PDAs (Dempsey, 2005). In addition, the potential impacts can also be greater—besides stealing information, malware may also corrupt and destroy data within the system, or indeed allow the system to be hijacked by a remote attacker.

Hackers may enter by all manner of means, including the possibility of using one of the aforementioned threats as an initial entry mechanism (e.g., phishing for a password, or distributing malware that opens a back-door on the target system). Depending on the level of access they acquire, they can potentially achieve unlimited control over the compromised system, and thereby exercise a full range of confidentiality, integrity, and availability-related impacts against the end-user.

In all cases, impact avoidance will typically rely on a suitable combination of technical safeguards on the system and appropriate behavior by the user, with neither being likely to suffice in its own right. As such, the users have a key role to play, and success will be closely related to their attitudes and awareness in relation to security.

THREATS FACING SERVICE PROVIDERS

For organizations offering online services, maintaining a trust relationship with the user community is clearly of vital importance. However, this could be severely damaged by security failings, and service providers must therefore be mindful of the potential for threats on several fronts. Indeed, attacks may occur that result in breaches of confidentiality, integrity, and/ or availability, all of which could be the trigger for an affected user to lose confidence in the provider. Indicative examples of such problems are highlighted in the paragraphs that follow.

Data Theft

Although end-users often perceive that their data is at the greatest risk as it travels over the network, it often finds itself being much more vulnerable at the remote destination, where hackers may break in and steal it en masse. Such opportunities may exist as a result of poorly configured or badly maintained systems that are vulnerable to hacker exploits, as well as systems that have not been designed to separate the storage of sensitive data from public-facing servers. Educational systems will inevitably maintain repositories of student records and other confidential files. As a consequence, they may be perceived as rich sources of personal information, and other details that may be extremely desirable for facilitating further crimes such as identity theft and blackmail. As an example of the problems that can occur, in 2004 San Diego State University was obliged to notify 178,000 students, employees, and alumni that their personal information may have been revealed following a hacker attack on one of their servers (Schultz, 2004). An even more significant incident occurred in 2006, in which approximately 800,000 students, parents, and staff from University of California, Los Angeles had to be contacted following the breach of a database containing names, Social Security numbers, dates of birth, home addresses, and other contact information (Lemos, 2006). Even if the data in these cases were not exploited further, the time, effort and cost involved in the notification process would still have represented a significant impact in its own right. As such, it is clear that data holders need to take appropriate measures to ensure that these assets are safeguarded against unauthorized disclosure.

Web Site Defacement (or Other Malicious Alteration of Content)

In this context, the content of the site is modified away from what the provider intended to serve, with the consequence that the integrity of the service has been breached (or, to use the parlance of the perpetrators, it has been "owned" by hackers). As the public-facing points of presence (in terms of both marketing and delivering services), Web sites represent common targets for attack. Indeed, defacement has become a significant problem, with sites running unpatched server software representing relatively easy targets, even for novice hackers (who are able to use scanning software to identify vulnerable systems, and then use similarly automated methods to exploit them). Indeed, sites may find themselves on the receiving end of attacks simply because they are vulnerable, rather than being specifically targeted for any other reason, and a look at a defacements archive (such as zone-h.org) will reveal all manner of targets, from government sites through to academic institutions. In terms of the resulting impacts, most publicized attacks involve very obvious changes to the content, with the consequence that visitors to the site are aware that an attack has taken place, and therefore, beyond the immediate disruption, resulting impact is focused around potential damage to the reputation of the provider. However, more insidious forms of attack are conceivable, in which attackers make more subtle modifications to content (e.g., in order to spread misinformation). In a service intended to deliver learning materials, such modifications would be unlikely to be noticed by the target audience (in the sense that they are accessing the information to learn from, and so would not be in a position to question its accuracy) and would have the consequence that they end up learning the wrong information.

Denial of Service

In the case of denial of service (DoS), an attacker attempts to intentionally impair or withhold access from legitimate users, and consequently has an impact upon availability. A DoS attack can be achieved by overloading systems such that they run out of resources (e.g., flooding a Web server with requests that serves to limit legitimate connectivity, or generating excessive traffic that consumes available bandwidth), or by instigating events that cause systems to fail altogether. Although a DoS attack does not result in disclosure or loss of data, there is still the potential for a significant impact, particularly if the unavailability of the site/service directly equates to a halting of business operations. An extreme example here is provided by the example of Cloud Nine, a U.K. Web hosting provider that went out of business in early 2002 as a result of a sustained series of distributed DoS attacks that targeted its key servers (T. Richardson, 2002). The general prevalence of DoS attacks is significant, with 25% of 436 respondents in the 2007 Computer Crime & Security Survey reporting that they had detected such an incident (R. Richardson, 2007).

Although these types of attack are most likely to be targeted against the providers, it is clear from the descriptions that many of the impacts would still be felt by end-users. As such, the occurrence of such incidents could easily be the undoing of any trust that has been established, with the consequence that users lose confidence and take their business elsewhere. The ongoing viability of the service provider would clearly be threatened if this was to happen on a large scale, and therefore it is in their interests to ensure that safeguards are employed. However, from the end-user's perspective much of this must be taken on trust, as they do not have any direct influence over the protection used at this level. Having said this, there are still a number of things that users can (and indeed should) do at the local level in order to protect themselves, and these issues are considered in the next section.

Addressing the Threats Facing End-User Systems

Given that they are often the intended targets, there are several things that end-users ought to know beyond the mere existence of the threats:

Why the Threats Might Affect Them, and What the Impacts Could Be (i.e., What Are the Implications if a Particular Threat Faces Their System?)

Example considerations here would be what spyware might be able to gather from their activities, or what would be available for malware to damage. Users also need to understand why they would be targeted, rather than assuming that there is no reason for it to happen. Bearing in mind the adage that robbers will target banks because that's where the money is, many end-users would conclude that there would be no reason for their systems to be attacked, because there is little of value to be found when compared to bigger targets. However, it is worth remembering that while many robbers may prefer banks, that does not stop them from robbing other places, too, with the lesser reward being offset by the easier target. The same can equally be true for hacking—depending upon the attacker's motives, a vulnerable end-user system may be a much more convenient and desirable target than a hardened corporate server. A good example here is provided by the rise of botnets (where a bot is a compromised end-user system, with the ability to be remotely controlled by a hacker), in which many participating systems are compromised end-user machines (Symantec, 2007).

The Possible Contexts in Which Each Type of Threat Can Be Encountered (i.e., Potential Attack Vectors)

Although e-mail is the main (visible) route for many of the threats, other avenues are also vulnerable and becoming more widely utilized. For example, instant messaging is now a viable option for the instigation of both malware infection and phishing attempts (Savvas, 2005). However, without advice to contrary, users may get the impression that they are safe as long as they are not using e-mail. Furthermore, virtually all threats are becoming more complex in terms of the techniques and tricks they use to dupe users, thus heightening the need for awareness amongst the possible victims.

The Capabilities of Any Technological Safeguards That May Be in Place (i.e., the Level of Protection They Can be Expected to Provide)

Users are presented with a potentially confusing array of technologies, such as antivirus, antispyware, antispam, and personal firewalls, and the need to understand how they relate to the various threats. In some cases, of course, the type of protection is clear from the name (e.g., antispam), but it is not always that straightforward. For example, protection against worms and Trojan horse programs is provided by software that is conventionally referred to as antivirus, which could cause some users to wonder whether the other forms of malware require additional solutions. Alternatively, knowing that antivirus programs can also be relied on to handle other forms of malicious code might cause users to overestimate the extent of the protection they are provided with (e.g., assuming that the same software will also act as a safeguard against spyware, which will not be true in all cases). Additionally, the name of the technology does not always indicate the threats that it deals with, and so the user is left to rely upon his or her own perception of what it does. For example, a user installing an "Internet security" package may assume that it protects them against all of the threats discussed in this chapter, but the reality is that only a subset may be covered.

Although nothing can be done to guarantee total protection, there are a number of steps that can be taken to provide a strong assurance against the impacts of attacks (several of which are increasingly found as part of the features provided as standard in the latest operating systems).

Personal Firewalls

The role of a personal firewall is to provide a selective barrier for traffic going to and from the user's PC from the Internet. An appropriately configured firewall can therefore prevent malicious incoming and (in most cases) outgoing connections from the user's system. As such, they provide a useful safeguard against incoming probes from hackers and malware, as well as restricting the potential for malware to spread outwards from the user's system.

Antivirus and Antispyware

In order to provide protection against malicious code threats, end-user systems require programs that can monitor and eradicate the problems. This includes the ability to perform full scans of memory and files, as well as to provide "on-access" protection when new content is opened or downloaded. Although many systems now come with suitable packages pre-installed, this is typically with a time-limited subscription that the user is required to renew (e.g., after 12 months). In addition, the effectiveness of the protection will depend significantly upon the malware and spyware signatures being continually updated to take account of the latest strains. As such, users have a responsibility to ensure that their protection is both enabled and up-to-date.

Antiphishing

Most Web browsers now include the ability to perform real-time checks of visited URLs against a list of known phishing sites, and so enabling this facility is likely to be worth the slight performance compromise that users will experience as a result. In addition, a level of healthy scepticism on the part of the user when reading unsolicited e-mails can provide a further safeguard.

Automatic Updates

Recognizing that bugs and vulnerabilities are regularly discovered in software that, if left unpatched, can be exploited by hackers and malware, it is important for users to keep their systems up-to-date in order to maintain protection. As a consequence operating systems and applications frequently include functionality to automatically download and install software updates as they become available from vendors.

Application-Level Security Features

Many of the applications that enable Internet access include features that can provide protection. For example, e-mail clients can be configured to filter spam and to block access to potentially harmful attachments. Meanwhile, Web browsers can block access to untrusted scripts and prevent pop-ups. However, in using these safeguards, users need to mindful that they may sometimes be blocking things that are actually wanted, and so this is a context in which a greater degree of awareness and judgement is likely to be required.

Backup

Although it cannot prevent a threat from occurring, having a backup of data is a very useful safeguard if the worst has happened and the original copy has been corrupted or lost entirely. Hacker and malware activities can clearly result in such consequences, but it is also worth noting that this is a valuable insurance against other threats, such as disk failure or physical theft or damage to the system.

Common-Sense Browsing

One of the most important things that users can do to help themselves is to exercise caution and discretion in the sites that they visit online. Although sticking to known, big-name sites is no guarantee that malicious content will not be encountered (e.g., even big-name sites may be attacked and temporarily compromised), it is certainly less likely for threats to be encountered than when visiting sites that are known to be serving content of a dubious nature (e.g., sites offering pornography and pirated materials being classic examples of where malware or spyware might be an unexpected part of the offering). Linked to this is the standard good practice of only opening and installing materials from known and trusted sources.

With appropriate technical safeguards, and a modicum of care and threat awareness, users can consequently go a long way to protecting themselves against otherwise significant dangers.

CONCLUSIONS

This chapter has outlined a number of the threats facing end-users and (to a lesser extent) service providers in the online world. Although it can clearly offer many benefits and opportunities, the unfortunate reality is that, without appropriate protection, cyberspace is certainly an unsafe place to be. Moreover, new threats will undoubtedly emerge in the future, alongside new online services and applications.

From the user perspective, it is important to ensure that the threats are viewed in a balanced manner. On the one hand, users should not be so concerned that it prevents them from making the most of the opportunities offered online, but at the same time they should not overestimate their protection and act in a cavalier manner. Even if security technologies are in use, there is still a residual risk from the threats, and misguided user actions can exacerbate the problem. As such is not only important to use the safeguards, but also to accompany them with enough awareness to ensure that unnecessary problems are avoided.

REFERENCES

Anti-Phishing Working Group. (2007). *Phishing activity trends: Report for the month of September.* Retrieved December 17, 2007, from www.antiphishing.org/reports/apwg_report_sept_2007.pdf

AOL/National Cyber Security Alliance (2005, December). *AOL/NCSA Online Safety Study.* http://www.security.iia.net.au/downloads/safety_study_v04.pdf

Dempsey, P. (2005, June). Hackers on the move. *Information Professional, 2*(3), 39-43.

Furnell, S. (2001). *Cybercrime: Vandalizing the information society.* Boston: Addison Wesley Professional.

Furnell, S. (2005, July). Internet threats to end-users: Hunting easy prey. *Network Security*, pp. 5-9.

Furnell, S. M., & Ward, J. (2006). Malware: An evolving threat. In P. Kanellis, E. Kiountouzis, N. Kolokotronis, & D. Martakos (Eds.), *Digital crime and forensic science in cyberspace* (pp. 28-54). Hershey PA: Idea Group.

Lemos, R. (2006, December 12). UCLA alerts 800,000 to data breach. *Security Focus*. Retrieved March 6, 2008, from www.securityfocus.com/news/11429

MessageLabs. (2007). *MessageLabs intelligence: 2007 annual security report*. Retrieved March 6, 2008, from www.messagelabs.co.UK/mlireport/MLI_2007_Annual_Security_Report.pdf

Mitnick, K. D., & Simon, W. L. (2002). *The art of deception: Controlling the human element of security*. Indianapolis, IN: Wiley.

Richardson, R. (2007). *CSI survey 2007: The 12th annual computer crime and security survey*. Retrieved September, 18, 2008, from www.gocsi.com

Richardson, T. (2002, January 22). Cloud Nine blown away, blames hack attack. *The Register*. Retrieved March 6, 2008, from www.theregister.co.UK/2002/01/22/cloud_nine_blown_away_blames/

Savvas, A. (2005, May 25). Sith attacks instant messaging users. *Computer weekly.com*. Retrieved September 18, 2008, from http://www.computerweekly.com/Articles/2005/05/25/210143/sith-attacks-instant-messaging-users.htm

Schultz, E. (2004). Security breaches threaten personal and financial data. *Computers & Security, 23*(4), 269-270.

Smith, C. (2007, November). *The state of spyware: Protect your network from evolving spyware trends*. Webroot Software, Presentation to British Computer Society South West Branch.

Symantec. (2007, September). *Symantec Internet security threat report. Trends for January-June '07, 12*. Retrieved January 12, 2008 from http://eval.symantec.com/mktginfo/enterprise/white_papers/ent-whitepaper_internet_security_threat_report_xii_09_2007.en-us.pdf

CHAPTER 15

REVOICING TXT

Spelling, Vernacular Orthography, and "Unregimented Writing"

Tim Shortis

CHAPTER OVERVIEW

This chapter offers an explanatory framework for the respellings associated with new technology text types such as e-mail, Internet chat, SMS (Short Message Service) text messaging, and instant messaging. I start by considering some of the features and patterns of U.K. adolescents' use of such writing and of the information and communication technology (ICT)-enabled semiotic resources of electronic text. I argue that ICT has enabled an extended set of orthographic resources that users can draw on to inflect their purposes and project their identities. It has offered an extended orthographic palette in place of the normative binary choices of print technology. I argue that such respelling is not new but recycles popular but relatively undocumented practices from trade names, popular culture, and children's transitional orthographies. In the second half of the chapter I go on to consider the contextual pressures that act on users' choices. ICT and the Internet have not so much changed spelling as

Connected Minds, Emerging Cultures: Cybercultures in Online Learning
pp. 225–243

reregulated what counts as spelling, and in so doing, there is a challenge to the official educational discourses of literacy, and particularly as they apply to orthography. In the globalized context there is a question beyond the reach of this chapter. Are these practices better thought of as localized to the experience of the complexities of the arcane English orthographic "system," or are they a case in a glob-localized disruption to orthography and literacy in the Internet and language paradigm that has followed the age of print?

INTRODUCTION

In this chapter I examine the use of respelling and vernacular orthography as found in digital communications including e-mail, chat, MSN, and text messaging. I offer an explanatory account of the nature of txt respelling, its linguistic features, and the contextual factors that motivate those features. In contrast to studies that have dwelled on the newness of such spelling as a netlinguistic phenomenon (Crystal, 2003, 2004), I argue that this orthography is better thought of as a digital recycling of preexisting popular practices that are all around us. Digital technology has diffused the use of respellings and orthographic principles which were in previous use in vernacular literacy practices including trade names, children's transitional "creative spelling," and graffiti, as catalogued by Cook and others (Cook, 2004b; Davies, 1987; Read, 1986). Such practices exist in collective consciousness even if they are not recorded in dictionaries. In contrast to studies which have dwelt on the microdistinctions between text messaging language and Internet chat (Crystal, 2004; Hard af Segerstad, 2002), I argue that txt spelling is generic: the spelling practices found in text messaging are similar to those found in Internet chat, instant messaging, e-mails, and other new media text forms.

The respellings of txt are "natural," functional, and uncodified, and are interpreted and replicated by immersion rather than by formal instruction. According to my interviewees, it is an orthography remade by users in their practices rather than one that depends on being received, learned, and directly replicated in the manner of the acquisition of standard language spelling accuracy. It reflects a shift in the stability of the identity positions we hold and the stability of the language conditions that have prevailed during the age of print (Carrington, 2005a). This functionality of ICT respelling, the capacity of users to recover meanings without recourse to glosses, sidelines the popular guides to netspeak and techspeak. In practice, such codification is superfluous, even misleading.

Following this, digital Internet has deregulated what counts as English spelling rather than altered spelling itself. It has not generally led to the invention of radically different new respellings and new orthographic principles, although it has diffused and magnified their use. My emphasis is less on the newness of the language and more on the newness of the literacy practices (Barton, 1994). Users are variably deregulating spelling and making idiolectal choices in relation to purposes, audiences, their own literacy identities, and technological constraints of the form/their own technoliterate competence.

As for the structure of this chapter, it starts with a definition of txt and an examination of one e-mail and two text message examples, before considering the extension of the spelling resources from which users draw in their respelling. I will develop a typology of this popular orthography and outline the factors that motivate these choices before offering a discussion of the theoretical implications.

DEFINING THE ENTITY TXT

For the purposes of this paper I am concerned with the spelling found in "txt"—that is, text entered on mobile phone pads and on keyboards in MSN Messenger and other ICT emergent text forms; related to txt used in (Internet relay chat) IRC and other digital computer-mediated communication contexts that are interpersonally and socially focused; characterized by, but not defined by, nonstandard orthography, especially in youth settings; emerging out of contexts of coconstructed interactive written discourse as distinct from composed longer documents to be read without intervening interaction; used primarily interpersonally and for socially orientated reasons rather than ideational functions in terms of Halliday's metafunctions (Halliday, 1979).

In this approach, txt respelling can be found in a number of different text forms. This working definition does not preclude teasing apart the techno-literacy modalities between e-mail and SMS, or between SMS and instant messaging, and to consider txt as an inflection of IRC chat. Any one subvariety will be better understood by situating it in the intertextuality of other ICT related emergent text forms but as I shall show in the data cited here, the differences between e-mail re-spelling and SMS respelling are less significant than the common denominators.

THREE EXAMPLES OF TXT RESPELLING

The e-mail message in Text A was written by a 12-year-old female student from Bristol to a friend using her new computer. It is an elaborate text which typifies the preparedness of young people to explore the possibilities of new digital literacies in order to present a distinctive sense of their individual and peer group identity (Carrington, 2003) and to animate written text with properties previously associated with the spoken mode (Baron, 2005). Its artful transgressions of standard English signal a covert prestige with the writer aligning herself with her peer group identity and seeking to distance herself from the conventions of standard forms, and thus from the conventions of teachers and parents. At the same time, this e-mail remains intelligible and straightforward in its referential meaning. We may not know who Pauline is, or why the writer is moving from topic to topic in such an abrupt way; we may infer the e-mail is written in response to a previous overreaction by the addressee (<Who let the dogs out?> implying "calm down" and also an allusion to a popular song of that time). But the difficulties in understanding this text lie in establishing the context of meaning in a context-dependent text that approximates the norms of informal conversation. At the level of orthographic realization the respellings are nonstandard but also conventional, accessible, and recoverable from context. There is also the sense of a text that has been designed and composed with some care. There are no casual misspellings. At points the writer is at pains to indicate missing letters with apostrophes.

The text exemplifies the kind of nonstandard orthography associated with new technology texts in general. It has been suggested that its consistent capitalization is in itself an allusion to text messaging which, in U.K. contexts in 2001, was often carried out using capital letters only. It is perhaps more extreme in its deviance than we associate with e-mail, now that e-mail has diffused into a mass practice. Other studies have shown how standard English in e-mail is shaped by its audience and purpose.

The e-mail typifies the mixed mode ICT text-type features found in e-mails, text messages, and chat, including features intimating spoken delivery: ICT conventions as initial points (trailing dots) for the kind of vague completion of utterance associated with the spoken mode; letter and number homophone respellings; phonetic spellings; graphical indicators of auditory paralinguistic features of pitch and volume; respellings suggesting accent, or at least pronunciation stylization, eye dialect ("bout"; "w'pauline"); and an alphanumerically constructed rebus showing a puzzled face.

In one subtle detail, the logos and symbols used in the signature are set out in a nonalphabetical "dingbat" font. When changed to an alphabetic font, it reveals the name of the writer (<◆⬤⬇⬆⬛⬛⬛> for <Jess>). The graphic works as a kind of code spelling.

This act of meaning-making would be severely misrepresented in a reset, spell-checked, cleaned-up typeset equivalent: the semiotic forms of the message are a part of its dramatic construction of interpersonal identity and ideational meaning.

This asynchronous e-mail was composed at leisure using a keyboard on a computer with a spellchecker. In contrast to the composed asynchronous e-mail with such facilities and ease of text entry, Text B features two "mundane" text-messaging interactions between 15-year-olds from south London. In the first, two 15-year-old girls discuss the events of the night before. In the second, one of the same girls has a social "conversation" with a boy she has met recently. Here there is a greater preponderance of nonstandard spellings, but without the compositional ingenuity and relish seen in the previous text. It is also noteworthy that one of these girls is using standard English and predictive text (<I'l> for <I'll> has been added by her to her dictionary), and the other is using manual entry. In spite of being close friends with many shared values, their practices in this respect are different. Both use the kind of slang associated with youth sociolect. In the case of the girl-boy interaction there is some inconsistency in spelling (e.g., the spelling of "school"). At the level of spelling this text is again very accessible and difficulties in understanding meaning relate to context dependency rather than orthographic obscurity. The motivation for the use of respellings will be affected more by the manner of text entry. The writers will have had less scope to compose their texts in the artful manner used by the writer of Text A. Here, skill in performance relates to sharpness in interaction. In many ways this text is utterly unremarkable text messaging spelling: nonstandard and inconsistent, yet intelligible and conventionalized. The deviant orthography is primarily driven by the technical conditions and the awkward manner of text entry. There is a minor key of affect. The shortenings may contribute to the sense of informalized digital tenor and teenager identity image. The single use of the winking emoticon allows a semiotic nuancing of meaning that moves outside the strictly linguistic, but this is the only instance of this. Taken as a whole, these two txt exchanges appear unselfconscious and routinized.

Text C is also a text message, but with a less verifiable provenance. It featured in many newspaper articles as the focus text for comments about the catastrophic effect of text messaging on young people's use of standard English. It is supposedly a text message homework response to an invitation to write about how the student spent the summer holidays. The nonstandard orthography takes a different pattern to that found in the previous two texts with a greater proportion of initialisms and graphical effects. Repeated testing of comprehension of this as a text message and in a survey of its respellings leads me to believe users see this as most unlike the kind of orthography they use in their routine text messaging and Internet chat. It is a verbal art performance stretching the conventions to the limits of intelligibility and possibly motivated by a distancing from the expectations of formal standard English as expected in school homework. While there is a certain pleasurable engagement with the ingenuity, meaning is not always recoverable from the combination of orthography and context. Several of the features are reported by my respondents as never seen before, whilst others such as <bro> are seen as vernacular respellings which would not be used in txting. This elaborated example shows by contrast the mundane intelligibility of most txt orthography of the kind found in Text B.

A TYPOLOGY OF TEXT RESPELLING

Although txt practices are heterogeneous, it can be argued the resources of nonstandard orthography are relatively homogeneous, as shown in the texts cited. In these texts and in the larger corpus from which they are drawn, there seems to be a finite set of orthographic principles that account for the overwhelming majority of txt respellings. These principles can be subdivided into three groupings that relate to motivational principles. Following the model developed by Werry's account of the linguistic features of Internet Relay Chat (Werry, 1996), there are three main motivations[1]:

- features for economy and text entry reduction;
- features for giving the respelling a simulation of spoken language; and
- features which involve a shift to multimodal visual and graphical effects and iconicity in which the linguistic sign is pushed into the periphery of meaning making.

In detail, each of these groupings consists of a number of orthographic devices. Features for economy and text entry reduction comprise such devices as:

- Omission of vowels (<gd> for <good>);
- Letter and number homophones (<r> for <are>, <2> for <to>);
- Initialisms and acronyms for key bindings and phrases (<G2G> for <got to go>);
- Clippings in which words are shortened by losing word ending (<congrats> for <congratulations>);
- Consonant reduction for medial double consonants (<imedtly> for <immediately>); and

- Respellings by analogy with other words with more straightforward sound-spelling correspondences (<thru> for <through>, <fone> for <phone>).

Features for giving the respelling a simulation of spoken language include

- Eye Dialect (<tuff> for <tough>);
- Accent simulation (<goin> for <going>, <wiv> for <with>);
- Semiotic features such as capitals to indicate paralinguistic details such as volume or emphasis (<AUFAUFAUF> for dog barking loudly);
- Stage directions in parentheses to indicate nuance (e.g., "Monsieur (said in a French accent)"); and
- Reduplication for stretched sounds for emphasis (<Soooooo>).

Features that incorporate graphical and kinaesthetic devices such as:

- Emoticons, sometimes from emoticon banks;
- Use of color, movement, pictorial imagery;
- Alphabetical rebuses such as (< @}-'-,-'--- > for a rose) (Werry 1996);
- Other special effects such as the use of text written in dingbats/web-dings or other nonalphanumeric fonts (which may come to mean in Roman alphabet when put into an alphabetical font, as in Jess's Text A e-mail signature above.

TXT ORTHOGRAPHY AS HYBRIDIZED TECHNOSOCIAL MEANING POTENTIAL

To argue that txt respelling is not new in its linguistic manifestation is not to deny the transforming meaning potentials of emergent txt forms. However, there are ways in which the linguistic trace is not altered much at the strict level of "spelling." From a social-semiotic perspective, text spelling is not simply a linguistic matter, and the electronic dimensions can function with significant semiotic potential. The language is not new, but the nature of the communication and the communication technology "literacy event" may be new. The communication practices around the events are also new, as is clear in the ethnographic and anthropological work done by Ito and others, which describe intricate practices not possible with previous technologies (Castells, Fernandez-Ardeval, Linchuan Qui, & Sey, 2004; Grinter & Eldridge, 2001; Ito, Okabe, & Matsuda,

2005; Ling & Yttri, 1999). At the level of linguistic detail the respellings and the orthographic principles underlying can be seen in other texts dating back at least to the nineteenth century. See, for example, "JC Olin Jewellery Store Contest" (1871).

MOTIVATIONS, FEATURES, AND EFFECTS OF VERNACULAR ORTHOGRAPHIES

The vernacular orthographies used in text spelling can be shown to have common features of respelling with five main mass-practice domains of use: trade names, popular culture, ICT practices, children's transitional "creative spelling," and specialized occupational shorthands. The uncodified orthographic principles underpinning the txt respelling draw from the patterns found in these popular resources and practices. These patterns and features show underlying principles although these are not codified rules. Free variation is possible whereby a word may be respelled differently by the same user in the same document.

Trade Names

There is a long-standing scholarly account of vernacular orthography and the kinds of typology associated with this. Txt spelling is amenable to the descriptive typologies found in this scholarship, most of which focuses on trade names, (Alexander, 1930; Cook, 2004a, 2004b; Davies, 1987; Pound, 1914, 1923, 1926; Praninskas, 1968). Those unfamiliar with this literature may be surprised to learn how old some of these respellings are. Alexander, writing in 1930, claimed that <U> for <you> was 30 years old then and was diffused by the use of this letter homophone in a mass market product called *Uneedabiscuit*. Pound carried out surveys of American trade names in 1913 and again in 1923 and noted an extraordinary blossoming of non-standard spelling in between her two studies. Her exemplified 1923 typology of trade names marks much the same orthographic territory as that used in text messaging and popular music.

Popular Culture

Related to trade names there is a frequent and conventionalized use of respelling in artifacts from popular culture including film, games, and music. These are popular culture domains in which nonstandard orthographic practices are common and appear to represent resistance and covert prestige. Their widespread use also demonstrates the intelligibility of these nonstandard forms to a nonspecialist mass audience. They amount to a cultural resource in collective memory, if not one much documented from the point of view of spelling. There is coverage of such spelling practices in graffiti, latrinalia, and Hip Hop (Adams & Winter, 1997; Androutsopoulos & Scholz, 1998; Romiti, 1998). More recently there has been work in developing a sociolinguistic account of orthography (Sebba, 2002, 2007).

To take the case of pop music, it is common knowledge that respelling is frequent. Millions of items of popular music media have been purchased by millions of people over the past 50 years. These media have routinely contained respellings and must be considered, along with trade names and advertising, to be offering a ubiquitous experience of vernacular spelling. From the current orthographic word play (for example around <parrowdice> for <paradise>) in Hip Hop and Grime, back to the documentary field recordings of *Negro prison songs* by Alan Lomax and others in the 1930s, pop music has been strongly influenced by African American and African Caribbean varieties, and the re-spelled representations of those varieties. These resources have been recycled by white European and U.S. artists so it is not just a Black vernacular English phenomenon. From Eminem's rap to *Get yer Ya Yas Out* and *Gimme Shelter* by the Rolling Stones, now nearly 40 years old, back to the respellings in early twentieth century African American genres, starting with work songs, blues, jazz, gospel, rhythm and blues, the White makeover of rock'n'roll, and the related genres of ska, rocksteady, dub, lovers rock, and reggae: pop music has consistently used re-spelling as a matter of course. It is not just hybridized African American and African Caribbean. It is seen too in the titles and lyrics of White working class groups such as the English 1970s group Slade (in itself playing on standard English <slayed>). These musical genres and their respelled documentary framings of artist names, collection and song titles, lyrics, and sleeve notes are in so many homes, though the phenomenon is little written about. Such studies as there are develop a sociolinguistic model in which nonstandard orthography allows the development of the kind of covert prestige associated with nonstandard accent and dialect features.

Children's Transitional "Creative Spelling"

There are many overlaps between the features of children's creative spelling and transitional nonstandard orthography (Bissex, 1988; Kress, 2001; Read, 1986; Treiman, 1993) and the linguistic coverage of trade-names referred to above. Children's creative spelling often locates the same pressure points in English, regularizing more complex phoneme/ grapheme correspondences: <nite> for <night>, <becoz> for <because>, <gnys at wrk> for <genius at work>.

Children's transitional orthographies are almost inevitable developmental experiences for every person literate in English. They are not just seen in other younger users but reside in memory as trace of personal biography. The experience is inevitable, because learning English spelling necessitates encountering "competing" spelling principles and illegal (non-English) letter string sequences of loan word etyma (such as <psy> for /si/ or <ph> for /f (Albrow, 1972; Carney, 1994; Cook, 2004b). The particular nature of etymological and morphological prioritization in standard English spelling makes for a double system of sound-spelling and morphological-etymological realizations.

Kress has demonstrated the creativity and confusion this causes in his close analysis of the challenges children encounter in "loan words" with etyma drawn from other orthographic systems (Kress, 2001). The agency of seventeenth century lexicographers and the deep orthography they created has bearings on what gets re-spelt in vernacular orthography and in txt. English spelling is often based on etymological and morphological motivation rather than simple sound spelling correspondences (Brengelman, 1980; Carney, 1994; Scragg, 1974). This leads to certain likely respellings in which a phonologically unlikely spelling attracts a regularization to phonetic correspondence. For example: <nite> for <night>, <wot> for <what>, <fone> for <phone>. Some of these respellings occur as conventionalized respellings in popular texts written for children, such as comics like *The Beano*.

Emergent ICT Text Forms

There is an orthographic intertextuality in spelling practices developed by users across a range of ICT emergent text forms including software programmers argot and the emergent text forms of e-mail, Internet chat, SMS, and instant messaging. These text forms may have situational constraints of awkward text entry or limitations in message size. As emergent text forms they have less determinate space and expectations of adherence to conventions than those expected in pen-and-paper letters. Carrington refers to one subvariety of this ICT-situated orthography as "squeeze text," a term used for spellings produced by the automatic production of shortened forms by software for abbreviated language use in specialized computer contexts which restrict the size of the message (Carrington, 2003). From a less technical standpoint ICT has spawned a variety of emergent text forms with new and unfamiliar contexts of composition, text entry, and interaction. In many cases these have been innovated by younger users and those with specialized technical knowledge. In many cases they have been associated with informalization and nonstandard spelling. The existence of this profusion of text forms has created an orthographic intertextuality by which users are aware of varied ways of spelling and more relaxed social attitudes toward spelling in emergent ICT text forms (e.g., SMS, MSN), especially given the relaxed digital tenor associated with these forms (Posteguillo, 2003). This context destabilizes existing expectations about the need to write using standard English spelling and formal tone. The respellings function as an interpersonal marker of informalized rapport.

Codified and Uncodified Shorthand

There is a fifth context in text-shortening practices adopted in specialized contexts. Codified varieties such as Pitman shorthand, the shortened language used in telegraphy and related contexts and identified by Sinclair as "basic English." Uncodified abbreviated respellings used in impromptu occupational procedures in which there is much repetition—the clippings and other shortenings used by teachers and markers of public examinations in their marginal annotations, to give just one example: <Punct> for punctuation and so on. Again, these shorthands are based on principles of simplification and reduction related to the kinds of shortening found in txt. These are longstanding practices not confined to ICT: in 1930 Alexander compared the shortenings of trade names with the shortenings used in simplified spelling schemes.

THE EFFECTS AND AFFECTS OF RESPELLING

In many accounts of respelling in ICT contexts, there is a practical emphasis on the value of respelling in reducing the demands of text entry: this is almost a default explanation (Hard af Segerstad, 2002). Respelling can also alter the meaning potential of the sign and invest it in dimensions of vivid engagement and affect that would not be available in standard forms. In her study of trade names, Praninskas cites a memorable image taken from I. A. Richards, likening the psychosocial effect of respelling to that of walking over flat, even ground giving way to difficult terrain, with all the attendant refocusing and emotional re-engagement (Praninksas, 1968). Katakoa has argued similarly about the effect of orthographic and graphological innovations and transgressions in informal letter writing (Katakoa, 1997, 2003). Respellings re-embody the linguistic sign, defamiliarize reading experiences formed mainly in practices which engage with standard English orthography, and can be powerful in eliciting active, engaged modes of rereading and decoding. In particular, respelling can embody text with simulations of spoken effects, often with complex psychosocial nuances of emotional affect (Besnier, 1993; Jaffe, 2000a). Respelling can index social, political and cultural stances and dispositions including oppositional stances and covert prestige (Androutsopoulos, 2000; Androutsopoulos & Georgakopoulou, 2002). It can take ludic forms that invoke delight and playful absorption in the manner of the popular appeal of word games and puzzles (Cook, 2000; Crystal, 1993). Respelling can be used as part of identity performance in the context of a society in which identities are multiple and managed (Carrington, 2005b; Carrington & Marsh 2005c; Smith & Kollock, 1999). Respelling nonetheless remains bound to its relationship with the standard orthographic iteration: it feeds off the formal linguistic patterns and naturalized social prestige connotations of the standard forms (Jaffe, 2000a, 2000b; Sebba, 1998, 2007). Spelling performance continues to act as a shibboleth that gatekeeps access to educational resources reproducing social class-differentiated access to resources and life chances through the meritocratic "playing field" of competitive public examinations and the looking glass world of social penalties for failure (Cameron, 1995; Carney, 1994; Carrington, 2003, 2004, 2005a).

THE NORMATIVE ORTHOGRAPHIC PALETTE
AND THE EXTENDED ORTHOGRAPHIC PALETTE

From the evidence of the texts examined here, and my collection of messages and interviews, txt respelling practices are far from homogeneous and there are marked variations between users, even within the practices of a single user, within and across their txts. My data sets show idiolectal variation over the sociolinguistic clines of class gender and ethnicity, and across the lines of age. To use a phrase like "the language of Txt" masks practices and events that are highly specific in their motivation in a particular instantiation. Txt spelling is a matter of options, but it is also a matter of choices made in the context of complex and varied day-to-day practices, identity positions and immediate practical discourse-in-place contexts.

I suggest the metaphor of "the orthographic palette" as a model for understanding the actual heterogeneity in the use of txt respelling conventions. That is, the choices available for spelling words. As I have argued, in disturbing the preexisting configurations of what counts as spelling, ICT/txt has disturbed the print standardization settlement by which only standard English spelling has recognition as an available choice in public writing: a binary with any other choice constructed as a deficit form, motivated by eccentricity, esoteric contexts, partial formation, or by incompetence.

To develop the analogy, the normative orthographic palette offers the normative options of the English writing system and its constituents as described by Carney, Albrow, and others. It is codified in dictionaries such as the Concise Oxford Dictionary or those found in spellcheckers. Other types of spelling such as prestandardization spellings, children's transitional orthographies, and spellings used in popular culture are not available for public writing and would be considered deficient spelling in terms of standard English accuracy. This ecology of orthographic varieties is a discarded option: seen but with no recognition of it as an available option except for private or low status contexts.

The frequency and ubiquity of txt language has moved this ecology on to the palette in a set of extended options for users. Standard English spelling is available, and often used, along with the options and meaning potentials of vernacular orthography and its provenances. As argued, re-spellings have different meaning potentials from those found in standard English (including consequences for effect, affect, and intertextuality).

THE "FORCE FIELDS" THAT ACT ON
USER CHOICES OF RE/SPELLING

In determining the choices of spellings to be made from the "extended orthographic palette," users are subject to a number of pressures or "force fields" that impact on their choices: "technoliteracy"; "literacy identity"; "audience and purpose"; and discourse-in-place constraints of time, place, and text entry convenience. These schematized "force fields" are now examined in turn.

"Technoliteracy": ICT Affordance/Potential Capability

The ICT affordances and enhancements made available and the user's "techno-literacy" in being able to access these features limit what can be done. They have inevitable consequences for orthographic control and choices. A measure of "technoliterate" familiarity with mobile phone procedures is necessary even to be able to enter text in a phone pad. Other determining factors include user's knowledge of, and access to, banks of emoticons, phone spelling dictionaries, or the device which determines whether the user is in predictive text mode. To give two specific instances: some of my users routinely entered their textisms into their mobile phone dictionaries and wrote in nonstandard forms using predictive text; other users were unable to use predictive text and were constrained to awkward manual entry and its pressure toward shortenings. These novice problems are there for all users at some point in their technoliteracy biographical trajectories and are shown graphically in truncated fragmentary/text messages and comments from absolute beginners.

Literacy Identity: Spelling "Stakes"

To learn to spell in standard English is not an easy accomplishment: the attainment has been compared with learning musical notation. Accurate standard English "performativity" is a key requirement and guiding objective of the literacy curriculum in school. Many users have notions of self-esteem and identity bound up in their literacy identity as a speller and the literacy dispositions of toleration and acceptance they show towards other people's spelling. Nonstandard spelling can be a matter of "high stakes" for personal and professional identity: an inhibition for the accomplished and less-accomplished. My respondents had markedly different attitudes towards their need to use standard forms. I am regularly told by academics that they make no use of non-standard forms in their txts. This may not be surprising given the value and currency of standard English accomplishment in academe. However, such choices were not necessarily related to age or literacy accomplishment in simple direct correspondence. Some younger users used predictive standard English text spelling, claiming they did not like the "gangsta" covert prestige of nonstandard respelling. Some older users, including those with higher degrees in linguistics, were happy to use extreme shortenings. Some teacher trainees were at ease with txt respellings, but were concerned to use punctuation and syntax with standard English accuracy. One linguistics graduate, working as a teacher, took an extreme and censorious attitude toward both nonstandard spelling and the use of nonpredictive text, believing these to be trivial and unevolved practices. The point is that txt respelling is an idiolectal choice related in part to attitudes and beliefs about the users' literacy identity, in turn related to beliefs about orthography, standard English, identity, and social (and technoliterate) accomplishment. There is a variation in these idiolectal choices that cuts across social clines of age, gender, and educational attainment.

Audience, Purpose, Context, Penalty

Audience, purpose, and context (social expectations of public discourse) all influence the level of insistence on the use of standard orthographic forms. In formal institutional and public contexts, there is a strong expectation that spelling will be "accurate" standard English and users may moderate their use of txt respelling in relation to audience. This accommodation may be surprisingly pragmatic and innovative. For example, taking the example of capitalization conventions rather than re-spelling, one university researcher reported that she used lower-case writing in all contexts except in her editing of a journal and when writing to academics whom she did not know. As a "touch typist," it suited her to write at maximum speed without the redundant markers of capitalization. As a researcher she was confident about her literacy identity: accommodation to the standard form was only necessary when there was a social penalty accruing from the audience and context. Given txt often occurs in dyadic informal exchange, this pressure is less marked in SMS and MSN than it might be in e-mail. But this account typifies the way users are mediating and filtering the affordances of ICT in relation to audience.

PHYSICAL CONSTRAINT OF TEXT ENTRY/TIME AVAILABLE

ICT technical contexts can carry situational constraints of awkward text entry, and the effort needed to "get things right" must be traded off against the practical exigencies of a situation. Earlier in the histories of ICTs, the keyboard itself would have been associated with a kind of skilled accomplishment particular to someone who had undergone specific training, as in the question "Can you type?" In some cases the need for speed arises out of social expectations that interactive written discourse in MSN will be "quickfire," short entries and in real time. Other times it is the raw physical difficulty of text entry. The practical constraints of the message construction may affect the use of respelling. Composing a txt message in a hurry on a train may lead to a different pattern of respelling than composing it comfortably at home with no time pressure.

DISCUSSION: STANDARD ENGLISH SPELLING, THE PRESCRIPTIVIST MODEL AND *"UNREGIMENTED WRITING"*

Standard language spelling has been ubiquitous in the age of print. As Cameron has shown, the expectation of a consistent standard language uniformity in spelling was a practice developed during the emergence of print literacy and the nation state regulation of a standard language (Cameron, 1995). Printing houses developed strict craft practices for ensuring consistency in spelling in the interests of what Cameron terms verbal hygiene. The variation in the spelling of words documented in historical dictionaries underwent a narrowing as the spelling of any word was cut down to a single acceptable form. Spelling was either standard and correct or nonstandard and deficient. This followed the linguistic pre-scriptivist model associated with the codification of language in the seventeenth and eighteenth centuries and attracted the notion of spelling performance as objectively measurable and freestanding from social motivations. This model of spelling could be considered as the orthographic instantiation of what Brian Street has termed "autonomous literacy" (Street, 1984, 1993).

In the postprint age of unregimented writing in informal contexts, the spelling practices associated with the age of print appear to be giving way to a looser, more permeable sense of what counts as spelling. Spelling is becoming a deployment of choices from a range of options including the standard English form among others. It is a matter of appropriacy and identity rather than a matter of rectitude and uniformity. It is a shift to a model of orthography as a semiotic resource adapted and inflected by users to re/make their meanings and identity positions. This is a model akin to Street's definition of ideological literacy in which literary choices can only be understood in terms of social functions and context, not autonomous regulation for its own sake (Street, 1993).

Users' choices from the orthographic palette are choices made from a range of spelling conventions and orthographic principles rather than choices from a palette of free variation in which all options are available. As Cook and others have shown, vernacular orthographies are seldom haphazard and often present logical alternative systems to those used in standard forms (Cook, 2004b). The patterns of respelling found in emergent ICT text forms—and there appears to be relatively little difference between the kinds of re-spelling used in the different forms—show a high degree of linguistic convention, logic, and commonality. Many of the spelling choices, the majority of words in most contexts, continue to follow a standard English default.

In this analysis the Internet, and digital communication generally, have not revolutionized spelling in the sense of altering the possibilities of respelling linguistically. But they have revolutionized what counts as spelling by legitimizing and popularizing longstanding vernacular orthographic practices found in popular and domestic culture but underrepresented in public, academic and media accounts of language use, and in linguistic corpora, that largely draw from texts spelt in standard English. There is not much new about vernacular spelling features such as vowel deletion, the use of homophones, phonetic spelling, accent stylizations, eye dialect, and the other features listed earlier.

The case of spelling has a bearing on how we may think of the impact of the Internet and netlinguistics. Some of the discourse around this prioritizes the historical discontinuity and novelty of the effect of ICT on language and linguistic study. In popular discourse much has been made of the analogy of revolution in such collocations as the *information revolution*: it may be more appropriate to think of the metaphoric force of deregulation, reregulation, and cultural flows associated with a networked society (Carrington, 2005a). The vernacular spelling used in netlinguistic and digital contexts is predictable, norm-related, ubiquitous, and culturally allusive. In considering the emerging development of Internet language, it is necessary to recognize the vast scale and immeasurable frequency of informalized interactive written discourse in txt. Such texts, which I term unregimented writing, are ungated by the institutional forces of traditional education, print technology, and employment. In analyzing data it is not easy to show how such language use is revolutionary, although aspects of it may be unexpected. However it is possible to make a case for the ICT disrupting and reconfiguring the cultural flows feeding into spelling choices and making spelling less of a prescriptivist expectation.

APPENDIX

Text A

WHO LET THE DOGS OUT?
AUF,AUFAUFAUFAUF!!!!!!!!!!!!!!

N E WAY 2 GET THE COOLSTUFF AT THE SIDE GO 2 FORMAT AND THEN STATIONARY THERES LOADS OF WICKED 1S

YES I DID NO 'BOUT ANDYS DAD TEACHIN U.................HM.

```
            33333
        { 0       0 }
            2


        _ _ _ _
```

SERIOUSLY U HAVE 2 CHANGE MY LIFE I DON'T CARE WHAT YOU DO JUST DO IT...........................

BOUT JUDE JUST GET HER ALONE AN SAY WHAT UVE BEEN SAYIN TO ME. SHE IS PISSED OFF W' PAULINE AS WELL U NO...........................

N E WAY BETTER GO HIT ME BACK YALL K?

LOTS OF HATE

ROSIE.... ☺ ⬱ ♦♦ .... ⬆ ☀⬇🏘️🏘️🏘️

Text B

MANA:
Hey Gems,how ru?How was last nite?Hope u had a gd time..;)I herd the party was rele bad...ppl had an awful time!I guess I shud b glad I didn't go afta all...tbXx
REPLY:
Hey babe I had a lovely time, i'l tell you about it another time...
Yeah I don't know how everyone managed to have such a shit time, thats the gorbeney girls way! Shall I call you tomorrow, and we can have a big us chat to make up for the last two weeks? X
MANA:
It's a date.Speak 2 u 2moz, beast Xx

JASON:
Urite its Jason from the comon.How r u? Wot u bin up 2 2day? Tb luv Jason
MANA:
Oh,hi!Im great thanx,u?Not alot,my day was ok,nothing special.how was urs?
REPLY:
Yeah same.was ok.what did u get up 2 after da party?where did u go?
MANA:
erm went sumwhere else 2 meet sum of my friends but we wer rele late so they had gone so then we jus went back 2 my mates house n stayed there.u?
REPLY:
Went 2 a pub 4 a bit...lol
MANA:
lol,u got served?so do u go 2 boardin school?
REPLY:
Na we got kicked out cuz it was closing. No I don't go boarding skl u?
MANA:
Aw shame.Nope, normal school.
REPLY:
Yeh I go normal skl 2.lol.
MANA:
anyways sorry but I g2g now.Nice talking, ill cya around x

Text C

My smmrhols wr CWOT, B4,we usd 2go2 NY 2C my bro, his GF & 3:- @ kds FTF, ILNY, it's a gr8 plc.
Bt my Ps wr so (:-/ BC o 9/11 tht they dcdd 2 stay in SCO & spnd 2 wkd up N.
Up N, WUCIWUG – 0. I ws vvv brd in Mon. 0 bt baas & ^ ^ ^ ^ ^ ^.
AAR8, my Ps wr ☺ - they sd ICBW, & tht they wr ha-p 4 the pc&qt...IDTS!! I wntd 2 go hm ASAP, 2C my m8s again.
2day, I cam bk 2 skool. I feel v O☺ BC I hv dn all my hm wrk. Now it's BAU

NOTE

1. Compare Thurlow "While young people are surely using their mobile phones as a novel, creative means of enhancing and supporting intimate relationships and existing social networks, popular discourses about the linguistic exclusivity and impenetrability of this particular technologically-mediated discourse appear greatly exaggerated. Serving the sociolinguistic 'maxims' of (a) brevity and speed, (b) paralinguistic restitution and (c) phonological approximation, young people's messages are both linguistically unremarkable and communicatively adept" (Thurlow, 2003). This paper follows Werry's and Thurlow's scheme.

REFERENCES

Adams, K., & A. Winter. (1997). Gang graffiti as a discourse genre. *Journal of Sociolinguistics, 1*(3), 337-360.

Albrow, K. H. (1972). *The English writing system: Notes towards a description*. London: Longman.

Alexander, D. M. (1930). Why not "u" for "you"? *American Speech, 5*, 24-26.

Androutsopoulos, J., & Georgakopoulou, A. (2002). *Discourse constructions of youth identities*. Amsterdam: John Benjamins.

Androutsopoulos, J. K. (2000). Non-standard spellings in media texts: The case of German fanzines. *Journal of Sociolinguistics, 4*(4), 514-533.

Androutsopoulos, J. K., & Sholz, A. (Eds.) (1998). *Jugendsprache- lange des jeunes-youth language: Linguistische und soziolinguistische perspektiven. VarioLingua non-standard-standard-substandard* [Linguistic and sociolinguistic perspectives: Varieties of language non-standard and substandard.]. Frankfurt, Germany: Peter Lang.

Baron, N. S. (2005). The written turn. *English language and linguistics, 9*(2), 359-76.

Barton, D. (1994). *Literacy: An introduction to the ecology of written language*. Oxford, England: Blackwell.

Besnier, N. (1993). Literacy and feelings: The encoding of affect in Nukulaelae letters. In B. Street (Ed.), *Cross-cultural approaches to literacy* (pp. 62-86). Cambridge: Cambridge University Press.

Bissex, G. L. (1988). *GNYS AT WRK: A child learns to write and read.* Cambridge, MA: Harvard University Press.

Brengelman, F. H. (1980). Orthopeists, printers, and the rationalization of English spelling. *Journal of English and German Philology, 79*, 332-354.

Cameron, D. (1995). *Verbal hygiene.* London: Routledge.

Carney, E. (1994). *A survey of English spelling.* London: Routledge.

Carrington, V. (2003). Texts and literacies of the Shi Jinrui. *British Journal of Sociology of Education, 25*(2), 215-228.

Carrington, V. (2004). Txting: The end of civilization (again)? *Cambridge Journal of Education, 5*(2), 161-175.

Carrington, V. (2005a). New textual landscapes, information and early literacy. In J. Marsh (Ed.), *Popular culture, new media and digital literacy in early childhood* (pp. 13-27). London: Routledge Falmer.

Carrington, V. (2005b). The uncanny, digital texts and literacy. *Language and Education, 19*(6), 467-482.

Carrington, V., & J. Marsh. (2005). Digital childhood and youth: New texts, new literacies. *Discourse: Studies in the cultural politics of education, 26*(3), 279-285.

Castells, M., Fernandez-Ardeval, M., Linchuan Qui, J., & Sey, A. (2004, October). *The mobile communication society: A cross-cultural analysis of available evidence on the social uses of wireless communication technology.* Research report prepared for the International Workshop on Wireless Communication Policies and Prospects: A Global Perspective, University of Southern California, Los Angeles.

Cook, G. (2000). *Language play, language learning.* New York: Oxford University Press USA.

Cook, V. (2004a). *Accomodating brocolli in the cemetary.* London: Profile Books.

Cook, V. (2004b). *The English eriting system.* London: Hodder Arnold.

Crystal, D. (1993). *Language play.* London: Penguin.

Crystal, D. (2004). *A glossary of netspeak and textspeak.* Edinburgh: Edinburgh University Press.

Davies, E. E. (1987). Eyeplay: On some uses of non-standard spelling. *Language and Communication, 7*(1), 47-58.

Grinter, R. E., & Eldridge, M. A. (2001, September). y do tngrs luv 2 txt msg? Paper presented at the Seventh European Conference on Computer-Supported Cooperative Work, Bonn, Germany.

Halliday, M. A. K. (1979). *Language as social semiotic: The social interpretation of language and meaning.* London: Edward Arnold.

Hard af Segerstad, Y. (2002). *Use and adaptation of written language to the conditions of computer-mediated communication.* Unpublished doctoral thesis, Goteborg University, Sweden.

Ito, M., Okabe, D., & Matsuda, M. (Eds.) (2005). *Personal, portable, pedestrian: Mobile phones in Japanese life.* Cambridge, MA: MIT.

Jaffe, A. (2000a). Non-standard orthography and non-standard speech. *Journal of Sociolinguistics, 4*(4), 497-513.

Jaffe, A. (2000b). The voices people read: Orthography and nonstandard representation of speech. *Journal of Sociolinguistics, 4*(4), 561-88.

JC Olin Jewellery Store Contest: Alphabetical and Pictorial Rebus Puzzle, from JC Olin Jewellery Store Contest. (n.d.). Retrieved June 3, 2006, from: http://theoldentimes.com/rebus2.html

Katakoa, K. (1997). Affect and letter writing: Unconventional conventions in casual speech by young Japanese women. *Language in Society, 26*, 103-136.

Katakoa, K. (2003). Emotion and youth identities in personal letter writing: An analysis of pictorial signs and unconventional punctuation. In J. K. Androutsopoulos & A. Georgakopoulou (Eds.), *Discourse constructions of youth identities* (pp. 122-149). Amsterdam: John Benjamins.

Kress, G. (2001). *Early spelling; Between convention and creativity*. London: Routledge.

Ling, R., & Yttri, B. (1999). Nobody sits at home and waits for the telephone to ring: Micro and hyper-coordination through the use of the mobile phone. Oslo, Norway: Telenor Research and Development.

Posteguillo, S. (2003). *Netlinguistics: An analytical framework to study language, discourse and ideology in Internet*. Castello De La Plana, Spain: Publicacions de la Universitat de Jaume.

Pound, L. (1914). Word coinage and American trade names. *Dialect Notes, 4*, 29.

Pound, L. (1923). Spelling-manipulation and present-day advertising. *Dialect Notes 5*, 226-232.

Pound, L. (1926). The kraze for K. *American Speech, 1*, 43-44.

Praninskas, J. (1968). *Trade-name creation: Processes and patterns*. The Hague, The Netherlands: Mouton.

Read, C. (1986). *Children's creative spelling*. London: Routledge and Kegan Paul.

Romiti, S. (1998). The mural writings of the young in Rome. In J. K. Androutsopoulos & A. Sholz (Eds.), Jugendsprache- lange des jeunes-youth language: Linguistische und soziolinguistische perspektiven. Variolingua nonstandard-standard-substandard [Linguistic and sociolinguistic perspectives: Varieties of language non-standard and substandard.] (pp. 281-304). Frankfurt, Germany: Peter Lang.

Scragg, D. G. (1974). *A history of English spelling*. Manchester, England: Manchester University Press.

Sebba, M. (1998). Phonology meets ideology: the meaning of orthographic practices in British creole. *Language Problems and Language Planning, 22*(1), 19-47.

Sebba, M. (2002). *Spelling rebellion*. In J. Androutsopoulos & A. J. Georgakopoulou (Eds.), *Discourse constructions of youth identities* (pp. 151-172). Amsterdam: Benjamins.

Sebba, M. (2007). *Spelling culture: Political, social and cultural aspects of orthography around the world*. Cambridge, England: Cambridge University Press.

Smith, M. A., & Kollack, P. (Eds.). (1999). *Communities in cyberspace*. London: Routledge.

Street, B. (1984). *Literacy in theory and practice*. Cambridge, England: Cambridge University Press.

Street, B. (1993). *Cross-cultural approaches to literacy*. Cambridge, England: Cambridge University Press.

Thurlow, C. (2003). Generation txt? The (socio-)linguistics of young people's text-messaging. *Discourse Analysis Online*. Retrieved June 22, 2008, from http://www.shu.ac.UK/daol/articles/v1/n1/a3/thurlow2002003-paper.html

Treiman, R. (1993). *Beginning to spell: A study of first-grade children*. Oxford, England: Blackwell.

Werry, C. C. (1996) Linguistic and interactional features of Internet relay chat. In S. Herring (Ed.), *Computer-mediated communication: Linguistic, social and cross-cultural perspectives* (pp. 47-63). Amsterdam: John Benjamins.

CHAPTER 16

THE CULTURAL IMPACT OF E-LEARNING AND INTRANETS ON CORPORATE EMPLOYEES

David Guralnick and Deb Larson

INTRODUCTION

The shift to e-learning in large companies has had a significant influence on employee culture, one that differs radically from how these same employees view and use technology in their everyday lives. Outside of work, the Internet has opened up a world of creativity and individuality for many; think of the success of blogs, MySpace, and YouTube. And thanks to text messaging, instant messaging, and blog comments, it has never been easier for people to communicate and collaborate. In corporations, however—and particularly in the e-learning world—quite the reverse has occurred: the emphasis has been on controlling employees by force-feeding them courses and information, as well as tracking their training.

Although e-learning has exceptional potential to foster creativity—for example, by enabling people to collaborate with one another and by using rich simulations to teach critical thinking—companies seldom put these approaches into practice. More often, learning management systems and page-turning courses predominate, complemented by an ava-

Connected Minds, Emerging Cultures: Cybercultures in Online Learning
pp. 247–260
Copyright © 2009 by Information Age Publishing

lanche of online information, little of which is structured or written to help employees work successfully. Thus, employees have come to perceive e-learning—and its digital sibling, the corporate intranet—as necessary evils at work: dehumanizing, rather than humanizing; limiting, rather than liberating.

In this chapter, we describe the current state of employee cyberculture and suggest that companies would be far better off to use a strategic design approach to e-learning and corporate intranets, one based on helping employees and engaging them in their work. By doing so, companies will be able to integrate technology into employees' work lives in a way that improves their performance and boosts their morale and commitment.

A BRIEF HISTORY OF CORPORATE E-LEARNING AND INTRANETS

To see how corporate e-learning has shaped employee cyberculture over the years, let's begin with a brief history of the online learning movement.

E-Learning Before the World Wide Web

In the early-to-mid 1990s, corporate e-learning was uncharted territory, populated by a handful of imaginative and impassioned course designers and their coconspirators, the progressive organizations that financed their efforts. These designers—often well-schooled in educational theory, computer science, cognitive psychology, and the emerging field of computer usability—invented custom e-learning initiatives to help client organizations achieve business goals (for example, "improving the speed and friendliness of front-line customer service") and teach employees specific skills (for example, "here's how to be fast and friendly").

Although this online instruction was based on accepted pedagogy, it was anything but conventional. Rich and robust simulations gave employees the chance to work through realistic job scenarios; sophisticated online reference tools dispensed procedural advice to workers in just the right doses; and storytelling systems allowed seasoned employees to pass their wisdom to the next generation. But no matter which educational approach designers chose, they unfailingly aimed to create learning experiences that were immediate, engrossing, and genuine.

To convey the essence of a job, designers dreamt up computer interfaces that expertly balanced form and function, style and substance. To create realism, they insisted on lively instructional writing and made liberal use of true-to-life video and audio. And to make sure these online learning products actually worked, they collaborated with computer programmers and testers before burning the final version to a CD-ROM or installing it on a hard drive.

The seminal products from this inspired and experimental period showed that e-learning could do more than just "train" employees:

- The Directory Assistance Training System, a learn-by-doing simulation described in Guralnick (1996) and Schank (1997), improved the speed of service employees delivered, which saved the sponsoring company five million dollars each year.
- The Boston Chicken Cashier Trainer, developed in 1991 and described in Guralnick (1996) showed that training for a mundane task—in this case, ringing up orders on a fast food cash register—could be both enjoyable and educationally effective.
- And finally, CD-ROM-based performance-support systems, such as ones used by IBM salespeople (see Schank, 1997, for more detail), provided just-in-time job assistance in a way that employees perceived as helpful to them.

To be sure, e-learning was not just educating employees; it was actually transforming their work lives. Learning with computers was cutting-edge and cool, action-packed and irresistible, and (dare we say it?) fun!

Despite these heady successes, the inventive era of e-learning had limited impact on the corporate world. Unfortunately, innovation is seldom widespread; it involves a dedicated and determined few who are willing to take sizable risks and stomach disappointing failures, all in the name of progress. Corporations often accept these risks to develop a product for the marketplace, but it takes a special company to do the same for an "employee" product, where measuring the return on investment can be difficult. Thus, in this nascent phase of e-learning, only companies with genuine commitment to employee learning and job performance ended up taking the leap of faith.

But for the few organizations that did believe, the rewards were substantial. They sold more products and served their customers better. They improved their day-to-day execution and saved more money. Their employees had more know-how and know-why. And above all, these organizations were enriching and elevating their workplace cultures. The future of e-learning, it seemed, held nothing but promise.

E-LEARNING AFTER THE WORLD WIDE WEB

In the late 1990s, when the World Wide Web exploded into ubiquity, companies quickly adopted this technology to create their own corporate intranets. In theory, the intranet was a well-organized virtual library where employees could find the information they would need to do their jobs. In practice, however, most were nothing more than digital labyrinths that led employees from one dead end to another.

The rise of the corporate intranet had profound and dramatic consequences for e-learning. All those lessons learned during the early trailblazing days—the importance of a goal-based approach, the need for educational soundness, the significance of fun—fell by the wayside, completely overrun by a new phenomenon: the mad (and maddening) rush to "put training online."

Eschewing strategic thinking for the specious benefit of "speed of implementation," companies took on the e-learning cause in an abrupt and odd way, mostly bent on replacing passé CD-ROM training with fashionable intranet learning. Almost overnight, e-learning went from entrepreneurial movement to enterprisewide institution, with these unfavorable consequences:

- *Data reigned supreme.* The emphasis of e-learning shifted from improving job performance—and enriching employee culture—to collecting cold, hard data. The learning management system (LMS), with its focus on tracking employee training and scheduling courses, became the cornerstone for many corporate e-learning "strategies."
- *E-learning turned into Big Business.* With visions of becoming the next Microsoft, players without any background in cognitive psychology, education, or computer usability—indeed, the very disciplines that made early e-learning so promising—rushed into the industry to grab a share of the revenue pie. In particular, technology companies and marketing firms gained dominant footholds.

Unfortunately, this techno-centric, business-first approach robbed e-learning of its very soul. The humanity and vitality that made up its essence disappeared, displaced by software applications that dictated when and how employees would learn. The bond that unified employees, company goals, and learning products ruptured and bled; the greater whole they had created withered away into nonspecific courseware that failed to inspire employees and elevate their workplace culture.

To illustrate this sad decline, one need look no further than the definitive vehicle for "putting training online," the page-turner. In these educational gems, employees were forced to read information on a screen, then click the Next button to do more of the same. Courses often had 50 or 60 screens; some pushed the tedium limit by surpassing the century mark. The most sophisticated page-turners had a few graphics or audio files interspersed throughout, and if employees were really lucky, the course might even feature "interactivity"—usually code for blocks of multiple-choice or true-false test questions.

Despite their pedestrian and educationally impoverished design, page-turners became a smash hit with many corporate training departments. Compared with the ambitious and imaginative online simulation, these read-and-click courses were simpler for trainers to conceptualize; easier for learning management systems and databases to track; mercifully devoid of "technically troublesome" video to stream on the corporate intranet; and less time-consuming and expensive to build.

But more often that not, page-turning courses ended up disappointing management and missing the mark with workers. Annoyed by their simplistic and often condescending approach, employees neither enjoyed nor learned from these online bore fests. As for management, it soon learned that although these courses were inexpensive to produce, they rarely helped improve employee job performance or the numbers on the bottom line—in short, they were bad for business. Most distressing, however, was that these page-turning courses and the learning management systems that tracked them turned employees (and many of their bosses) against e-learning. Cynicism superseded hope, and employee cyberculture took a giant step backwards.

E-LEARNING IN CORPORATIONS TODAY

After having lived through the dark ages of "putting training online," it seems that many companies are now searching for a bit of e-learning enlightenment. Encouragingly, they have railed against the exorbitant pricing and overwrought functionality of learning management systems, and they have come to recognize that that the dreary online courses in use today are not doing much for employee performance or morale. So even though the strides are small, we have some forward movement.

But to recapture the magic from the halcyon days of early e-learning, companies need to recognize that today's e-learning still suffers from two major problems:

First, *e-learning disproportionately emphasizes technology*, and does so at the cost of sound educational theory, clear and compelling writing, and a goal-based approach to designing online learning. Information technology (or IT) departments often play an influential role in intranet and e-learning work, but the problem is that they lack expertise in adult education and computer usability. Thus, e-learning products and intranet sites seldom suit the tasks employees need to perform, and both are rife with foolish design consistencies, such as the use of nested hierarchical menus for content structures that are way too large in scale and depth.

And second, *e-learning continues to fixate on upfront training*, or training that takes place before employees are on the job. Workers are getting way too much education way too soon, and when they return to the job, they have already forgotten most of what they've learned.

Thanks to this near obsession with technology and training, most employees have now come to adopt one of these attitudes toward online learning and information:

- Intranets and e-learning could be good, but right now my company's approach isn't addressing my needs.
- Intranets and e-learning will never be able to help me, so I'd rather not deal with them.

What's most striking—indeed, shocking—here is the stark contrast between how employees perceive the Web at work and how they see it outside of corporate walls. How can the former be boring and useless, while the latter is inexorably linked with fun and personal empowerment?

The answer, it seems, can be found in how people relate to technology. People get excited about new technology when it helps them do something they care about, in a way that makes them feel good; indeed, the product fulfils a visceral, rational, and emotional human need (Norman, 1988). For example, consider the iPod. You can do something you want to do (take lots of music with you), and you can do it in a way that connects with you, makes you feel comfortable. The same is true of Google (the search is something people want to do, and it works simply and easily) or Facebook (it lets people connect and communicate with one another in an enjoyable and elegant way). What creates all these positive feelings is excellent design: not only does the product look and feel right to you, but it also lets you do you want to do—quickly, easily, successfully.

Unfortunately, we have found few corporate intranets or e-learning products that people similarly embrace, yet there's no good reason for this paucity of affection. In fact, one could argue that the opposite should be true: it should be much *easier* to conceive and build first-rate online experiences for employees (as compared with society as a whole), because designers are dealing with the restricted context of a work environment, one where it is much simpler to zero in on employee needs and preferences. But somehow, companies fail to see this, and insipid online products remain the corporate norm.

What companies must understand is this: (1) your employees want your intranet and e-learning products to improve their work lives and make them feel good; (2) if your technology can achieve these goals, your employees will be more productive and fully engaged in your business;

and (3) both your corporate culture and bottom line will be strengthened as result of your actions.

Why Are Things the Way They Are?

When it comes to the key factor in getting employees to embrace e-learning—that is, its design—most companies still tend to make three philosophical mistakes.

To begin with, *organizations overvalue completeness.* For whatever reason, companies feel they must have everything online, at all levels of detail. But all information is not created equal and shouldn't be treated as such. That's why companies need to worry less about having stuff online, and more about the structure of their online information.

Moreover, *companies undervalue the presentation of content.* Organizations do not pay nearly enough attention to the manner or style in which they present information to employees. More specifically, they fail to recognize the benefit of clear, concise instructional writing and the value of visual explanations such as photos and charts. The result is too much job information that's confusing or downright unusable, often resulting in lower employee productivity and accuracy. To fix this situation, companies need to invest more time and effort into writing, editing, and presenting information.

And finally, *organizations persist in subscribing to a training rather than a performance view.* Companies spend far too much e-learning effort on training (e.g., courses and training tracking), rather than on job performance (e.g., just-in-time tools that answer employees' procedural questions). E-learning and corporate intranets must be designed to help employees perform their jobs well, as well as connect them to the company's vision, mission, and goals.

Exacerbating this situation is technology itself, which actually "enables" people to unintentionally create inferior online products. Because the technical tools and systems used to build e-learning and corporate intranets are designed around the concept of data, instead of end-user goals, it's much easier to create, say, a cumbersome and confusing online reference site rather than an elegant and effective one.

All this bad design can make employees feel indifferent, skeptical, or downright jaundiced about the online "help" they're receiving. In fact, it is not uncommon to hear employees describe intranets and e-learning in these terms:

- It's watching me and reporting back to my boss.
- It's blind to my needs and preferences.

- It's giving me more work to do.
- It's impersonal and treats me like a drone.
- It's full of inaccurate and patronizing information.
- It's boring and wastes my time.

The good news, however, is that companies can still turn the tide and begin to give their employees valuable online learning and information. Let's see how.

A PLAN FOR RIGHTING THE CORPORATE SHIP

In order for e-learning and corporate intranets to reach their potential and resonate with employees, companies must reclaim the wonderful qualities of early e-learning, as well as adapt the best ideas from today's popular Web sites. The trick, however, is to bring the goodness of these products to the corporate environment without losing any of the entre-preneurial spirit that fuelled their invention. That's one tall order, but we believe the strategy we're about to outline can help.

Let's start here: companies must focus their intranet and e-learning initiatives on things to help employees do their jobs better, in all senses of the word—that is, more efficiently, more easily, and more enjoyably.

The concept of "enjoyable" e-learning is worthy of further definition, for there's a fair amount of online instruction that *is* entertaining—such as an amusing video or an addicting game—but it has nothing to do with the employee's work. These diversions are not the type of "enjoyable" we're championing, just as we would never propose that people use MySpace at work, or that companies have people listen to their iPods at the office because it "improves morale." Instead, we're suggesting that within the context of the work environment, companies must embrace this thinking: if you can build a comfortable online space that helps people do their jobs better, you'll demonstrate that you understand what your employees need and want, and that's good for organizational productivity and morale.

It is within this realm of enjoyment that e-learning and intranets have such vast, untapped potential. After all, we see Web sites and technology products that resonate with people in their everyday lives; now, we're looking for companies to do the same for their employees, but *within the context of work*. In a certain sense, we're recommending the technological equivalent of Google's physical "Googleplex" offices (see Levering & Moskowitz's 2008 *Fortune* magazine article on the top 100 companies to work for)—that is, an online space to help create an authentic and uplifting workplace.

How To Get There

In order for companies to build these enriching and enjoyable online environments, we suggest they follow five core principles:

1. *Adopt the philosophy that most employees want their corporate intranet and e-learning initiatives to do more than just package and push company information.* Employees want their online spaces to help them perform at the highest level, in a way that totally absorbs them in their work. Instead of being instruments of corporate command and control, intranets and e-learning need to become tools of employee engagement.

2. *View technology as something that can bring out the best in people; that is, if it is designed well.* Technology can foster creativity and collaboration, unite people around a common goal, and create shared experiences to strengthen a company's culture.

3. *Focus on improving employee performance, rather than employee training.* Employees do not want to sit in virtual courses, earn printed certificates, and build some sort of training transcript for posterity. They want to contribute to the company, be a part of the action, and learn in an organic way. Therefore, companies need to invest in building just-in-time job assistance tools or, better yet, integrate these online tools with business processes.

4. *Staff intranet and e-learning initiatives with in-house people or external consultants who have expertise in the design of e-learning and corporate intranets.* Not only do these designers need strong backgrounds in cognitive psychology, computer usability, and educational theory, but they also need to be imaginative problem solvers. In short, companies can no longer allow IT departments to drive intranet and e-learning design; they must shift the IT role to technical implementation instead.

5. *Push for the development of software tools that build engaging, pedagogically-principled e-learning.* It's time to stop buying authoring tools that allow employees to do little more than read and click.

The first three principles require a significant shift in organizational attitudes (and may ask companies to slay a sacred cow or two); the last two are strategic imperatives companies can add to their existing intranet and e-learning approaches. But when taken together, all these principles ask companies to view technology and employees in a way that should encourage them to create the right online tools to improve job performance and enrich employee cyberculture.

In the next section, we describe one successful corporate e-learning initiative.

RETAIL PERFORMANCE IMPROVEMENT:
A SUCCESSFUL STRATEGY

For the purposes of illustration, we will now describe one corporate-culture success story from our own experience (Guralnick & Larson, 2007), a performance-based e-learning strategy we implemented in a large retail company in the United States. Built to serve the needs of employees in over 1,500 retail stores, this strategy included online training and performance support, along with an e-learning authoring tool. Ten years after the initial rollout, this suite of products is still going strong.

Back in 1998, we were asked to "create some kind of online training" (yes, the direction was that general) for our target audience: employees who held one of the key management jobs found in every store. Each of these managers was responsible for a major operational area—for example, the sales floor with its merchandise displays, the "front end" with its cash registers, or the "back room" with its inventory.

Through our research, we discovered that these employees had two primary needs:

- *Better job information:* Even the most seasoned managers were perplexed by the numerous, detailed, and often changeable procedures relating to their job. Managers wanted a faster, effortless way to get this information, as well as assurances it would be current.
- *More purposeful training:* Managers asked for more engaging and job-relevant training, but only for tasks deemed critical to the daily operation of their area.

In short, these employees were asking us to cut through the clutter, save them time, and help them do their jobs better. They were not interested in some sort of training curriculum to help them learn; they wanted innovative tools to help them *perform*. This insistence on performance propelled us toward the e-learning solution we eventually created, a suite of online products that included:

- *Information-reference sites:* These sites housed current job procedures and made scores of manuals, booklets, videos, and job aids obsolete. With well-organized and clearly-written reference information, the sites soon became the source for credible, current, just-in-time job information.

- *Coaching training:* Because managers were also responsible for coaching their employees, we created training to help them learn this complex "soft" skill. Using our "Watch, Rate, and Compare" model, managers watched a video of someone in their role in a coaching situation, rated the coach's performance on key criteria, compared their ratings to those of experts, and then saw the same scenario performed well, so they could model their own behavior.

- *Technical training:* This product taught people how to use the "Radio Frequency (RF) Units"—handheld devices needed for many daily business activities, such as keeping track of store inventory. Our learn-by-doing simulation enabled managers and their employees to practice using RF units to complete realistic, everyday job tasks.

Managers accessed these products via direct links, but could also search the entire suite to find all items—text information, videos, or training scenarios—to help them address a particular performance issue. For example, a frustrated checkout manager could type "my cashiers are slow" into the search, and get quick tips for increasing cashier speed, as well as a link to a relevant coaching training scenario. In addition, all products included a "Tell Us What You Think" feature, allowing managers to send feedback to headquarters.

Our consulting team wrote the content for the first rollout of each model, but then the client's trainers at headquarters were given a specialized authoring tool called the Encompass E-learning Toolkit to update sites, manage content, and create new e-learning. The toolkit included these features:

- *Authoring:* Trainers and subject matter experts were able to create rich training scenarios and reference information, using the intuitive authoring component of Encompass.

- *Internal content management:* Encompass served as the central knowledge base for the headquarters team, housing both job training and job procedures. Its content reports allowed trainers, subject matter experts, and others to review content.

- *Sensible content reuse:* Encompass allowed content to be customized and reused across different audiences; it also enabled reuse across different products, such as in a training scenario and an information page.

- *Usage data:* Encompass tracked each action users took in the product suite, but gave this information to headquarters in aggregate form, so trainers could learn how store employees were using the products.

This comprehensive e-learning strategy was both employee and performance-focused, while being firmly connected to the company's business goals. It addressed the educational and practical needs of the learners (store employees), as well as the people charged with providing the learning (the trainers and subject matter experts at headquarters).

Results

Although our client declined to undertake a formal study of performance improvement, we were able to gauge the success of this e-learning initiative by gathering feedback from the employees who used the product suite, as well as the headquarters people who evaluated job performance in the stores.

In the end, our data showed that each job position performed more efficiently, by a minimum of 5 minutes per 8-hour work shift. That resulted in a savings of over $15 million per year for the company.

We also learned that the product suite really did resonate with employees. It quickly became the most frequently used site on the company's intranet and was soon elevated to the position of e-learning standard and internal company "brand."

Why This Strategy Worked

We believe three key factors contributed to the success of this e-learning strategy:

- First, *a central group with specific expertise in e-learning conceived and built the learning and system* architectures, while also leading the design and development process for each product. The role of computer programmers was restricted to the technical implementation of the products.

- Second, *the Encompass toolkit was designed for the goals of its audience.* Easy to use, it allowed people to focus on content rather than technology, which helped its headquarters audience create effective online training and reference for store employees.

- And finally, and perhaps most importantly, *the products were "right" for their users*. Each was designed for the goals and style of the audience, to help them do their work successfully. More specifically:

  o The products were designed to be used in short bursts of time, which fit perfectly in the fast-paced, action-oriented world of store employees.

  o The information references were not only searchable, but also organized by the high-level business goals each manager needed to achieve.

  o The writing in the information reference was lively and personable, but also clear and actionable. People enjoyed what they read, understood it, and were able to put it into practice.

  o The technical training was designed around real-life tasks employees faced (for example, "You're out of laundry detergent…what do you do?"), rather than out-of-context procedural steps.

  o The coaching training was engaging and fun because the situations and dialogue were realistic and interesting. The "fun" was never gratuitous or unrelated to the employee's job.

  o Employees felt emotionally connected to the products. Everything from the writing style to the graphical look was designed to make the employees' work lives easier and more enjoyable, and this resonated with them.

In short, this product suite delivered a high return on the company's investment, as well as high employee satisfaction. More significantly, it became a cornerstone of the employee cyberculture, much in the way that an iPod has out in the world.

CONCLUSION

Corporate e-learning and intranets have had a significant influence on employee cyberculture, and for the most part, this influence has not been positive. Outside of work, the Internet has opened up a world of creativity and individuality for many; yet in corporations, and particularly in the e-learning world, quite the reverse has occurred. The focus has been on tracking employee training and giving them simplistic online learning that fails to help them perform better or make them feel good about their employer.

The time is right, however, to draw on the success stories from the early entrepreneurial era of e-learning, as well as from today's most compelling technology. We can mine both for ideas and inspiration not only to help transform the style of corporate intranets and e-learning, but also to make these online experiences become the defining part of a healthy and optimistic employee cyberculture.

REFERENCES

Guralnick, D. (1996). *An authoring tool for procedural-task training*. Evanston, IL: Northwestern University.

Guralnick, D., & Larson, D. (2007, January). A successful e-learning strategy for a large U.S. retail organization. Paper presented at the i-Learn Forum 2007, Paris.

Levering, R., & Moskowitz, R. (2008, February 4). 100 best companies to work for 2008. *Fortune*, pp. 61-70.

Norman, D. A. (1988). *Emotional design: Why we love or hate everyday things*. New York: Basic Books.

Schank, R. C. (1997). *Virtual learning: A revolutionary approach to building a highly skilled workforce*. New York: McGraw-Hill.

CHAPTER 17

IMAGINED WORLDS, EMERGING CULTURES

Steve Wheeler and Helen Keegan

INTRODUCTION

We live in an age in which mobile technology keeps us constantly connected, and where ubiquitous computing enables quick access to a treasure house of knowledge. It is hard to imagine a world in which there are no digital technologies, and this is acutely the case within the education systems of Western industrialized nations. Technology has enriched and enlivened modern life, with mobile technologies enabling us to keep in touch constantly and access information where and when we require it (Ager, 2003). The rapid evolution of social networking spaces on the Internet has facilitated massive and rapid multiple connections between students across a spectrum of intensities, from the superficial to the closely intimate (Ellison, Steinfield, & Lampe, 2007). Technology may now be an indispensable component of modern life, but it generates its own problems, even within familiar contexts. Many of society's long established mores, conventions and rules are being challenged, undermined, and even supplanted as a result of mass interest and engagement with the virtual world. We locate these experiences in "imagined worlds'" due to

Connected Minds, Emerging Cultures: Cybercultures in Online Learning
pp. 261–276
Copyright © 2009 by Information Age Publishing
261

the nature of the virtuality. It is often the fantasy component and the freedom to let one's imagination run riot that first attracts adherents. Imagined worlds facilitate a number of experiences that could never be conceived as possible in the real world, but they also mediate familiar experiences. One familiar feature of the human experience—friendship—is increasingly mediated through new technologies and social spaces. For some, even this fundamental human experience may need to be reconceptualized.

VIRTUAL FRIENDSHIPS

Social networking sites can encourage virtual promiscuity, allowing the "friending" of strangers at the click of a mouse. Some friendships blossom into deeper relationships while others simply wither and die. Tenuous or outdated connections survive simply because no one has bothered to delete a hyperlink. Relationship may become superficial and individuals are reduced to a postage stamp image on a screen. The boundaries between "real" and "virtual" friends become increasingly blurred when so many people spend large proportions of their time connected to, and communicating with, others through the imagined world of the Web. Some friendships may maintain strong ties, while many more will be superficial with weak ties. Boyd and Ellison provide clues to the nature of "friendship" in their commentary on social networking sites:

> What makes social network sites unique is not that they allow individuals to meet strangers, but rather that they enable users to articulate and make visible their social networks. This can result in connections between individuals that would not otherwise be made, but that is often not the goal, and these meetings are frequently between "latent tie.s" (Boyd & Ellison, 2007, p. 210)

Spare time exerts a major influence on the intensity and extent of virtual friendship. There are a finite number of hours in the day, ensuring that time is always a precious commodity. While easy and visible virtual connections to others result in the formation of weak ties, relationships in the here-and-now may suffer at their expense. Such shifting notions of community and identity when communicating across boundaries in an increasingly networked and information-rich, but time-poor world may result in the weakening of previously strong real world ties in favor of nurturing online relationships. We socialize with "virtual" acquaintances, while we neglect our "real-world" friends.

It is, of course, reasonable to argue that friendships formed online may be no less valid or enduring than those formed in the real world; from an ontological perspective the distinction between "real" and "virtual" friendship may become problematic if based purely on the physical, due to our increased connectivity resulting in many genuine friendships taking place online. Nevertheless the ease with which we are able to connect to a globally distributed kinship group adds a complexity to life. The complexity arises because most people are restricted to the number of networks within which they can actively participate at any one time. Many universities and colleges are not asleep to the possibilities, and are investing heavily in the implementation of managed learning environments, but errors are being made. In striving to bring communities of learners together in formalized online learning management systems (LMS), colleges and universities are competing with the extremely popular online social networks where learners have already established elaborate cultural practices. These include services such as MySpace, Friendster, Bebo, Facebook, and picture-sharing sites such as Flickr and Picasa. While the "net-generation" is fairly comfortable living much of their lives online, the ease with which users can participate within, and transit between, online communities can be bewildering. Where institutions try to engage students in online learning, the potential blurring of the boundaries between work and play can become problematic. Moves by institutions away from the structured LMS into the uncertain terrain of popular social networking sites will meet with varying degrees of success, but more probably will hit a wall of resentment, because students see the likes of Facebook as their own territory. Furthermore, social networking sites impute a culture of information "grazing," where learning is superficial due to the availability of "too many networks, and too little time." They are almost certainly incompatible with the ethos of the institutionalized LMS.

A CLASH OF CULTURES?

Are we then witnessing a clash between old established, and new emerging cultures? Is the LMS incompatible with social networking? Institutions would certainly be advised to take a backward step and appraise the current landscape. There have been significant cultural changes in the last 15 years, many of which derive directly from the effects of emerging technologies. The changes have altered people's perceptions about business (e-commerce), education (e-learning), communication (mobile technologies) entertainment (the Internet) and many other regular activities in modern life. Such cultural upheaval inevitably creates consternation, perhaps reminiscent of the "future shock" predicted by Toffler (1970). Toffler offers that future shock is a personal perception of "too much change in too short a period of time," but the personal perceptions of several people, if similar, begin to pervade the social consciousness. Technology has driven a distinct shift in social perception where information has been radically transformed from atoms to bits (Negroponte, 1995) or, in other words, from the physical to the electronic. The common practice in the Western world of business, education and governance is now to e-mail rather than to post a letter or send a memorandum. We thereby witness a significant, sustained, and incremental migration from the physical to the virtual in almost all contemporary social practices. It is a shift that has influenced all aspects of modern life, including the production and provision of education and the connections between people. The evolution of delivery technologies does not necessarily change the content they convey (but see Kozma's alternative view, 1994). Yet they offer powerful encouragement toward a convergence of thinking and a change in cultural perceptions.

Recent research evinces a clash between old media and new media cultures (Jenkins, 2006); not merely between the physical and virtual, but also between those who espouse Web 1.0 against those who champion Web 2.0. One vociferous critic of Web 2.0 is Keen (2007) who argues that the social Web with its free and open content encourages the undermining of professional expertise. Keen's perspective may be interpreted as unashamedly capitalist, espousing the notion that knowledge is a commodity and that it is devalued when all and sundry can contribute freely to it. Such conservative views are countered by the more liberal arguments of O'Reilly (2005), Surowiecki (2004), and others, who hold that social Web applications encourage creativity, freedom of speech, and support an environment within which the combined knowledge of the masses—the "wisdom of the crowd"—can be made available to all, and for free.

Such reconceptualization of media will draw out the inevitable tensions between bona fide journalists, who have traditionally published in paper format, and those who publish their views of current affairs online at "blog speed." It could be argued that both cultural artefacts have elements of face and opinion in them, but who determines which is the most valuable or which provides the truth? The same argument applies to encyclopedias and other receptacles of "knowledge."

Wales, one of the founders of Wikipedia, declares: "Imagine a world in which every single person on the planet is given free access to the sum of all human knowledge. That's what we are doing." The ultimate aim of Wikipedia is to "create and distribute a free encyclopedia of the highest possible quality to every single person on the planet in their own language" (Wales, 2005). This is, of course, an ambitious goal, and one that will inevitably encounter several problems and criticisms. Interestingly, Sanger, Wales's erstwhile colleague and Wikipedia cofounder, recently declared at an education conference that Wikipedia is "broken beyond repair" (Thomson, 2007)

COPYRIGHT AND OWNERSHIP

One key problem emerging from the clash of new media with a long established culture is that of ownership and protection of intellectual property. There is a conflict between this old culture and the new social Web culture where "everything is free and open." Resulting disputes are played out very publicly. At the time of writing there are media reports that YouTube is being sued by several old media companies for breach of copyright, with many music videos and other cultural artifacts being freely uploaded to its site so that they can be publicly viewed. This will not be the last court case. Ownership over the photographic images of movie stars such as Marilyn Monroe and James Dean, political figures such as Ernesto "Che" Guevara and Winston Churchill, or pop stars such as John Lennon and Elvis Presley are hotly disputed by their estates, yet millions worldwide trade in the images of these cultural icons with alacrity. Implicitly, the reputations and lifestyles of these cultural icons are up for sale, as entrepreneurs freely use their images to promote their own ideas and sell their wares.

The rapid and libertine exchange of images and artifacts deemed in the predigital age to be "owned" has perpetrated an overt transgression of previously maintained cultural boundaries, in this case the accepted codes of practice. These practices are partly legitimized by the appearance of new and more liberal tribal ground rules, such as creative commons, anticopyright (indicated by a reversed image of a copyright sign), and others. Such emergent cultural contrivances challenge many of the long established social mores of ownership and poses fundamental questions about the nature of intellectual property, copyright protection, and other legal issues. One American academic, Lessig, is a highly vocal proponent of the view that copyright restrictions should be reduced, particularly for technology applications. He has recently turned his attention to a crusade against political corruption, and addresses these issue using radical approaches. Lessig has set up a wiki so that anyone who has any information on political sleaze can post it for public scrutiny. In the best traditions of democracy, he has also set up an "Anti-Lessig" wiki so that his opponents can voice their opposition to his ideas. Although these are risky strategies, open to abuse, and potentially ripe targets for litigation, the Lessig wikis are displayed openly on the Internet—the first window of information for the digital generation—arguably the most democratically powerful information dissemination tool ever.

"Broadcast yourself" is the epithet of video sharing site YouTube. It is a strap line that has fomented a number of legal and cultural issues. Most YouTube users would see no problem in copying, editing, and posting video clips from a feature film, television show, or other copyrighted sequence. The copyright owners take a different view. Legal battles are the result, and reconceptualization of the law may be the only recourse. Significantly, property theft is only one dimension of the issues surrounding the social Web. We must also consider issues of privacy.

STAR WARS KID

In 2002, a Canadian teenager recorded a video of himself energetically swinging a wooden stick around his head, copying the Darth Maul character from the Star Wars film *The Phantom Menace*. He recorded the tape in his high school studio, and then it was left forgotten in a school storeroom. One day, a classmate found it, viewed it, and considered that it was amusing enough to share with his friends. Between them, they made several copies, and eventually the clip was uploaded as a file onto the Internet. The video then spread rapidly and virally, through friends telling friends, sending links, texts, and via the sharing of files. Within a few weeks, the video had been downloaded and viewed by several million others. Soon other versions began to appear on the Internet, some with overdubbed music and sound effects, others parodying *Star Wars*, and then other films such as *The Matrix*. Some versions are embellished with sophisticated visual effects, spectacular glowing light saber overlays and other clever editing tricks, so that an entire suite of "*Star Wars* Kid" videos is now viewable online.

It is estimated that collectively, the various versions of the "*Star Wars* Kid" clip have now been downloaded over a billion times, notably from social network video sharing sites such as YouTube. Soon several versions of the clip found their way onto mainstream broadcast television. But most viewers of the video forget that someone was hurt by the video. Ultimately, the teenage boy's unsought Internet and television publicity led to prolonged embarrassment and exposure to harassment and mockery that became unbearable for him. He was reported to have undergone long-term psychiatric care. In 2006, the Associated Sun Press reported that the boy's family had successfully reached an out-of-court settlement with the families of his classmates for a sum of over 350,000 Canadian dollars.

CULTURAL PATTERNS OF USAGE

Discernible patterns of usage emerge when we observe activities on social networking sites. There is for example, a subtle difference between the personae projected by those using the photo-sharing site Flickr, when compared to those using the social networking site Facebook.

Flickr can be viewed both as a macro- and as a microcommunity that increases in granularity as subgroups form out of larger groups, where memes emerge from the sharing of social discourse in a hybrid cultural space. As relationships develop and life histories are shared, so the members coalesce into smaller and more intimate groupings. Mirroring the patterns of socialization that we observe in everyday life, friendships and rivalries may be formed; groups are joined and left (sometimes users leave groups dramatically in acts that may be equivalent to the proverbial "baby throwing his toys out of the pram"), and people experience emotional responses to others in the community on the basis of their comments or, indeed, lack of comments.

As in Facebook, friendships and relationships are formed that then transfer over into face-to-face meetings. People organize "Flickr Meets," where groups of Flickrites get together in real-life, and friendships develop between fellow Flickrites from different countries or parts of the same country who meet up with others in their neighborhood. There are also Flickr weddings, Flickr affairs—and Flickr fall-outs. Essentially anything that happens when people get together happens on Flickr, and in this respect it is far more than a photo-sharing network. It has become a massive and vibrant online community.

In Facebook by contrast, many friendships and relationships already tend to exist prior to links being made on personal Facebook sites. Old friends and classmates can be searched for, and then links are made. Subsequently, a friend's friend list can be viewed, and secondary friendships can be initiated. Facebook may be less intimate than Flickr in many ways, with many acquaintances and "friends of friends" on one's list, but few with strong social ties. This is paradoxical, given that Facebookers tend to use their real names and images, while it is the accepted culture of Flickrites to use pseudonyms and representing images. Some initial Facebook research suggests that users employ this service predominantly to find out more about people they meet in the real world, and they are less likely to use it to initiate new connections (Lampe, Ellison, & Steinfield, 2006). Gross, Alessandro, and Heinz (2005) reported that many Facebook users are exposed to potential attacks on various aspects of their privacy, and showed that only a small percentage of users changed their highly permeable privacy preferences. The laissez-faire culture of Facebook strengthens some Facebookers' perception that their space can be viewed only by their "friends." Recent press reports suggest that potential employers and university admission staff check out Facebook sites to find out more about applicants. Several have fallen foul of this emerging practice, in which their own comments, images, and other on-screen exploits militate against them.

THE LEARNING CONTEXT

We hope we have convinced you that there are emerging cultures in the social networking communities, and we should expect them to emerge. Wherever people gather, whether physically or virtually, shared social meanings are evolved that serve to identify that group as distinct, and perhaps even define them as unique. We are interested, in this volume, in exploring the educational meaning and context of these digital tools and the cultures they propagate, so the section discusses some ideas around this.

One of the many challenges facing educators today is how to abstract the elements of online communities that "work" and apply these to their own professional practice. There are tensions between top-down and bottom-up approaches to teaching and learning; for example, centralized versus decentralized models, formal versus informal learning, traditional versus new forms of assessment. In many Web-based communities, learning often occurs informally and "ferally." The concept of feral learning (Nunan, 1996) is particularly apt when considering the types of learning that take place in networked society/online communities, where learners are less restricted by structure, gathering knowledge through roaming across hyperlinked texts, creating their own pathways according to their personal interests.

One of the most important dichotomies in the context of education exists in the tension between formal learning (as observed in colleges, schools, and universities) and informal learning (most commonly seen in online chat-rooms, through social networking sites, and in massively multilayer online role playing games or MMORPGs). Teachers need to be aware that the student experience is increasingly volatile and that emerging technologies are changing the culture of study. Young people bring their own cultures—set of values, expectations, and linguistic codes—with them to the university or college, and they employ specific technology tools to support these cultures. There is a growing distance between the inchoate culture of youth and the conservative culture of the university that often results in dissonance.

SPEECH CODES

Culture needs to be learnt, often through language and speech codes, and this can only be achieved by immersion in that culture. This requires new users to sometimes remain on the periphery of the digital environment until they are certain that they have enough tribal knowledge to be able to more fully participate. Digital tribes can often be recognized by their specific linguistic codes, much in the same way street gangs or social groups exhibit their identity through specific word invention, dialect, and accent. We were both already members of one community (Steve on Facebook and Helen on Flickr). When we transitioned across and signed up to the alternative service, the subtle shift in linguistic conventions and communication styles across the platforms became clearly apparent to us both in a number of ways.

Flickrites largely use pseudonyms on Flickr and real names on Facebook. Whereas Flickr is used by the author's community mainly as a recreational online social space, Facebook friends include colleagues, and therefore a greater degree of transparency (and professionalism) is expected. It became an unspoken rule that different naming conventions would be adhered to across the two platforms, and Flickr friends would not divulge one another's identities on Facebook—such as, address people by the name they use on that particular platform.

In terms of communication styles, there are some interesting and useful examples of shifting dialogue across the two platforms. When commenting on Flickr images, all dialogue takes place around one image (i.e., the users come to the image in order to converse). Cross-referencing does take place across what may be seen as "visual boundaries" (i.e., the static image), but this only works on the community level among groups with stronger ties in the sense of shared humor and comments.

In contrast to this, Facebook users can leave public messages on "walls" for their friends to read. Tribal custom suggests the acceptable practice is to respond by going to the friend's wall, and in order to view to dialogue as a whole the user must view it "wall-to-wall." While commenting on actual photos in Facebook operates in a similar manner to Flickr (people can leave comments on photos is they wish), in reality Flickr comments are reminiscent of Facebook wall scrawling, and therefore it was interesting to note the ways in which users from different platforms would use the comment wall in Facebook. MySpacers migrating to Facebook were comfortable leaving comments the Facebook way, where viewers only see one side of a conversation at one time, whereas Flickrites had to adapt to this paradigm shift, as they would instinctively respond to comments on their own walls in response to the comments of others, keeping the conversation in one place—which actually goes against Facebook protocol, which decrees that the user leaves comments on the walls of others, but that it is not normal practice to leave messages on their own walls.

Another example of shifting linguistic codes used by different digital tribes can be illustrated by the reaction of one of the author's friends to a certain style of comment in Facebook. The friend, while not an active Flickrite, had viewed the author's photos and comments on Flickr on many occasions and so was familiar with the language and communication style used by the Flickr subcommunity. When the author left a comment in Flickr style on a photograph in Facebook, the friend responded by teasingly commenting "You're not in Flickr now, you know."

This demonstrates that such subtle linguistic differences are indeed evident to passive observers across platforms, and that in some cases code-switching and code-mixing may be viewed as cliquey and exclusive, discriminatory, or even offensive. This ties back in to the idea of impression management and the use of separate accounts for separate communicative spaces; what is seemingly amusing banter amongst a kinship group could in fact be rather offensive to outsiders, and this is one of the difficulties of a life lived online. Words do not disappear into the ether; rather, there is permanence in textual dialogue that gives the words/conversation more weight, and this that can create tensions further down the line.

We can contextualize this within education. It is highly likely that the more platforms we communicate across, the more diverse range of linguistic codes will be used, and some may be more appropriate than others. Recent work from the University of Durham has demonstrated one tutor's way of harnessing the communication across different online spaces in ways in which benefit both her and the students. Having noticed a distinct drop-off in module cohort communication in the discussion board areas of the institutional VLE, the tutor set out to investigate the reasons behind this, as communication had previously remained lively on the traditional VLE forums. It became apparent that the students were now active on Facebook, and were spending time there instead. The tutor joined Facebook and was swiftly invited by the students to join the group that they had set up (independently from the VLE in a bottom-up approach) to discuss her module. When she then began to explore the discussion areas of the group, she found comments such as "wasn't that lecture boring," which students would never have written in the formal (VLE) discussion areas. However, she also found that the students were discussing the module and realized that this was where they were "hanging out." They were choosing to communicate and discuss the module in their own private space, as opposed to the top-down implemented institutional space. This shift in the locus of control from the institution to the learner is indicative of the generally agreed-upon notion of the learning paradigm shift in education in an increasingly networked society in which social software use is in the mainstream.

In the case described above, while the tutor found some of the content of the students' private space to be inappropriate for the institutional VLE, and the linguistic codes used to be far less formal (highly vernacular, in some cases), the ideas were still there. Some students they found it easier to express their ideas in the more relaxed virtual space on Facebook, and so the tutor began to act as a "broker," reading discussions between the students on Facebook and then inviting them to elaborate on strong ideas in a more formalized way on the discussion areas of the institutional VLE. This approach worked well in this case, although it must be said that the tutor and students have a very positive relationship. In other cases it is not difficult to imagine scenarios where students resent tutors entering what they see as being their private space. However, the concept of brokering between platforms and styles could be useful for educators in developing new conceptions of (and practices in) how to "educate" and learn in an increasingly networked world.

GAMES AND VIRTUAL SIMULATIONS

While online gaming has become a fabric of youth culture, and is viewed by many as the preserve of "leisure time," games and virtual worlds also offer exciting possibilities for education (Jenkins, 2006 Prensky, 2001). Although the educational value of immersion has been well-documented (Dede, 1995; Dede, Salzman, & Bowen Loftin, 1996; de Freitas, 2006), we are now witnessing the mainstreaming of virtual worlds such as Second Life (SL), which are potentially fertile ground for the development of innovative and immersive educational spaces. Within these spaces, avatars can participate in role-play and historical re-creations and re-enactments—for example the Arden project, which is an immersive virtual reality based on the world of the works of Shakespeare (http://swi.indiana.edu/), and immersive language environments, such as *Virtual Morocco*.

Increasing numbers of users are experiencing SL as a social platform that can be used for formal learning purposes, and can involve attendance at events in which some sort of streaming is involved. One examples of this is *Jokaydia* (an island owned and run by the University of New South Wales in Australia). It is fast gaining a good reputation as a virtual venue for educational technology-related events, such as the e-Learning 07 Conference and the International EduBlog Awards (2007). Creative online events such as these link virtual and physical spaces, hosting live events with virtual participants in-world. Much of the real value of meetings and conferences lies in the informal chatting before and after the "main event," and online virtual worlds populated by avatars lend themselves conveniently to this type of interaction—perhaps more readily than the traditional Web conference.

Web-conferencing across platforms and spaces provides exciting new ways to communicate. When some kind of visible, tangible presence is employed within the event, the result is often a much more immediate and meaningful experience. Another key motivating factor for those who are interested in using virtual worlds as learning spaces is that of enhanced presence through avatar interaction when communicating and collaborating across spatial and temporal boundaries. Online friends and colleagues can meet in virtual spaces, which afford a level of presence and realism that is seen to be more engaging than 2-D online environments.

There are many psychological issues to contend with within the imagined world. We contend here that it is likely that mixed reality will be the dominant user experience for those who are regularly immersed in multi-user virtual environments such as Second Life. The seductive lure of co-presence and the appeal of creating digital alter-egos (avatars) of oneself that are visually attractive and void of any blemish or what in the physical world may be seen as a handicap or disability ensures that many serious SLifers spend a lot of their time and energy (and sometimes hard cash) on creating facial features, exotic clothing, jewelry, and hairstyles. Such activities combine to ensure that many millions of users are regularly sucked into what Wallace has called a "time sink" (Wallace, 1999). Earlier in the chapter we discussed the possibility that some immersed users may develop friendships in-world and neglect to maintain their real-world friendships. It is possible that many cases of relationship breakdown due to digital technology will be reported in the coming years as imagined worlds become more attractive than reality.

There are many implications of imagined worlds and the social networking services for education. Students will be expected to multi-task and transition between multi in-world environments to keep pace with events, connections, and resources. As a result, a sort of "information grazing"—superficial knowledge acquisition—will occur, the value of which will need to be determined. Students engaged across multiple online platforms may be subject to continuous partial attention, and they will need to manage their multiple identities, distributed presence, and multiple, asynchronous conversations. They may also need to take care over what they consider is "real" and all the potential transgressions into the "imagined."

While MUVEs, particularly SL, are increasingly being used and explored within educational contexts, practical issues such as hardware and bandwidth requirements and a significant learning curve should be considered. First-time visitors to SL for example, need to learn to walk all over again, and also learn how to transport their avatar using alternative and exotic forms of transport such as "flying" and "teleportation." They must learn the new culture of SL, which prompts when to interact with other avatars, what is permissible and what is frowned on. Avoidance of social gaffes in-world is reminiscent of the cultural rules of digital communication cultures, such as avoiding typing e-mails in uppercase letters, which is considered to be "shouting." The inception of almost every new technology raises challenging issues about exclusion and inclusion, particularly for those who have physical disabilities or cognitive impairment. The move toward Web-based "platform agnostic" imagined worlds such as MetaSpace holds potential to break down such barriers, and as MUVEs become increasingly available and usable, we suggest they will also become more democratized.

VIRTUAL AND IMAGINED WORLDS

First place—the space in which we and our family resides, and second place—our place of work—are both replete with digital technology. Now computer-based artefacts have colonized our "third place" of habitation— a space where there is neither home nor work, but a place in which we might spend our leisure and friendship time (Oldenburg, 1999). Traditionally, the third space has been a richly social experience, normally within a coffee bar, pub, hair salon, or other public place. For Oldenburg, the third place is located at the very heart of society, and becomes a cultural reference point. Increasing numbers of people are turning away from traditional third places, and migrating toward imagined environments within which they can experience virtual relationships, electronic contact, and digital simulation of human experiences.

SOCIAL SPACES AND CULTURAL CAPITAL

We move on to a brief exploration of the ways in which social spaces such as blogs and wikis are driving cultural changes. We are witnessing a surge in popularity in extrainstitutional social spaces such as Bebo, MySpace, and Facebook. Young people view such sites very much as a part of their territory, and often treat them as their first port of call when they need to communicate with their circle of friends. We are unsure how social sites will affect education, but institutions ignore this phenomenon at their peril. One of the key questions that will need to be addressed focuses on the implications for formalized education, and its relationship with informal learning. We also need to know whether a cultural disparity is emerging between the generations. One significant criticism of social spaces such as Wikipedia is how to distinguish between fact and opinion. The wisdom of the crowd (Surowiecki, 2004) is an essential feature of social spaces, particularly when social tagging and collaborative filtering is used. Of course, there is a fine balance between Web content that coalesces due to the wisdom of the crowd, and that which is perpetrated by the stupidity of the masses.

According to Bourdieu, it is possible to accrue power and status in any social setting by gaining access to cultural capital—the accumulated cultural knowledge of that society (Bourdieu & Passeron, 1973). We argue here that the process of tagging pages and other digital artefacts through the use of utilities such as Del.icio.us in itself evolves into a form of cultural capital. It is the equivalent of a tribal member making a mark to delineate his territory. Another means of gaining cultural capital may be to gather an impressive list of "friends" on your personal social space. Facebook, for example, provides users with an attractive visual representation of their list of friends, called the "entourage." Features such as this may partly explain the popularity of social networking services for young people.

MANAGING DIGITAL IDENTITY

Personal identity is as important online as it is in real life, but identity in social online spaces can differ in its manifestation. The representation of self incorporates a number of attributes including the management of one's impression. This is an increasingly complex task in the digital age, taking a multiple digital identities into account, as well as granularity—the extent to which digital identity is managed in any given context. One user may employ several different icons to visually represent themselves within multiple accounts, and will often need to remember a number of different passwords and user names. A deeper treatment of these issues can be found in the Miller and Arnold chapter in this volume.

CONCLUSION: EMERGING CULTURES

In this chapter we have presented perspectives on cybercultures in education and have specifically focused on how emerging Internet social spaces impact on individual perceptions and practices. We paid particular attention to the social networking and multiuser virtual environment cultures, where imagination can be unleashed, but where friendship may be superficial. We dwelt on the tensions observed between old and new media cultures and the shift in perception that emerges regarding issues such as ownership, intellectual property, copyright, personal identity, and privacy.

We discussed how cultural values such as privacy, identity, and ownership are being redefined. There was an exploration of how "imagined worlds" are currently used and how tribal cultures develop around and through them. Questions were posed about the shape and practice of education in a technology-rich culture in which the ubiquitous and pervasive computer has enabled personalized, participative, and aggregative learning to rapidly become the standard in formalized education. We highlighted two "digital clan" cultures—Facebookers and Flickrites—and examined their mores and practices of sharing and communication, with particular emphasis on cultural values. In a digital age where values are constantly shifting and identities and relationships are being redefined, one of the few things communities have left to rely on is the familiarity of their tribal culture. New and emerging versions of this shared, symbolic understanding will in turn shape the technologies that create our imagined worlds.

REFERENCES

Agar, J. (2003). *Constant touch: A brief history of the mobile phone.* London: Icon.

Bourdieu, P., & Passeron, J. -C. (1973). *Cultural reproduction and social reproduction.* London: SAGE.

Boyd, D. M., & Ellison, N. B. (2007). Social network sites: Definition, history and scholarship. *Journal of Computer-Mediated Communication, 13*(1), 210-230.

Dede, C. (1995). The evolution of constructivist learning environments: Immersion in distributed, virtual worlds. *Educational Technology, 35*(5), 46-52.

Dede, C., Salzman, M. C., & Bowen Loftin, R. (1996). ScienceSpace: Virtual realities for learning complex and abstract scientific concepts. In *Proceedings of the 1996 Virtual Reality Annual International Symposium* (pp. 246-252). Washington, DC: VRAIS, IEEE Computer Society.

de Frietas, S (2006). Learning in immersive worlds: A review of game based learning. *JISC.* Retrieved January 20, 2008, from http://www.jisc.ac.uk/media/documents/programmes/elearninginnovation/gamingreport_v3.pdf

de Kerckhove, D. (1997). *The skin of culture: Investigating the new electronic reality.* London: Kogan Page.

Ellison, N. B., Steinfield, C., & Lampe, C. (2007). The benefits of Facebook "friends": Social capital and college students' use of online social network sites. *Journal of Computer-Mediated Communication, 12*, 1143-1168.

Gross, R., Alessandro, A., & Heinz, H. J. (2005). Information revelation and privacy in online social networks. In *Proceedings of the 2005 ACM workshop on privacy in the electronic society* (pp. 71-80). New York: ACM Press.

Jenkins, H. (2006). *Convergence culture: Where old and new media collide.* New York: New York University Press.

Keen, A. (2006). *The cult of the amateur: How today's Internet is killing our culture and assaulting our economy.* London: Nicholas Brealey.

Kozma, R. (1994). Will media influence learning? Reframing the debate. *Educational Technology Research and Development, 42*(2), 7-19.

Lampe, C., Ellison, N., & Steinfield, C. (2006). A Face(book) in the crowd: Social searching vs. social browsing. In *Proceedings of the 20th Anniversary Conference on Computer Supported Cooperative Work* (pp. 167-170). New York: ACM Press.

Negroponte, N. (1995). *Being digital*. London: Hodder and Stoughton.

Nunan, T. (1996). Flexible delivery: What is it and why is it part of current educational debate? In *Higher Education Research and Development Society of Australasia Annual Conference Proceedings*. Retrieved September 10, 2007, from http://www.lgu.ac.uk/deliberations/flex.learning/nunan_fr.html

Oldenburg, R. (1999) *The great good place: Cafes, coffee shops, bookstores, bars, hair salons, and other hangouts at the heart of a community*. New York: Marlowe.

O'Reilly, T. (2005). *What is Web 2.0? Design patterns and business models for the next generation of software*. Retrieved October 9, 2007, from http://www.oreilly.com/pub/a/oreilly/tim/news/2005/09/30/what-is-web-20.html

Prensky, M. (2001). Digital natives, digital immigrants. *On the horizon, 9*(5), 1-6.

Surowiecki, J. (2004). *The wisdom of crowds: Why the many are smarter than the few and how collective wisdom shapes business, economies, societies and nations*. New York: Doubleday.

Toffler, A. (1970). *Future shock*. London: Random House.

Thomson, I. (2007, April 12.). Wikipedia "broken beyond repair" says co-founder. *IT Week*. Retrieved March 7, 2008, from http://www.itweek.co.uk/vnunet/news/2187672/wikipedia-broken-beyond-repair

Wales, J. (2005, March 8). *Wikipedia is an encyclopedia*. Retrieved February 7, 2008, from http://wikipedia-l@wikimedia.org

Wallace, P. (1999) *The psychology of the Internet*. New York: Cambridge University Press.

ABOUT THE AUTHORS

Graham Attwell is the director of the Wales-based independent research organization Pontydysgu (the Bridge to Learning) and presenter of the "Sounds of the Bazaar" podcast. His research interests include the informal- and work-based learning and training of teachers and trainers. Much of his work focuses on the development and use of open source software and social software for learning, and on the use of new technologies for knowledge development and sharing. Over the last year he has been working on the development of e-portfolios and what is now being called personal learning environments. Graham is a regular speaker at seminars and conferences internationally and has published his thoughts extensively in books and journals. However, his preferred means of communication is story telling through his blog, the "Wales Wide Web," which can be found at: http://www.pontydysgu.org/blogs/waleswideweb/
E-mail: Graham10@mac.com

Jill Arnold is a senior lecturer in psychology at Nottingham Trent University. Her educational work, teaching, and researching has been in all sectors of adult, continuing, and higher education across the East Midlands. Her teaching has included women's studies as well as critical feminist approaches to social and individual psychology, which currently includes the psychology of self and identity in the cultural and material world. She has recently developed teaching interests to include wider political, geographical, and cyber aspects of identity. Jill's research has ranged from qualitative studies of student experiences of learning in higher education to the social psychology of new technologies, particularly the presentational aspects of gendered cyber identity. More recently,

using discursive and visual methodologies, she has been developing her work on the experiences and portraits of women in their middle years. Jill is also a photographer and the nurturer and/or controller of her walled garden.
E-mail: jill.arnold@ntu.ac.uk

Palitha Edirisingha is a lecturer in e-learning at the Beyond Distance Research Alliance at the University of Leicester, United Kingdom. Palitha is coinvestigator of the HEA funded IMPALA and IMPALA 2 podcasting projects. His research interests include mobile technologies, Web 2.0 applications, and learning technologies in developing countries. His recent book, a volume he has coedited with Gilly Salmon, is titled *Podcasting for Learning in Universities* and was published in 2008 by the Open University Press. Palitha's Web site can be visited at: http://www2.le.ac.uk/departments/beyond-distance-research-alliance/About%20Us/staff/pal
E-mail: pe27@leicester.ac.uk

Steven Furnell is the head of the Centre for Information Security & Network Research at the University of Plymouth in the United Kingdom, and an adjunct professor with Edith Cowan University in Western Australia. His research interests include computer crime, security management, user authentication, and security usability. Professor Furnell is a fellow and branch chair of the British Computer Society (BCS), a senior member of the Institute of Electrical and Electronics Engineers (IEEE), and a U.K. representative in International Federation for Information Processing working groups relating to information security management (of which he is the current chair), Network security, and information security education. He is the author of over 180 papers in refereed international journals and conference proceedings, as well as the books *Cybercrime: Vandalizing the Information Society* (2001) and *Computer Insecurity: Risking the System* (2005). Further details of his work can be found at: www.plymouth.ac.uk/cisnr
E-mail: sfurnell@plymouth.ac.uk

Ken Gale is a lecturer in education working in the Faculty of Education at the University of Plymouth in the United Kingdom, engaged in various forms of research and in developing and teaching on a range of programs from certificate to master's level. His particular teaching and research interests are located within the philosophy of education and in the study of poststructural theory and narrative practices as they may be applied to postcompulsory teacher education. In this respect his current research involves consideration of the ways in which creativity, in the form of narrative inquiry and auto-ethnographic practices, may be applied to

enhance the theory and practice of teacher education. As well as his work in creativity he has published papers in the areas of educational management, online learning, triadic assessment, and writing as methodology. He has written and currently teaches modules on the integrated master's program on the philosophy of education, discourse theory, narrative inquiry, gender studies, and the enhancement of practice in postcompulsory teacher education. Ken is married to Helen, has three children, Katy, Reuben, and Phoebe, and lives in Cornwall (U.K.).
E-mail: K.J.Gale@plymouth.ac.uk

David Guralnick is president of New York-based Kaleidoscope Learning and is an adjunct professor at Teachers College at Columbia University, in the United States. His work has been featured in *Wired* magazine, *Training* magazine (as an Editor's Choice), and the *Wall Street Journal*, and he is the recipient of numerous e-learning design awards. He is also chair of the International Conference on E-Learning in the Workplace; president of the International E-Learning Association; senior editor of the *International Journal of Advanced Corporate Learning*; and e-learning chair for the New York chapter of the American Society for Training & Development. More about David's work can be found at Kaleidoscope Learning's Web site, http://www.kaleidolearning.com/
E-mail: dguralnick@kaleidolearning.com

Leon James is a professor of psychology at the University of Hawaii, Oahu. He has published books and articles in the fields of psycholinguistics, language learning, and driving psychology. His current research interests include cyberpsychology, information literacy, and theistic psychology. He teaches research seminars for undergraduates majoring in psychology. He maintains a driving psychology Web site at www.DrDriving.org and is considered one of the world's foremost experts on road rage. His articles are available online at: http://www.soc.hawaii.edu/leonj/leonj/leonpsy/leon .html
E-mail: leon@hawaii.edu

Helen Keegan is in the School of Acoustics and Audio Engineering at the University of Salford. Her initial role in the school was as a developer of CAL materials, having previously worked as a freelance multimedia designer and producer/developer of enhanced CDs for national and international clients including The British Council, Futuresonic, *Flux* Magazine, Castlefield Gallery, and Fred Perry. Helen's interest in the evaluation of learning technologies led to her taking on a wider role within the university in the area of e-learning, heading the evaluation team for the University of Salford e-learning pilot project (2000-2002), the result

of which was the establishment of a Learning Technologies Centre to support the development and application of learning technologies throughout the university. Helen's Web site is at: http://www.acoustics.salford.ac .uk/profiles/keegan/
E-mail: H.Keegan@salford.ac.uk

Mark A. M. Kramer is an emerging scholar, participatory observer, and informed critic of mobile information and communications technologies. Currently, Mark lectures at several universities in Austria while conducting his doctoral research in the fields of e-learning and m-learning. Mark spends a great portion of his time between Vienna and Salzburg, travelling an average of 24 hours a week on the Austrian Railway. This time is spent in part writing his thesis while conducting real-world research and developing strategies for extreme-mobile learning scenarios. Mark is an active mobile-blogger and can be reached at the following coordinates: http://www.mamk.net
E-mail: mark@kramer.mobi

Deb Larson works for Kaleidoscope Learning in the United States, and has been a practitioner in the organizational development field for over 25 years, specializing in the design and development of innovative and pragmatic initiatives to improve employee job performance, increase employee engagement, and bring results to the bottom line. Her contributions to the world of digital learning include spearheading the strategy to introduce e-learning and just-in-time performance support to over 250,000 employees at a major American corporation. Deb was educated at the University of Minnesota. She lives in Minneapolis with her son, Teddy.
E-mail: deblarson@mac.com

Gorg Mallia lectures in communications and instructional technology at the Centre for Communication Technology, University of Malta. He holds a PhD in education from Sheffield University, U.K. His main areas of interest are print and presentation media, branding communications, new media technologies and social software impacts, and transfer of learning. or is also a media practitioner. He is a published social cartoonist, a writer and illustrator of children's books, and a media personality in his own country, as well as being the chairman of Malta's National Book Council. He is a member of the scientific and organizing committees of a number of learned conferences, including ICICTE, Greece, and has published extensively in his areas of expertise. or's most persistent area of research revolves around the concept of hypertextual processing: the change induced by immersed usage in new media technologies. He lives

in Malta, but lectures regularly in other universities abroad, predominantly the University of Lund, Sweden. His Web site can be found at: http://www.gorgmallia.com
E-mail: gorg.mallia@um.edu.mt

Hugh Miller is a principal lecturer in psychology at Nottingham Trent University. He has been teaching on design degrees as well as psychology courses for many years, and has given many presentations on the overlap between psychology and design. He has been interested in the use of IT in learning and teaching since the early 1990s, partly because of a wider interest in how technology is involved in people's social lives. He is currently researching design for well-being, and the social psychology of objects generally. He lives in the East Midlands with a soon-to-be-retired teacher, a cat, several bikes, and far too many books. All the children have left, but there still isn't enough space for the books.
E-mail: hugh.miller@ntu.ac.uk

Howard Rheingold is the author of: *Tools for Thought, The Virtual Community* and *Smart Mobs*. He served as editor of *Whole Earth Review* and editor of *The Millennium Whole Earth Catalog*. He was founding executive editor of *Hotwired* and founder of Electric Minds. Howard was also a nonresident fellow at the Annenberg Center for Communication, USC, 2007. He has taught participatory media and collective action (UC Berkeley, SIMS, Fall 2005, 2006, 2007), virtual community/social media (Stanford, Fall 2007, UC Berkeley, Spring 2008), Toward a Literacy of Cooperation (Stanford, Winter, 2005) and digital journalism (Stanford University Winter, 2005, 2006, 2007). Howard is currently a visiting professor at De Montfort University, in the United Kingdom, and his projects include The Cooperation Project, Participatory Media Literacy and is a HASTAC/MacArthur Foundation grantee. Howard's thoughts on mobile technologies can be found at http://www.smartmobs.com and http://vlog.rheingold.com
E-mail: howard@rheingold.com

Tim Shortis is the author of *The Language of ICT: Information Communication Technology*, published by Routledge. He was formerly the head of English at a British sixth form college, the chief examiner of the AQA 'A' Level English Language, and the Language consultant on the British Library's Texts in Context project. Tim researches and writes about language and ICT and has a keen interest in the emergent languages and respellings within mobile texting cultures.
E-mail: timshortis1@mac.com

John Traxler is a reader in mobile technology for e-learning and director of the Learning Lab at the University of Wolverhampton. He works with the university's Centre of Excellence in Learning and Teaching, looking at innovative technologies to support diverse communities of students and with the university's Centre for International Development and Training, exploring ways of using appropriate innovative technologies to deliver education in developing countries, in especially sub-Saharan Africa. John has cowritten a guide to mobile learning in developing countries and is coeditor of the definitive book on mobile learning with Agnes Kukulska-Hulme, titled *Mobile Learning: A Handbook for Educators and Trainers*, published by Routledge. He has been invited to present at the South African national science festival, SciFest, at Rhodes University, and by Microsoft to the Mobile Learning Summit in Seattle, and the Canadian government to the ICTD conference in Bangalore. He publishes regularly, evaluating and embedding mobile learning, and is interested in the profound consequences of universal mobile devices on our societies. He is jointly responsible for national workshops on mobile learning for U.K. universities and has delivered similar workshops to university staff in Germany, Kenya, South Africa, Canada, and India. He advises U.K. universities on mobile learning projects. He advises the Swiss BioVision Foundation on appropriate technologies to support Kenyan farmers and continues to work with the Kenyan government implementing national support for teachers' in-service training using mobile phones and video. He has links with South Africa's Meraka Institute and Avallain AG, one of Europe's leading e-learning system developers. He lives in a market town in rural Shropshire in England with his wife.
E-mail: John.Traxler@wlv.ac.uk

Viv Tucker has more than 20 years experience working in FE and HE contexts and has been working as a full-time lecturer in education for the University of Plymouth for the last 10 years. Viv trained as an artist and has taught still photography and filmmaking. Her interest in digital technologies has led her to develop an online learning community of practice for trainee teachers in post-16 education. Acutely aware of the personal worlds we all dream of and inhabit, Viv decided to leave the university in July 2008 to focus on making visual- and text-based works of art to express the way in which she experiences her world. She is still pursuing her academic research, which focuses on narrative inquiry, wellbeing, identity, and cyberculture, but feels the need to work outside a large organizational structure for a period of time.
E-mail: imagination@zetnet.co.uk

Vasi van Deventer is an associate professor in the Department of Psychology in the College of Human Sciences at the University of South Africa. His first degree in mathematics, computer science, and physics provided a good foundation for his interest in technology. But it was the journey through psychology and philosophy that opened up the world of abstract theory and metaphysics, allowing him his much-loved oscillation between the practical world of the "engineer" and the abstract world of the "theorist and philosopher." The opportunities to consult in business and industry provide constant motivation to explore the practical application of psychometric theory, e-learning design principles, and protocols of information management. His academic teaching and research interests are continuously informed by these exposures to practical experience. Vasi currently teaches on a number of undergraduate and postgraduate programs including a master's program in research consultation and a doctoral programme in consultation psychology. His professional registration category is clinical psychology. Vasi is an active member of national and international psychological societies and regularly serves on the organizing and scientific committees of academic conferences. He lives in Pretoria, Gauteng, the economic and industrial heartland of South Africa.
E-mail: vdevesh@unisa.ac.za

Steve Wheeler is a senior lecturer in education and information technology in the Faculty of Education at the University of Plymouth in the United Kingdom. He has worked with educational media and learning technologies since 1976, predominantly in the fields of nurse education and teacher training. His current research interests include e-learning, creativity in learning, distance education, and the social Web. His first degree in psychology fueled his interests in human responses to technology, and this is now the main focus of many of his studies. He has published over 100 scholarly papers and articles in the fields of e-learning and educational technology. He teaches on a number of under- and post-graduate programs for the university and regularly gives lectures, workshops, and seminars at other universities across Europe. Steve sits on the committees of several international learning technology conferences, and serves on the editorial boards of seven peer-reviewed journals, including *ALT-J, Interactive Learning Environments,* and *IRRODL.* His most recent book, titled *The Digital Classroom: Harnessing Technology for the Future* (co-authored with Peter John) was published in January 2008 by Routledge. Steve's Web site is at: http://www2.plymouth.ac.uk/distancelearning and his e-learning blog, "Learning with 'E's," can be found at: http://steve-wheeler.blogspot.com. He lives in the South West of England with his wife Dawn and their three school-age children.
E-mail: swheeler@plymouth.ac.uk

Nicola Whitton is a research fellow in the Education and Social Research Institute at Manchester Metropolitan University. Having worked in learning technology for the past 10 years, she has recently completed a doctorate in the area of collaborative computer games for learning, and now specializes in researching game-based learning in the higher education sector. Nicola's Web site is at: http://www.playthinklearn.net/Index
E-mail: n.whitton@mmu.ac.uk